The Crisis of Islamic Masculinities

Also Available From Bloomsbury

Islam and the Veil edited by Rabiha Hannan and Theodore Gabriel
PB: 9781441135193
HB: 9781441187352

Muslim Youth edited by Fauzia Ahmad and Mohammad Siddique Seddon
PB: 9781441119872
HB: 9781441122995

Bloomsbury Companion to Islamic Studies edited by Clinton Bennett
9781441127884

The Crisis of Islamic Masculinities

Amanullah De Sondy

B L O O M S B U R Y
LONDON • NEW DELHI • NEW YORK • SYDNEY

Bloomsbury Academic
An imprint of Bloomsbury Publishing Plc

50 Bedford Square
London
WC1B 3DP
UK

1385 Broadway
New York
NY 10018
USA

www.bloomsbury.com

BLOOMSBURY and the Diana logo are trademarks of Bloomsbury Publishing Plc

Hardback edition published 2013
This paperback edition published 2015

British Library Cataloguing-in-Publication Data
A catalogue record for this book is available from the British Library.

ISBN: HB: 978-1-7809-3616-1
PB: 978-1-4725-8714-5
ePDF: 978-1-7809-3693-2
ePub: 978-1-7809-3744-1

Library of Congress Cataloging-in-Publication Data
A catalog record for this book is available from the Library of Congress.

Typeset by Newgen Knowledge Works (P) Ltd., Chennai, India
Printed and bound in Great Britain

Dedicated to the memory of
Glasgow's Bonnie Lass, my friend
Miss F. E. Mc Glade (Mac, b. 1915–d. 1993)

Contents

Acknowledgments

There are many people I wish to thank for supporting me with constant encouragement with regard to this book project. Parents shape the thoughts of their children in more ways than imagined; love always to my Mum, Nasim Akhtar, and my late Dad, Inayat Ullah. They arrived from Sialkot, Pakistan, and settled in Glasgow, Scotland, in the 1950s, and so my connection to my heartlands must also be acknowledged—beautifully split, as the prolific Scottish author Lewis Grassic Gibbon famously charged in *Sunset Song*, 'nothing endures but the land.'

My utmost gratitude goes to Lloyd Ridgeon, who supervised me closely in all matters technical but also spent considerable time listening to my meandering critical thoughts and questions. A supervisor of this caliber is hard found, and for that I will forever remain indebted. I am also thankful to Julie Clague, George Newlands, Alexander Broadie (the regular musings at the French coffee shop near Glasgow University on Scottish Enlightenment were greatly appreciated, and the tradition continues), Mona Siddiqui, and Fr. John Bollan for helping me refine my thoughts during my time at the University of Glasgow. Thanks must also be given to my editors, in particular Lalle Pursglove of Bloomsbury Academic and Katie Van Heest—thank you for having faith in this project.

There are a number of people who helped me transition from Scotland to the USA, I am grateful to the support of Vincent Cornell, Abdullahi An-Naim, Mary Keller, Richard King, Kecia Ali, Aysha Hidayatullah, Ahmet Karamustafa, Asma Barlas, Norman Johnson, Amina Wadud, Naeem Inayatullah, Sorayya Khan, Rachel Wagner, Elizabeth Castelli, Randall Styers, Zayn Kassam, Tazim Kassam, Omid Safi, Ayesha Chaudhry, Rumee Ahmed, John Fitzgerald, Nargis Virani, Juliane Hammer, Scott Kugle, Zahra Ayubi, Dan Boucher, Karl Niklas, Ed Cobb, Sakina Cornell, Rkia Cornell, Adele Reinhartz, Sadiyya Shaikh, Laury Silvers, Tudor Parfitt, Olivia, Whitney Bauman, and Iqbal Akhtar.

I heartily acknowledge the support I have received from dear colleagues at the University of Miami, in particular Michelle Gonzalez Maldonado,

Dexter Callender, Stephen Sapp, David Kling, Henry Green, Bill Green, Dan Pals, David Graf, Traci Ardren, Steven Butterman, Ralph Heyndels, Sumita Chatterjee, Richard Godbeer, Bill Walker, Koichi Tasa, Christina Civantos, and Teresa De La Guardia.

My brothers and sisters all deserve acknowledgment and thanks, Hadayat, Asmat, Rafaqat, Asma, Asfa, and Asea; and their partners, Shakeel, Mehmood, Samia, Serwat, and Samina; and their children, Ameerah, Hafsa, Nafeesah, Hira, Nabeeha, Fariha, Safa, Mohsin, Shoaib, Ehsan, Hassan, Hisham, Haider, Umber, Aneesa, Uthman, and Ayaan.

Good friends have been necessary companions on this journey, too. I am blessed with Zaheer Sadiq, who has not only been a friend since primary school but a confidant and critic when I most needed one, at times receiving the brunt of my anxieties and tensions. I am also grateful for the friendship of Chris Foxon, Margot Rhead, John Xander, Frank Wilson, Shoket Aksi, Imran Hussain, Shabana Naz, Maria Rathore, Manveer Sangha, Noorah al-Gailani, Iain and Kathleen Morrow, Natalie and Emma, Mark and Craig, Darren Waite, Alana Vincent, Marta Mejia, Ghalib Dhalla, Arifa Farooq, Alina Mirza Tim Rhead, Toby Rhead, Rev. Kenny Macaulay, Natalie Ghosn, Mahnoor Campbell, Kamran Campbell, Narmeen Mushtaq Khan, and Sana Akbar. I would also like to thank all the staff and producers at the BBC Radio Scotland for allowing me to broadcast on Thought for the Day which has been ongoing since my graduate studies at the University of Glasgow. I learnt that a complex thought is useless if one is unable to present it with clarity and in concise language.

And finally, thanks for the inimitable voice of Pakistan, Madam Noor Jehan (1926–2000). The famous Pakistani poet Faiz Ahmed Faiz (1911–1984), gifted her his famous *nazm*—'Mujhe se pehli si mohabbat meray mehboob na mang', 'Don't ask me for that love I once offered that was ignorant of the world's realities . . .' I remain plagued by this day and night.

Introduction

No matter: she was not happy, and never had been.
Why was life so unsatisfying?
Why did everything she leaned on instantly crumble into dust?
But if somewhere there existed a strong,
Handsome man with a valorous, passionate and refined nature, a poet's soul in the form of an angel,
a lyre with strings of bronze intoning elegiac nuptial songs to the heavens,
why was it not possible that she might meet him some day?
No, it would never happen! Besides, nothing was worth seeking, everything was a lie!
Each smile hid a yawn of boredom, each joy a curse, each pleasure its own disgust;
and the sweetest kisses only left on one's lips a hopeless longing for a higher ecstasy.[1]

~~~

Masculine identities are lived out in the flesh,
but fashioned in the imagination.[2]

While they arise for complicated sociopolitical reasons, rigid notions of masculinity are causing crisis in the global Islamic community. As a result of harsh political realities—regional instability, colonialism—that threaten Islamic communities, theocratic inflections of the religion are resurging. These theocratic Islamisms idealize an entrenched masculinity defined through familial dominance and shows of power, sometimes expressed as militarism. The rigidity of the masculinity that emerges prompts a certain exodus from religious Islam[3] to a secular, if still in some ways culturally Muslim, identity. Some Muslims who do not agree with narrow construals of manliness feel forced to consider themselves secular and therefore outside the religious community, which Muslims call the Ummah. Those rigid ideas of gender tend

have 2 be secular b/c don't like gender role
~~~

to be articulated in Qur'ānic commentary and through historical precedents relating to societal, religious, and familial obligations, which are therefore the sites that must be engaged in an evaluation of the validity of any singular, ideal Islamic masculinity. This book is an exploration of key figures from two broadly defined sources—the Qur'ān and Indian–Pakistani history—which exposes the tendentious and precarious nature of severe constraints on Muslim manhood.

Living religious communities are never as monolithic as their spokespeople and reformers might suggest. However diverse Muslims are, they have to live with the spectres of legalist Islam and centuries of interpretative tradition over them. Many individuals cannot find themselves in the most codified image of Muslim manhood that has accreted since the Prophet Muḥammad's time: single men, women, non-heterosexual men, and transgender individuals. Islam itself is hardly homogeneous. Most basic discussions of Islam are centered on its five pillars[4] as if they were the hallmarks not just of every Muslim's practice but of every Islamic society. The intricate layers and nuances held within Islamic traditions and lives are often lost in our very twenty-first-century desire to understand them as quickly and neatly as possible. This often leads to bewilderment when one is faced with real Muslims who do not fit neat pictures. A nonfasting Muslim during the month of Ramadhan, for example—perhaps one who is drinking from an alcoholic beverage[5] in one hand and holding a pork sausage[6] in the other—may still hold his faith in Islam as a Muslim. How is one to reconcile simplistic approaches to Islamic traditions (and the simplification can come from within or outside the Ummah) and the diverse lifestyles of Muslims in various cultures and societies?

We must begin by accepting that one cannot literally speak of one Islam but only of Islams. Karamustafa has argued that a "civilizational" approach is needed for such a debate on varieties of Islam:

> A civilizational tradition, simultaneously in and above specific cultures, is fundamentally interactive with and inclusive of culture. As an ongoing civilizational discourse, Islam is an interactive and inclusive tradition: it interacts with the cultures it comes into contact with and, where it takes root, reshapes and reforms cultures inclusively from within. As a result, there are numerous different Islamic cultures on the globe, and they are all

> equally Islamic, equal partners in the making and remaking of the Islamic civilizational tradition.[7]

Pakistan in particular can claim a fraught but mutually reinforcing relationship with the construction of Islamic masculinity because "from its inception the Pakistani state has had to confront questions of religious identity-politics."[8] For some reason, patriarchy has taken particular hold here; it is certainly, unmistakably shaped by geopolitics and the history of colonialism in the region.[9] Multitudes of sociological and anthropological studies on Muslims throughout the world explore the connections between geography and religious expression. However, a cardboard-cutout understanding of Islam will ultimately lead to a flat understanding of men and women. The way in which Pakistan, as a sovereign state, has politicized issues of gender and sexuality, through its various parties, often leads to overlooking the way in which its diverse citizens live and understand Islam. These political and nonpolitical expressions of Islamic understanding and practice are deeply rooted in approaches to authority. This is evident in the debates surrounding "Muslim women" who are often understood as a single figure stereotypically related to a form of "Islamic" oppression and degradation, usually with respect to veiling, which is itself practiced in multiform ways. As the veil is politicized, its commentators lose sight of how personal the relationship is between Muslim women and their veil, in all its expressions.[10]

In much the same way that the notion of a Muslim woman conjures a certain image, discussions surrounding Muslim men are also limited to essentialized forms of masculinity—either ideal or reviled, but usually always relating to an Islamic patriarchal society. Such narrow understandings of Islam and Muslims then commandeer questions relating to sexuality: a lesbian veiled Muslim woman or a transsexual Muslim person in the mosque is a variance that many sociologists and anthropologists may highlight for the shock-and-reveal factor, but Islamic theologians have often dismissed these figures as un-Islamic and far removed from Muslim traditions. Is this truly the case? Can such alternative forms of masculinities and femininities not be encompassed in Islamic traditions? These are some of the questions that this book aims to discuss and elaborate upon.

Turning to the non-Islamic world, it is evident that the West is not understood in the same restrictive way to which the "Islamic world" is subjected to. The West itself, and its image outside its boundaries, has been open to issues relating to diversity, especially in challenging idealized notions of gender and sexuality. Raising such questions has led to a detailed debate on masculinities in the West; however, so far such debates have not received reciprocal attention in Islamic theology and practice. As the English and Film Studies professor Lahoucine Ouzgane has observed, "dominant masculinity in Islamic cultures has so far remained an unrecognised category that maintains its power by refusing to identify itself. There are very few studies that make Muslim *men* visible as gendered subjects and that show masculinities have a history and clear defining characteristics that form and integral part of the gender relations in Muslim cultures."[11] An emerging variety of narratives present various images of gender and sexuality in novels and travel writings on homosexual Muslims[12] (almost always male)[13] or the personal writings of Muslim women in patriarchal society, a focus taken up later in this book. Unfortunately, these are most often left at the fringes of an "un-Islamic" discussion on masculinity and femininity because mainstream Muslims and the powers that be dismiss these narratives as unacceptable.

Placing special focus on India and Pakistan further destabilizes any monolithic image we (both inside and outside Islam) may have of the Muslim man as Arabic or Middle Eastern. If one is to seek varieties of Islams or Islamic masculinities, then one must seek an alternative image of Islam beyond the Arab lands, which have often dominated discussions on Islam. This could be due to the fact that the Qur'ān was revealed in the Arabic language and the last prophet of Islam, Muḥammad, was located in Arab lands, too. However, belief in the oneness of God, a central Islamic teaching, is not limited to a geographical location, as is mentioned in the Qur'ān itself:

> O men! Behold, We have created you all out of a male and a female, and have made you into nations and tribes, so that you might come to know one another. Verily, the noblest of you in the sight of God is the one who is most deeply conscious of Him, God is all-knowing, all-aware. (Qur'ān 49:13)

In critical and Qur'ānic terms, then, South Asia is fruitful grounds for counterexamples that allow us to read against the grain of mainstream Islamic tradition to expose its inner workings and make sense of diversity, which need not be itself contradictory.

The case studies of diverse Islamic expressions of masculinity that fill this book make clear that lived gendered experiences are manifold; what also becomes clear is that there is room to play with the *ideal* of Islamic masculinity, too. Whatever Islamic history, tradition, text, and law have to say about masculinity, the fundamental core of Islam is to be found in its very name: submission. Some of the groups and individuals explicated in these pages overtly draw on the centrality of submission in order to destabilize gender construction as usual, but many only gesture in that direction.

A multiform approach

This study aims to evaluate constructions of masculinities in Islamic traditions, chiefly the Qur'ān,[14] and the impact such notions have on the lived realities of Muslim men (and women) in India and Pakistan between the eighteenth and twenty-first centuries. Difficulty and tension arise when discussing Islamic masculinities, so let us be clear that this book aims to trace—but not enter—a theological debate. Since there is no one form of homogenous Islam, it is not an aim of this research to defend or apologize on behalf of a monolithic religious culture. In fact, within Islamic theology God is understood as "the greatest"—someone or something that does not need a defence, be it from a sociologist, an anthropologist, or an Islamic-studies perspective. Instead, the approach is historical and metainterpretive; it reads the silences, works against the grain, and reads negatively to expose what is hidden, what is operative but not acknowledged in terms of lived masculinities within Islam. This is a natural mode for a study that takes unearthing variety and discontinuities as its aim. It is therefore important that this book not be read as or claim to be a seamless product or statement.

In much of the previous academic work on masculinity it has assumed to be a "monolithic unproblematic entity, with patriarchy attaining a universal status as the single cause of the oppression of women."[15] In response, the Western study of masculinities has pushed to understand nonpatriarchal masculinities, but "the terms 'masculinity' and 'patriarchy' are closely linked in a historical sense, since both were taken up by socialists and radical feminists during the late 1960s as part of the process of theorising male dominance."[16] So, until recently, masculinity has tended to be absent from mainstream academic research. This was largely due to the "unitary notion of masculinity" which was often employed in studies largely concentrated on women and girls.[17] However, men's studies cannot be regarded as a new focus of research since the current interest in gender arose in response to the fact that social disciplines had previously been concerned almost exclusively with men.[18] Discussions surrounding patriarchy and masculinity *in Islam* have not flourished, and so there are immense possibilities for research on Islamic masculinity and Islamic masculinities; this book is one starting point for such discussions.

In broaching this topic of masculinities in Islam, one runs the risk of committing orientalism or making other colonizing moves. Although Edward Said's critique *Orientalism* won him many high accolades, it has, at times, made an uncomfortable task of critical scholarship on Islam (or Muslims), especially by non-Muslim or Western scholars who may forever be labeled as orientalists looking to study the "Islamic East," a charge which dismisses not only their work but also their questions. Such sentiments are increasingly finding their way into contemporary studies that aim to "correct" the perceptions of Muslims by "Orientalists."[19] Studies that use Said's Orientalism as a key research method tend to strengthen the divide between the "East" and the "West" using a postmodern, postcolonial argument to create some form of legitimacy. The effects of such are now being felt on the ensuing discussions and debates on Islamic masculinities studies. The Iranian social scientist Shahin Gerami questions whether masculinity studies are a form of "cultural imperialism" on Islamic societies:

> When we incorporated feminist ideas in our women's movement, we were addressing injustice, exploitation, and the dehumanization of women in the name of tradition, religion or authenticity. That is different from masculine or even social cleavages, but we are still a long way from claiming any victory for women's rights, despite incremental gains. We, the others, have accused the Orientalists of being intellectual thrill seekers, the upper-class equivalent of soldiers of fortune or academic bungee jumpers. Since feminism frowns upon exploring the other for our thrills, what can be gained from masculinity research in cultures struggling with basic human rights for women.[20]

Gerami seems to overlook the way in which idealized notions of an Islamic masculinity have played an essential role in restricting the basic human rights of women—or Gerami may be separating masculinity discussions from Islam. Such separations have led some to adopt a more "secular" approach in their work on gender and sexuality in societies and cultures without seeking answers from Islamic traditions.

Certainly, lived masculinities and femininities have been an interest for sociologists and anthropologists mostly from the West, and their methods and presentations of diversity have not explored such realities theologically—at least where Islam is concerned. This could be due to the limitations of the work of sociologists and anthropologists, but one of the core reasons for this is due to prevalent understanding that such discussions and debates are located in the West and in imposing such discussions on the Islamic world a new form of Orientalism is taking place.

My commitment to this research, even though it walks a cultural line we have been told is very delicate, also emerges from my own split identity—divided between Scotland and Pakistan. If one were sympathetic to sociologists who raise objections to questioning masculinities on the grounds that such interrogation is another form of Western imperialism or is orientalist, one may still be open to research like this. I aim to bridge that divide by raising the debate from a mixed-identity standpoint; I appreciate equally both worlds as complements within the study of Islam. In fact the cultural and intellectual similarities between Scotland and Pakistan never cease to amaze me, so I resonate with the concerns that the prolific Islamic law expert at UCLA Khaled Abou El Fadl has voiced:

> The problem is only exacerbated by concerns over the infiltration and dismantling of the Islamic intellectual heritage by Western values and foreign systems of thought. Some of my teachers, for instance, tended to brand the use of non-customary or unfamiliar methods of analysis as part of the Western cultural invasion. Admittedly, some of these methods did, in fact, originate with Western writers. At other times, however, at least from my point of view as a student, I would sincerely believe that my method was simply original and unprecedented, and was honestly my own. Nevertheless, the method would be stigmatised as Western simply because it was unprecedented or different.[21]

Although this research is written from the perspective of a Muslim believer, it does not preclude any question in terms of masculinity.

I originally conceived of this work as an inquiry into Qur'ānic masculinities specifically, and that appealed to me because, unlike laws that have since been drafted and codified, the Qur'ān forces self-reflexion. Narrative invites individuals to appreciate the contours of life and other people's lives in a way that law does not. This is especially true with Islamic law in that it actually aims to do the work of applying the Qur'ān to lived experience in a blanket way. So, following the Indian modernist Sir Syed Aḥmed Khān (1817–98), this research focuses extensively on the Qur'ān itself, not commentaries or Ḥadīth (sayings attributed to the prophet Muḥammad). Khān thought, and I agree, that "the Qurān stands on its own, requiring only the application of a dedicated and enlightened mind for its understanding."[22]

This book, on the other hand, does not quite stand in a field of its own. Lahoucine Ouzgane has edited a collection of essays in a book entitled, *Islamic Masculinities*, which is the only current book that deals with Islamic masculinities.[23] His book has three sections, "masculinities and religion," "masculinities and the Palestinian–Israeli conflict," and "masculinities and social practice." Ouzgane outlined the rationale and aim of his book as such and indeed it complements the driving current within my own book:

> Islamic masculinities adopts a social constructionist perspective and is premised on the belief that men are not born; they are made; they construct their masculinities within particular social and historical contexts. Thus, masculinities in Islamic contexts emerge as a set of distinctive practices defined by men's positionings within a variety of religious and social structures.[24]

This book explores the way in which Islamic traditions continue to uphold the sex role theories surrounding an Islamic masculinity. The term *Islamic masculinity* then assumes a single trend of masculinity, which is rarely the case, for "it is clear from the new social research as a whole that there is no pattern of masculinity that is found everywhere. We need to speak of 'masculinities,' not masculinity. Different cultures, and different periods of history, construct gender differently."[25] The plural term *masculinities* is then a word that goes against the grain but requires serious consideration in the study of Islam and Muslims. Often we find that it has become politically correct or timely to celebrate diversity, but I have found that at times those advocating in such a way do so at a superficial or sensationalist level. There is a great danger to this approach, as it can easily solidify exclusivist understandings without appreciating voices and lives that are the opposite. For example, I have found many Muslim men and women live warm, happy, and fruitful lives in accordance with what some may deem as a fundamentalist, even extremist, Islam, yet certain forces who believe they uphold modern Islam, often equated with words such as *liberal* and *progressive*, don't just dismiss those fundamentalists' lives but fail to see them for what they are.

Muslim masculinities, ideal and authentic

A course I took early on in my undergraduate career at the University of Stirling in Scotland—Race, Ethnicity, and Gender: Building Blocks for the Critical Study of Religion with Mary Keller and Jeremy Carrette—helped me realize that these identity markers and pluralism are the categories that are sorely needed for interrogating the Muslim experience in the world we live in today. Many young boys, including Muslim boys, are bombarded with masculine role models to emulate. Sociologists have found that this dominant form of masculinity "influences boys and men's understanding of how they have to act in order to be 'acceptably' male, and that this dominant mode is associated with heterosexuality, toughness, power, and authority, competitiveness and the subordination of gay men."[26] While there may be no centralized effort in Islam or in other societies made to shape men in the form of some ideal masculinity, masculating processes occur in quotidian, repetitive social interactions. As Raewyn Connell, the pioneer sociologist of masculinities studies argued, "Masculinities are configurations of practice within gender relations but requiring a structure that includes large-scale institutions and economic relations over and above the face-to-face relationships and sexuality." While masquerading as a personality trait, masculinity has a de facto institution backing it.[27]

The way in which Islamic traditions play a role in shaping and policing masculinity in Islamic societies affects not just social interactions but also understandings of Islam. With great emphasis on the pursuit of knowledge in Islamic traditions,[28] the prophet Muḥammad, understood as a teacher, and his sayings as lessons are then also key in producing Islamic norms of masculinity, a focus of this book. In one ḥadīth it is stated,

> Yahya related to me from Abdullah ibn Abd ar-Rahman Ibn Ma`mar Al-Ansari that Ata Ibn Yasar said that the Messenger of Allah, may Allah bless him and grant him peace, said, "Shall I tell you who has the best degree among people? A man who takes the rein of his horse to do Jihād in the way of Allah. Shall I tell you who has the best degree among people after him? A man who lives alone with a few sheep, performs the prayer, pays the zakat, and worships Allah without associating anything with him."[29]

This prophetic tradition places emphasis on the valiant and heroic forms of Islamic masculinity above the more softer form of Islamic masculinity, yet reading against the grain also highlights that there is no prescription of marriage, family, or procreation—crucial location points of upholding hegemonic Islamic masculinity. This shows that exemplifying particular forms of masculinity and femininity from texts and traditions is always partially subjective to suit the needs and desires of individuals who choose as they desire. Idealized masculinity would lead to an understanding that every man is happily married to a wife who bears him children. It is then not just masculinity that society idealizes but also "the wife," "the child," and "the family." This reality is not always the case and shatters the myth of masculinity. It is the understanding of this book that gender and sexuality are constructed through a range of individual experiences and abilities, be they biological or social. This book makes no attempt to justify the gender or sexuality of believing Muslims as "right" or "wrong" as such a discussion is rooted in an understanding that there is an "ideal" gender and sex and that all must be constructed upon such understandings.

The construction of masculinity is dependent upon the notion that it has an opposite. Generally, this counterpart is assumed to be women, who are construed as the "opposite sex," and even gender studies largely consider femininity to be the chief, if not only, foil for masculinity:

> Theories of identity have come to value the concept of alterity. Alterity refers to the "otherness," one's status as an outsider. The implication is that identity formation occurs through a process of "othering"—marking groups as different and excluded. . . . Ever since classical Greece, we have defined and understood gender as a series of binary polarities. For example, in order to

> have a paternalistic masculinity, it is necessary to have an image of women in need of protection from the harsh world of business and politics.[30]

Such images are also prevalent in Islamic traditions, namely through the story of Adam and Eve. What emerges from their creation story is the basic premise that man stood for all of humanity until woman came into the picture. Woman is the other, the abject, the foil. Also in a sense deviant, effeminate men and female masculinities[31] in the West have justifiably and compellingly been addressed by scholars, and a recent book even situates itself as a defining statement on the status of homosexuality in Islam.[32] All underscore this phenomenon whereby genders are constructed *against* other constructs. Indeed, as Connell stated, "Without the concept such as 'masculinity' and 'femininity' we would be unable to talk about the questions of gender ambiguity that have been so important."[33]

Surely, the empowerment of women has been associated with whatever masculinity crisis *in the West* is associated specifically with Western ways of knowing:

> In the west heterosexual men have responded to the challenges of feminism and gay liberation in different ways, but they have left many men feeling uncertain and confused about what it means "to be a man" as we approach the millennium. There seems to be a crisis of masculinities initiated through the feminist questioning of traditional forms of male power and superiority that have been structured into the very terms of an Enlightenment vision of modernity.[34]

But in Islam the Ummah's crisis of masculinity is predicated in a different way. Conveniently, Islam, while diverse, does have a basic or core orientation or worldview that its members must in some sense agree with or accept as their own. So we can identify with some confidence a small constellation of alterior others against which Islamic masculinities takes shape. Women certainly figure here, but so do God and the West (with its unruly women). Instead of accepting a simplistic divide between Islamic femininity and Islamic masculinity, then, the case studies that this book undertakes paint the picture of Islamic *masculinities* holding their own—or trying to—explicitly *against* not just the difference that women represent but also in contrast to God and the non-Islamic world. Islamic masculinities are anything but monodualistic. If anything, they are polydualistic, and the battery of binaries in which they are engaged produces manifold variance.

The first case study in this book is meant to take as its subject the most rigid, the most contemporarily relevant, and foundational spin on Islamic masculinities. Where Muslims are oppressed, a strictly gendered Islamism—politically inflected, theocratic—becomes attractive. A pivotal figure in Islamist thought and one who responded to the political realities of post-imperial India, Syed Abūl A'lā Mawdūdi was effective in influencing a certain segment of Muslim society that remains globally influential to this day. A twentieth-century political Islamist, Mawdūdi hardened the conceptions of Islamic masculinity by aggressively interpreting scripture, collapsing it with historical precedent, and presenting his own opinions and ideas as theology—as tantamount to *God's* opinions and ideals. Mawdūdi powerfully constructs the binaries that we will see Islamic masculinities working within and against throughout this investigation, those bêtes noires being God, the West, and women.

Muslim feminists since the latter part of the twentieth century have responded to not only Islamic but also Mawdūdiesque *Islamist* masculinities that push them into abjection. Muslim women feminists take the opportunity to respond primarily by challenging the exegeses underpinning the discourses that position constrained gender as the basis of a strong Ummah. (Mawdūdi, in fact, worked diligently on a Qur'ānic commentary to support his political agenda.) These groundbreaking feminist scholars reorient the binaries—man and God, man and woman, Islam and the West—by focusing more on nondichotomous tenets against which few Muslims could argue. Submission, or surrender, is chief among these overarching concerns that feminists convert into tools of liberation. The chapter dedicated to Muslim feminist work places special emphasis on scholarship coming from India, Pakistan, and women of those backgrounds, such as Asma Barlas, who charges herself with "un-reading patriarchy from the Qur'ān." But other leading Muslim feminists, such as Amina Wadud, who are not specifically from South Asia have also been used extensively to highlight the debates and questions characteristic of Muslim feminist writings writ large. South Asian Muslim feminist women are not thinking among themselves alone. This chapter reveals the tension that many Muslim feminists have in challenging patriarchy through submission to

God as they do not dismiss patriarchal structures, such as the significance of the family, but negotiate their position within them.

Muslim feminist thinkers tend to prefer arguing textual interpretation and experience rather than challenging the familial structures that are meaningful to them even though Islamists have so thoroughly coopted those domestic relationships. So the feminists direct us to the scriptures themselves, where we immediately find that the narratives about the prophets depict extremely varied familial situations producing no discernible singular Qur'ānic masculinity, at the very least with respect to social and kinship responsibilities. The Qur'ān is considered a divine text by the more than one billion Muslims globally, and so its messages are inextricably bound to historical and contemporary Muslim lives. In critically analyzing the Qur'ānic world's messy and even dysfunctional Islamic masculinities, we see how they complement lived realities, which in a way makes the text seem more human, more difficult to domesticate. To further push the feminist scholars' interest in submission or surrender, this critical overview of Qur'ānic masculinities identifies the diverse, even on some levels incongruous, ways in which the prophets demonstrated their obedience to God.

Returning to India and Pakistan, we take a Mughal example of what would essentially be perceived as a hedonistic Islamic masculinity in the life and work of Mirzā Ghālib, the renowned eighteenth- and nineteenth-century Urdū and Persian poet who raises a tension between his spiritual existence and the Islamic norms prevalent in his day. With his fondness for alcohol and courtesans alongside his perhaps laissez-faire perspective on the taking of young male lovers, Ghālib began to see himself as un-Islamic. He certainly was not the picture of Muslim masculinity that Mawdūdi would later draw. He was a paragon of a poet who was characterized by a certain hedonism—a search for love that expressed itself in pleasure seeking. He did fulfill marital and childrearing obligations, too, though, so he actually maps for us a viably Islamic alternative masculinity because he satisfied social responsibilities in addition to his outside pursuits. His struggle to identify within the Islam that he actually held so dear foreshadows the predicament that the Ummah finds itself in today, so we do well to linger in Ghālib's Mughal world for a bit.

Although he never characterized himself as a spiritualist, many of Ghālib's thoughts, practices, and experiences align him with Ṣūfism, the mystical branch of Islam. In some ways, Ṣūfism represents something not ungendered but actually *feminine* with respect to the other divisions within Islam:

> To the extent that mysticism can be considered the "inner," "private" and "hidden" dimension of religion, it can be regarded as its feminine expression. As the counterpoint to a more public, outer, moralistic, codified expression of religiosity, its doctrines and practices tend to focus more on the experiential dimension of the divine, rather than the cerebral explanation.[35]

Particular emphasis is placed on the social relationships that such Ṣūfī doctrine has constructed, namely that of the *Murshid* (master) and *Murid* (disciple), which may trouble the binaries already identified as operative—man–God, man–woman, man–West—or it may just add another dynamic to the list. Defined by a similar and single-minded quest for ultimate love, Ṣūfism allows otherwise obligatory social relationships to bend around this one preoccupation or simply fall away. Shah Hussayn, a sixteenth-century Ṣūfī saint challenged Islamic conformism through his unruly "spiritual dance" and his romantic relationship with a Hindu boy. The Qalandari Malangs provide an extreme and therefore useful site for analysis, too. They are essentially wholly abject, often property-less, and wayward. Malangi men sometimes begin to take on the appearance of women through clothing, accessories, and affect. Something of a trend in recent scholarship attempts to proffer Ṣūfism as a resolution for all issues of restricted gender and sexuality, but the Malang movement is still largely a male one, and they have trouble shaking all of the trappings of patriarchy. It is perhaps too much to expect that any community could do that much, and Ṣūfis like the Malangs do show that more fluid gender can come from an unswerving dedication to communing with the beloved—with the one, with God. However, this case study also tests the limits of the hope that simple commitment to submission will uproot systems of social dominance and constrained ideals of gender.

I have written this book to explore the many possibilities of Islamic masculinities in relation to Islamic texts, traditions, and societies. This book is not trying to argue for any "best" form of Islamic masculinity but is trying to fathom how men and women have constructed their gender and sexuality in the pious belief of an unseen God. The implications of opening up this debate have left me unable to write a book from an ivory tower with high gender theory or intricate detail on Islamic texts and linguistics. Not that I have omitted their significance but I have tried to bridge discourse to lived Muslim realities. The challenge for Muslims in the past and in the present is how to embody the letter of the text to their lived reality, their human experience. At times I've been left rather perplexed after reading academic studies on Islam thinking "and so what?" This book, if I may state so boldly, has taken on board that "so what" question at every step of the way and hopes to open up a debate among academics and nonacademics who realize how important and significant it is to understand the complexities of Islamic masculinities.

1

The Knot Mawdūdi Tied

By far the most dynamic and well-organized challenge modernist Islam has been facing in India, and especially in Pakistan, is that of the revivalist writings and preachings of Abu'l Ala Mawdūdi and his well-knit, monolithic, almost totalitarian religio-political organization, the Jammāt-I Islami.[1]

One of the most polarizing figures in discussions relating to Islam in Pakistan, if not the world at large, Syed Abūl A'lā Mawdūdi, a Muslim theologian, journalist, and statist, has perhaps done more than any other figure to ignite the political application of Islam that has concerned the world of late. Categorically standing firm on the claim that "God has ultimate power" is inalienably about gaining power and control. Terms such as "Islamist" and "political Islamist" are today thrown around to describe a variety of phenomena, and this chapter on Mawdūdi is concerned with the way in which his thought shaped a particular form of Islamic masculinity that clearly resonates with other charismatic Muslim men who led political Islamic movements. Mawdūdi's foundational book *Purdah* uses Islamic traditions to present his vision for an ideal Muslim woman, but in doing so he also, sometimes unwittingly, charted his vision for an ideal Muslim man.[2] Most effective in strengthening his argument is its invocation of God because it roused the spiritual sentiments of every Muslim, regardless of education, and encouraged them to unite. While it would be difficult to argue that his work could be seen, even now, as conventional, Mawdūdi's ideas do have traction and have been pushing Islam from the radical outside inward, toward the Muslim mainstream. Islam is now defined by how it handles what he set in motion in the first half of the twentieth century. But evaluating the development of political Islamism globally, its positives and negatives, is beyond the scope of this book. The essential question is whether political Islamism has played a part in moulding an Islamic masculinity, especially in India and Pakistan.[3]

Mawdūdi, this magnainfluential figure, accomplished pivotal things in no small part because he came of age in pivotal times. Born on September 25, 1903, in Aurangabad, Hyderabad State, Mawdūdi grew up in pre-partition India[4] in a religious family. Mawdūdi was even connected ancestrally to Muḥammad.[5] He was set up to be an independent thinker by a tragedy: the death of his father, Ahmad Hassan (born 1855), interrupted his studies, and he was thereafter self-educated with the occasional help of accomplished educators. His language skills—in not just Urdu but also Arabic, Persian, and English—enabled him to read widely on the subjects that interested him most.[6] All of this set him up to start his career as a journalist around 1918 for various Islamic publications and in 1920 became the editor of a newspaper, *The Taj*. His establishment of a political party called the Jammāt Islāmi (Islamic party) around 1940 shaped the way Islamism would be rooted in Pakistan and, by extension, India.

Prior to his formal forays into affairs of the state, Mawdūdi had shown an interest in politics from an early age and was said to be a part of a Khilafat movement, a secret society, and also a movement known as *Tahrik-I Hijrat*, which opposed British rule and encouraged mass migration to Afghanistan.[7] However, Mawdūdi did not have a long tenure in any of these organizations and isolated himself in his academic and journalistic endeavors. Mawdūdi's first book was titled *Al-Jihād fī al-Islām* (Jihād in Islam) and published in 1930.[8] Thereafter he began working on a commentary on the Qur'ān. It would seem apparent that Mawdūdi's thought and writing was driven by the political realities that Muslims found themselves in, and much of that had to do with influence—constructive and constraining—from the West.[9] The Qur'ān, as the literal word of God, and his affiliation to it were to become his greatest source of power as he moved toward engineering his vision of an Islamic society.

The family, for Mawdūdi, was to become the glorified cornerstone of society because of its strict gender roles. Men were expected to be the breadwinners and women the homemakers. Such a system would keep things in an Islamic order. This was not necessarily something new or novel, as most Islamic commentators and jurists have found issues of gender and sexuality challenging and hence continually striven to strengthening ways of controlling them—augmenting family, marriage, and procreation through written prescriptions. Yet we must also be aware of the social, economic, and political climate in which Mawdūdi was driving his ideas: it comes as no surprise that his views were palatable to Muslims reacting to non-Muslims within India and from Great Britain at the time.

During his career, he was imprisoned in spells totaling four years and eight months.[10] Most notably for his scathing attack on the Ahmadiya Muslim denomination that he classified as a heretical movement that had nothing to do with Islam. Incarceration failed to spark a change in Mawdūdi's views, and he remained firm in his conviction that the only way forward was to establish an Islamic state, which led him becoming even more outspoken on all things he deemed un-Islamic. Mawdūdi believed that sovereignty lay with God and was not willing to allow "the people" to rule in an Islamic state, pitting Western-style democracy against Islam, which "by encouraging indiscriminate westernization, this attitude threatens to erode the Islamic identity and to rob Islam of its effectiveness as a force guiding the life of man."[11] He stood by his principles when martial law sentenced him to death in 1953. Charged with having created propaganda about a reformist movement in Pakistan, he did not appeal the judgment, saying, "if the time of my death has come, no one can keep me from it; and if it has not come, they cannot send me to the gallows even if they hang themselves upside down in trying to do so."[12]

Mawdūdi believed in an Islamized culture without geographic boundaries because "Islamic culture is based on a covenant between God and his creature, man. Its norms are set for all times. They are valid for all humanity, irrespective of national frontiers, race, color, or language."[13] But what he observed in the world around him were Muslims that he did not consider sufficiently Islamic. Mawdūdi aimed to psychologically bully many Muslims into believing that they were below par when identifying as Muslim:

> This huge crowd, which is called the Muslim nation, is such that 999 out of 1000 have got neither any knowledge of Islam, nor are they aware of the distinction between truth and falsehood. From the father to the son, and from the son to the grandson they have just been acquiring the name Muslim. Therefore they are neither Muslims, nor have they accepted the truth by recognizing it as truth, nor again rejected falsehood by recognizing it as falsehood.[14]

And Mawdūdi used every possible means to propagate widely his vision of a strict political Islamism. He astutely recognized that economics play a role in shaping thought and practice, and so to create an Islamic sovereignty that obeyed religious laws and leadership, he needed to make sure that wealth did not bring liberties that would overshadow the state's law.

It was for this reason that Mawdūdi attacked capitalism and socialism, arguing that capitalism was created because of "liberalism": "the economic system based on the liberal theory of uncontrolled economy came to be known as Modern Capitalism."[15] Mawdūdi felt that that such modern capitalism leads to a hands-off government, a sense of entitlement to personal property, work motivated by profit, competition, different rights for workers and their superiors, the idea that progress is a natural process, and "right of unhampered struggle—the rights of the individuals to use their resources, individually or in groups in any field they like, the gains accruing thereby or the losses incurred were their own concern."[16] If capitalism was too self-centered, then this was also the case with socialism, which he believed it was "collectivism, a term coined as an antonym of 'individualism' of the neo-capitalistic order."[17] He stated that the new "creed" of socialism became a "novel idea of a few adventurers":

> But the craze of originality is one of the very interesting defects of the western mind, especially when such originality is utterly devoid of sense and its authors presents it in a thoroughly dashing style, trampling principles, and arranges his hypothesis scientifically enough to make it look like a "system."[18]

On the basis that the West's promotion of such economic systems was flawed, Mawdūdi disputed capitalism and socialism at length. It was in his concluding remarks, which inferred God as the solution, that he presented the "puzzle" and the "Islamic solution."[19] Mawdūdi reshaped the Western models of economics by adding his notion of ultimate accountability lying with God. His ideal Islamic economic system would be based on the fundamental value of the "individual" since, unlike a "party, nation or society," an individual is "accountable to God."[20] Mawdūdi therefore advocated an economic system in which the individual was free, stating that "individuality and perfect development of personality is not possible without freedom of thought and action."[21]

Even with that economic freedom for the individual, his understanding of "accountable to God" led back to his political Islamist ideology. Mawdūdi highlighted an example from the life of the prophet Muḥammad that led him to believe that the individuality which he so earnestly promoted must ultimately be controlled:

> He (the prophet) was apprised of the soaring prices of commodities and requested for their official control. He declined, saying, "I want to meet my Lord (God) in such a state that there is no complaint of injustice against me from a single soul." It does not mean that he left dearness to take care of itself and did nothing to remedy it. What he disapproved of was the official intervention in the market prices and disturb the whole complicated system. Leaving it alone, he devoted all his energies to the moral reform of the businessmen and by continuous preaching brought home to them the fact that voluntary rising of prices is a great sin. His preaching had the desired effect and price index came down to normal before long.[22]

He was unwavering in his devotion to (his understanding of) God's law and required that all Muslims adhere to this law, even recommending severe regulation: "Industries and business adversely affecting morals and physical health of masses should be banned. If any of these is considered essential from a certain point of view, there must be due restrictions."[23]

In its central function of distinguishing what is Islamic from the non-Islamic, Mawdūdi's political framework starts with theocentricity and works through revelation and a divinely ordained authority structure. *Tawḥīd*, the ultimate monotheistic precept, is understood by Mawdūdi to be the belief that "God alone is the creator, sustainer and master of the universe and of all that exists in it—organic and inorganic."[24] This motivates his written works. *Risāla* is "the medium through which we receive the law of God" and related this to two things specifically: the Qur'ān—and the Prophet Muḥammad's life, which acts a paradigm for the requirements laid out in the Qur'ān—and *Sharī'a* (law).[25] For example, he based his vision of a borderless Islamic society on textual record: "besides the ignorance of Kufr and Shirk, if there was an enemy of Islam it was the Satan of *watan* (nationhood) . . . if you pick up the books of *Aḥādīth* you would find how the Prophet fought against distinction based on blood, soil, colour, language and social status."[26] Through this political framework he envisaged an Islamic state, "a theocracy, or rather a theodemocracy where the Kingdom of God—the only legislator—is administered by the whole community of Muslims."[27]

Sharīʿa (law) is understood as the logical culmination of Qur'ānic and prophetic requirements. Accepting and following Islamic law is likened to submitting to God alone, yet often lost in this faithful act is the central fact that the law is legislated and derived through human endeavor, almost always by Muslim men. At a time when Muslims felt oppressed by the British ruling power and demanded their own state, an indigenous, Islamic political formula was appealing to the oppressed both politically and spiritually. Without clarifying the complexities of Islamic law's origins and development, Mawdūdi often conceived of Islamic law in its most monolithic form. He writes:

> It is a principle of Islamic law that *Iman* (belief) consists in adherence to a certain set of doctrines and anyone who accepts those doctrines becomes a *Mu'min* (believer). No one has the right to call such a man a disbeliever or drive him from the fold of the *Ummah* (one Muslim community, often understood to be global), unless there is clear proof that faith has been abandoned. This is a legal position. But in the eyes of the Lord, *Iman* is only valid when it entails complete surrender of one's will and freedom of choice to the will of Allah. It is a state of thought and action, coming from the heart, wherein man submits himself fully to Allah, renouncing all claim to his supremacy.[28]

The way in which Mawdūdi invokes "law" is in a fashion similar to the way he invokes "God" and the "Qur'ān" as binding and unequivocal. This has often been the practice of political Islamists who aim to lay a claim so strong and with "divine" strength that no one dare hold it in contempt. For Mawdūdi, doctrine and belief are clearly defined on issues of ethics and morality—so clearly that legislation is not more than a step away:

> In other words, it is God and not man whose will is the primary source of Law in a Muslim society. When such a society comes into existence, the Book and the Messenger prescribe for it a code of life called the Shari`āh, and this society is bound to conform to it by virtue of the contract it has entered into. It is, therefore inconceivable that a real Muslim society can deliberately adopt any other system of life than that based on the Shari`āh. If it does so, its contract is *ipso facto* broken and it becomes "un-Islamic."[29]

To discount any opposing Islamic ideologies, he asserts his assumption that justice, courage, and truthfulness—as opposed to "falsehood, injustice, dishonesty and breach of trust"—have always found praise among human beings. He bemoaned those who still oppose such simple premises of society, saying that without clearly delineated roles related to morality, no society can prescribe a compelling and intelligible code for behavior. He was also concerned that what prompts individuals to be moral is not the basis for these other legal ideologies, so that there's a mismatch between motivation and the follow-through required. The only explanation for such an incongruity, Mawdūdi found, was from "conflicting views and concepts of the universe, the place of man in it, and of man's purpose on earth."[30] Such was the power of Mawdūdi's concept of *Risāla*.

Khilāfa, the last pillar of Mawdūdi's thought, refers to the religious authority that each individual holds. It is a radical equality that comes of this humanity-wide caliphate; it puts every person in direct relationship with God, a relationship that has integrity despite any external, socially imposed bounds. Mawdūdi therefore considered the state as an extension of the authority of individuals. In some ways, his vision was democratic:

> [The individuals'] opinion will be decisive in the formation of the Government, which will be run with their advice and in accordance with their wishes. Whoever gains their confidence will carry out the duties of the caliphate on their behalf; and when he loses this confidence he will have to relinquish his office. In this respect the political system in Islam is as perfect a democracy as ever can be.

Mawdūdi himself articulates the key difference between this kind of "perfect democracy" and that of the capitalist societies he rejected: "In Western democracy the people are sovereign, in Islam sovereignty is vested in God and the people are His caliphs or representatives."[31] He saw citizen-run democracy as a liability because faulty human whims could undermine the Islamic underpinnnings of such a society:

> Philosophically, democracy is a form of government in which the common people of a country are sovereign. Laws are made with their opinions and can be amended only with their opinion. Only that law can be implemented that they want, and the law which they do not want would be removed from the statutes.[32]

Although his reliance on *Tawḥīd*, *Risāla*, and *Khilāfa* was deployed in a uniquely effective way, Mawdūdi used self-authorizing tactics that are largely consonant with what other Islamist leaders have done. Such an individual may construe himself as either a revitalizing force or a divinely ordained one:

> Some of these leaders would assume the role of *mujaddid* (renewer of the faith), while others would seek to effect a radical sociopolitical transformation through militant messianic movements as *mahdi* (a saviour sent by God). In their ideological formulations and political actions, these leaders would legitimise themselves by invoking Qur'ān, the Prophet's traditions (*Sunnah*), and historical precedents reaching back to the early Islamic community.[33]

Charismatic and influential men tends to be the heart of what triggers the revivals, but political Islamism's development throughout the world has been anything but uniform.

Influenced by local and regional politics, geography, and history, each Islamist movement has brought a distinctive set of values to the oversimplified principles that all things "un-Islamic" need to be corrected by reverting to "Islamic" ideals. The political scientist Richard Hrair Dekmijian traced the historical period of these revivalist responses from the Ummayad rule through to the "contemporary crisis milieus" which he lists as "Muslim brotherhood 1930s," "Iran's Islamic revolution and Shi`ite resurgence" and "Sunni resurgence (1970s–90s)."[34] With the benefit of such an expansive view, Dekmijian has presented a framework for understanding the development of such movements in various historical periods in the Islamic world: he calls it the "cyclical dynamic of crisis and resurgence." Mawdūdi reflected on what he understood as the crisis and his Islamic political formula to revitalize Muslim society toward and Islamic resurgence against not just the British but anyone who disagreed with his branding of Islam and Islamic.

The crisis which becomes the focus of these movements can be expressed as a series of "dialectical perspectives in Islamic society," says Dekmijian.[35] These include:

> Secularism vs. Islamism, Islamic modernism vs. Islamic conservatism, establishment Islam vs. fundamentalist Islam, ruling elites vs Islamist militants, economic elites vs. Islamic radicals, ethnic nationalism vs. Islamic unity, Ṣūfism vs. Islamism, traditional Islam vs. fundamentalist Islam,

> religious revivalism vs political Islamism, gradualist Islam vs. revolutionary Islam, Dar al-Islam vs. Dar al-Harb (territorial domain of Islam vs. rest of the world).[36]

The first conflict between secularism and Islamism is a "central dialectic in all Muslim societies"[37]—a dialectic that Islamists first cast as a crisis and then solve through their constructive use of history.[38]

Dekmijian highlights some of the core understandings of Islamism, which he drew from the teachings of Mawdūdi along with Hassan al-Banna (1906–49, founder of the Muslim brotherhood in Egypt),[39] Syed Qutb (1906–66, understood to be a leading thinker in the Muslim brotherhood movement, with his many publications including a commentary on the Qur'ān),[40] Sa`id Hawaa (1935–89, a leading ideologue in Islamism in Syria),[41] Muhammed Abd al-Salām Farrāj (1954–82, the founder of the organization known as Jammāt al-Jihād, or Society of Jihad, in Egypt said to be behind the assassination of President Anwar Sedat in 1981),[42] Fathi Yakan (b. 1933, the head of the Islamic action front in Lebanon),[43] and Juhayman ibn Muḥammad ibn Sayf Utaybi (1936–80, renowned for his takeover of the holy Mosque in Mecca because he felt that the Saudi regime was corrupt and imitating the West).[44] Dekmijian finds that Islamist ideology is based on several components and has the sole aim of a "return to basics—to the puritanical foundations of faith."[45]

Dekmijian defines the central tenets of Islamism through seven key points beginning with a very basic tension between secularism and religion. The Western solution to that potential conflict is not acceptable to Islamists, whose experiences of oppression by Western incursion lead them to differentiate themselves by merging state and faith. This becomes (1) the central concept of *Din wa Dawlah*, believing that in "Islam, unlike Christianity in the West, the separation of the faith (*din*) and the state (*dawlah*) is inconceivable." (2) Rule (*hukm*) is the notion that the Qur'ān and Sunnah alone give the law, and the state must enforce the law. *Hukm* thus brings textual precedence into the mix, bolstering a belief that Islam is the "final truth" and "final revelation"; as the possessors of truth, the Muslims' primary missions in life are worship (*ibadah*) and transmitting Islam (*da'wah*) in order to secure God's commitment. (3) The nostalgic idea of a return to the straight path (*Sirāt al-Mustaqim*) has developed a sixth pillar, *Jihād*, that is understood at times as a physical struggle to establish an Islamic order as a religious duty. (4) The notion that there is a universal *Ummah* widens the market for Islamism, bringing with it the idea that the aim of every "good Muslim should be the establishment of Allah's sovereignty over the whole of mankind." (5) Islam considers the life of man as a spiritual and material unity, which is understood as "social justice" and is linked to "moral behaviour." Here, the subject is policed and the moral collapsed into the political. Islamists also seek (6) a legitimate rulership based on Islamic law "principles and precedents reaching back to the Prophet and his four 'rightly guided' successors." This would then lead to the establishment of the *khilafah*, or caliphate, system. Under that operationalized order, (7) the *Ummah* "should be a puritanical society based on *salafiyyah* maxims," which are usually understood as a strict adherence to the message of Islam and the Prophet's paradigmatic example. Islamists believe that when these tenets are upheld then the Islamic state has the God-given right to "enforce what is good and to prohibit what is objectionable."[46]

From Dekmijian's definition, the key point in Islamist thought and practice becomes clear—the aim is to achieve the utopian ideal of "Islamic," which allegedly has been lost through un-Islamic practices and thoughts. The many movements that Dekmijian highlighted in various parts of the world show how widespread Islamist ideology is.[47] Such a mass movement is led by the vision of a united Islamic world in which all Muslims are led by the same set of tenets. Strict gender roles, especially in Mawdūdi's hands, have become a major marker of adherence to Islamist principles. While Mawdūdi was not in his day and certainly is not now the only advocate of intensely political Islam, his reactions to his mid-twentieth-century contemporaries contextualize him both in a poignant political moment and in a conversation about religion and governing that continues to this day.

Iqbal and Jinnah: Mawdūdi's contemporaries and his whetstones

The implications of Islamist doctrine on gender construction are evident in those parts of the Islamic world that have tried to reach for Islamist ideals. Islam has been a controlling and guiding factor from the beginning in the creation of Pakistan, for example. However, not all of the burgeoning country's early leaders agreed on the role of Islam in the new republic. In order to

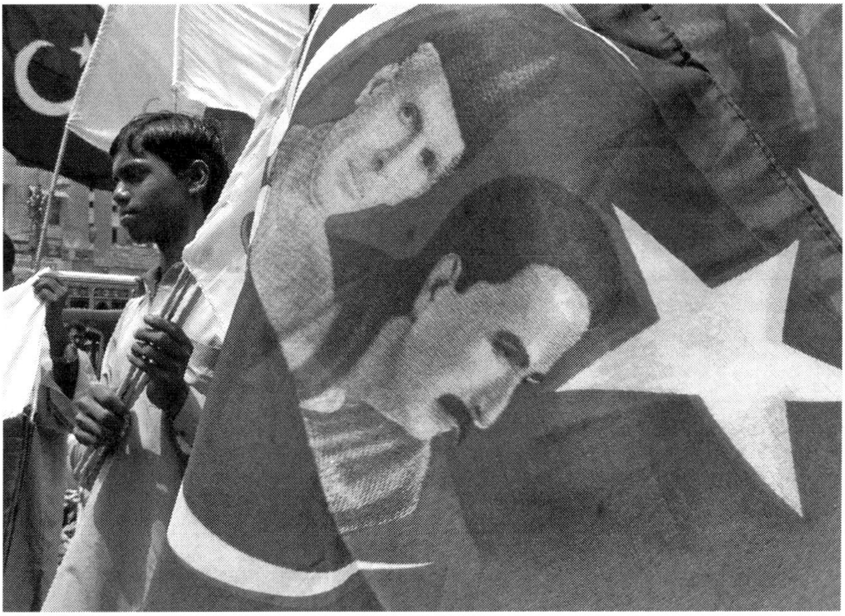

Figure 1.1 Jinnah and Iqbal's image dons the Pakistani flag upheld by a Pakistani boy

locate Islamist thoughts and ideals in the work of Mawdūdi, one needs to seek the alternative male voices that were emerging during this time too. If masculinity is shaped through an interaction with all that surrounds it, then those surrounding Mawdūdi are essential gendered roles he envisioned (Figure 1.1).

Pakistan attained independence under the leadership of Muḥammad Ali Jinnah (1876–1948), and throughout the partition discussions and final independence of what was to become the Islamic Republic of Pakistan he was supported by the renowned poet and philosopher Allama Sir Muḥammad Iqbal (1877–1938), with his religious standing. However, it was not primarily Jinnah's or Iqbal's vision which was established in the new state. The modernist influence of Syed Aḥmad Khān's (1817–98) Aligarh movement and the revivalist writings of Shah Waliullah (1703–62) played considerable roles.[48] Analyzing Iqbal and Jinnah's work contextualizes Mawdūdi with respect to the prevailing intellectual thoughts of Indian Muslims before the partition.

Allama Sir Muḥammad Iqbal was a renowned poet, philosopher, and academic in pre-partition India. Iqbal was born in Sialkot, India on November 9, 1877 (or 1873; dates vary) into a religious family. Iqbal studied for a degree in philosophy at Cambridge University and his PhD in philosophy in Munich from 1905 to 1908.[49] In his doctoral thesis, "The Development of Metaphysics in Persia," he traced the metaphysical thoughts of Persians from Zoroaster to Baha'ullah and there is also a chapter within his thesis that deals with the controversy between idealism (Ash'ari philosophers) and realism (Aristotelian Najm ad-Din al-Katibi).

It was on his way to Europe that his teacher from Lahore, Sir Thomas Arnold, advised him to visit the mausoleums of Khwaja Nizamuddin, Amir Khusrau, and Mirzā Ghālib. Iqbal was greatly influenced by the poetry of Mirzā Ghālib, the subject of this book's fourth chapter, and it is said that when Iqbal visited his burial place, someone began to recite his poetry, at which "Iqbal sobbed bitterly and embraced Ghālib's grave."[50] In his book *Stray Reflections* Iqbal stated, "I confess I owe a great deal to Hegel, Goethe, Mirzā Ghālib, Mirzā Abdul Qadir Bedil and Wordsworth. The first two led me into the 'inside' of things, the third and fourth taught me how to remain oriental in spirit and expression after having assimilated foreign ideals of poetry, and the last saved me from atheism in my student days."[51]

Iqbal was influenced by Western culture—he was fluent in English as well as Persian and Urdu—but was cautious about adopting European ways which he connected with paganism, "European Christianity seems to me to be nothing more than a feeble translation of ancient paganism in the language of Semitic theology."[52] However, he has been said to have "admired the British lifestyle and stated that the well-being of India depended upon good relations with Britain."[53] Iqbal was then seen to be a strong bridge between those who opposed the West wholeheartedly and those who held it dear to their hearts,

> The only standard by which Iqbal might be hung would be a universal one, one that not only did not exist but that, in Iqbal's view, could not emerge from either the reason ("brain malady") of the West or the mysticism ("heart-malady") of the East. It could only have been the sort of standard that Iqbal himself eventually proposed, a standard of individual truths that turn out to converge.[54]

Iqbal welcomed the abolition of the caliphate, saying that it had been a "corrupt institution since the beginning of Umayyad rule in 661 AD" and further stated that he supported the Ataturk decree calling for Turks to don Western clothing and write the language in roman script—he believed that Islam, as a society, had no commitment to any particular dress or language.[55] But Iqbal also made statements on gender and dress that effectively supported gender conformity, albeit a little less harshly than did Mawdūdi: "our young prophets of social reform think that a few doses on western lines will revitalize the dead Musalman woman and make her tear her ancient shrouds. This is perhaps true. But I fear, finding herself naked, she will have once more to hide her body from the eyes of these young prophets."[56] He did not see the fall of the caliphate as a weakening in the strength of Islam because his thoughts were still reaching for a utopian ideal, "a free Islamic world . . . composed of a group of independent republics ruled by their peoples through their elected representatives."[57]

Any broad alliance among all Muslims would be achieved, Iqbal thought, by each Muslim culture organically addressing its own challenges. Of the Islamic world's internal disconcertion and its lack of agreement even in terms of moral issues, he wrote this poem, reproduced here in its entirety:

> The poppy heard my song and tore her mantle;
> The morning breeze is still in search of a garden.
>
> Ill lodged in Ataturk or Reza Shah,
> The Soul of the East is still in search of a body.
>
> The thing I am may merit chastisement;
> Only—the world is still in search of a gibbet.[58]

Iqbal felt that Islamic law, as formulated by medieval jurists, needed massive reorientation and revision to be relevant to a Muslim community's needs.[59] This at least was a moderate bridge between the West and the East. Iqbal was not pleased with the narrow interpretations of Islam that Muslims were presenting; indeed, he thought that landmasses splintered into myopic nationalisms were much to blame for Europe's troubles.[60] Most of his reflections on Europe and the West in general were penned upon his return from Germany in 1910.

For Muslims to start redressing the ills of society, Iqbal encouraged Ijtihād, creative independent reasoning that leads to behavioral precepts. Any notion that Ijtihād was no longer useful or used (sometimes called "the door of Ijtihād closing") was totally rejected by Iqbal: he called that notion "pure fiction" that "especially in the period of spiritual decay, turns great thinkers into idols."[61] Iqbal's statement on Ijtihad may not be seen as "open to all" as one may lead to believe as he was advocating and hence his view was not dissimilar to that of Mawdūdi's, who stated, "Only those who had faith in the Shari'āh; had knowledge of the Qur'ān, the prophetic traditions, and other sources of religious law; and were proficient in Arabic would practice Ijtihād."[62] The issue was not so much on the principle of Ijtihad, as both men needed this to advocate their positions; the issue was which of the two were more "Islamic."

Iqbal's vision greatly influenced the creation of Pakistan because he presented views that reflected East and West. He understood the colonialism of Southeast Asia as, in part, caused by Islamic culture's inability to live up to its tradition:

> When Iqbal compared the living tradition of Islam with Islam of the Qurān and the Prophet, he found it wanting in daring, in valour, in imagination, and in heroism. That Muslims should have been drawn toward European ways demonstrated the debility of the living tradition. He saw clearly that imperialism had encroached not just upon territory but upon ways of being, and for that he blamed Muslims themselves as much as Europeans. Muslims had become sheep, accepting not just economic and political but psychological dependence.[63]

Iqbal's most famous poetic masterpieces speak to this disconnect between what he saw as Muslims' potential as a group and their lived realities. The two poems, known as *Shikwa* (*The Complaint*, 1909) and *Jawab-i-Shikwa* (*The Answer to the Complaint*, 1913), are interconnected.[64] Iqbal begins his "complaint" by detailing the achievements of Muslims and questioned God as to why His wrath was upon them:

> Before our time, a strange sight was the world You made:
> Some worshipped stone idols, others bowed to trees and prayers.
> Accustomed to believing what they saw, the peoples vision wasn't free,
> How then could anyone believe in a God he couldn't see?
> Do you know of anyone, Lord, who then took Your name? I ask
> It was the muscle in the Muslim's arms that did Your task.
> Here on this earth were settled the Seljuqs and the Turanians,
> The Chinese lived in China, in Iran lived the Sassanians
> The Greeks flourished in their allotted regions,
> In this very world lived the Jews and the Christians.
> But who did draw their swords in Your name and fight?
> When things had gone wrong, who put them right?

Of all the brave warriors, there were none but only we.
Who fought Your battles on land and often on the sea.
Our calls to prayer rang out from the churches of European lands
And floated across Africa's scorching desert sands.
We ruled the world, but regal glories our eyes disdained.
Under the shades of glittering sabres Your creed was proclaimed.[65]

Iqbal is lamenting the lost power of Muslims in a fashion not dissimilar to the Islamist calls for a utopian Islam. In the context of Iqbal's India, this approach may have been a means to herald the sentiments of Indian Muslims not just against the power of colonial rule but also against the Hindus.[66]

The way in which Iqbal sought to unite Muslims is also evident in his own "answer to the complaint":

You are one people, you share in common your weal and woe.
You have one faith, one creed and to one Prophet allegiance owe.
You have one sacred Kaaba, one God and one holy book, the Koran.
Was it so difficult to unite in one community every single Mussalman (Muslim)?
It is factions at one place; divisions into castes at another.
In these times are these the ways to progress and prosper?

Who abandoned Our Chosen Messenger's code and its sanctions?
Who made timeserving the measure of your actions?
Whose eyes have been blinded by alien ways and civilisations?
Who have turned their gaze away from their forefathers' traditions?
Your hearts have no passion, your souls are of spirit bereft,
Of Muḥammad's message nothing with you is left.[67]

It is clear that he believed that Muslims were in a sense suffering because they had lost sight of "codes" and "sanctions" that God had sent to human beings. But he held strongly to his affiliation with the West, stating, "most of my life has been spent in the study of European philosophy, and that viewpoint has become my second nature. Consciously, or unconsciously I study the realities and truths of Islam from the same point of view."[68] Iqbal's vision of Islam was then ambiguous; these poems show him floundering between East and West in his poetry and thoughts.

Iqbal's support of Muḥammad Ali Jinnah, Pakistan's first national leader, makes his complex viewpoint all the more consequential. Jinnah wanted to establish a state that would be rooted in religious diversity. Like Iqbal, he was European educated: Jinnah studied law in London in 1892 and at the age of nineteen was called to the bar in England. During his time in London, he became interested in politics and returned to India to become a successful lawyer in his home country. Jinnah led the All India Muslim League's struggle for an independent state for Muslims. In his first official address to the constituent assembly in Karachi, Governor-General Jinnah offered freedom of religious worship and practice to all and stated that everyone was a citizen of the state of Pakistan. Jinnah mentioned his desire to see terms such as *Hindus* and *Muslims* come to have little significance, not in the religious sense but in the political sense, so that everyone held their own beliefs but their national identity overrode such factors. This address was strongly criticized by the Islamists, who felt that Jinnah was embracing those aspects of Western that opposed the very foundations of their idealized Islamic State.[69] Mawdūdi lambasted Jinnah's vision, saying,

> Not a single leader of the Muslim League from Jinnah himself to the rank and file has an Islamic mentality or Islamic habits of thought, or looks at political and social problems from an Islamic viewpoint . . . Their ignoble role is to safeguard the material interests of Indian Muslims by every possible manoeuvre or trickery.[70]

Some commentators have argued that such Islamic sentiments actually supported Jinnah's ambitions: "It is true that Jinnah's great role was a highly important contributor factor, but without intense religious fervour and zeal for an Islamic state on the part of the Muslim masses, Jinnah could not have achieved Pakistan."[71] To this end Jinnah reassured a religious leader in the North-West Frontier Province that Pakistan would be led by Islamic law by virtue of the fact that the major legislative body would be made up predominately of Muslims.[72]

Over his tenure in government, Jinnah's views continually enraged the Islamists, who were displeased not just with his vision for Pakistan but also with the way he conducted his personal affairs. Jinnah married a girl 24 years his junior from an elite Parsi family in Bombay.[73] This marriage was not well received by the Parsi community or the Islamists, who started a chant saying, "For a *Kafir* (infidel) women he left Islam. Is he then a great leader or a great infidel?"[74] His appointment of Jogendra Natha Mandal, a Hindu, as Pakistan's first minister of law and labor, did not change the perception that Jinnah's actions alien to the environment that he called his own.

Four movements opposed Jinnah's vision. The Deobandi Jamiatul Ulama were a part of the Indian National Congress and worked against the Pakistan movement; the Majlis Ahrar-i-Islam was strong in the Punjab and worked in Congress against the Muslim League; the Khaksar movement was a military movement opposed to the concept of Pakistan to the extent that its adherents were implicated with an assassination attempt on Jinnah; and the Jammāt-i-Islāmi, founded in 1941 and led by Mawdūdi, who pushed for a theocratic state in Pakistan.[75] Jinnah remained true to his word and stated in his inaugural speech that one may belong to any religion, caste, or creed as this has had nothing to do with the business of the state.[76] But proponents of the Mawdūdi's brand of theocracy were able to make real progress after Jinnah died in 1948, just a year after Pakistan's independence.

Jinnah and Iqbal constituted something of a united front:

> The founding fathers of Pakistan, Iqbal and Jinnah were both liberal democrats aiming at reorganisation of the Islamic community in accordance with known principles of democracy, and to a certain extent wished to change the economic system on socialistic lines. In any case they envisaged the community of the Muslims as a community of free individuals, totally independent of the authoritarianism and diktat of monarchs, feudal lords, priests, capitalists and imperialists.[77]

Jinnah and Iqbal represent a middle ground between a society that was totally secular and a theocracy. Although Jinnah and Iqbal had created a strong alliance between the two of them, their views were not entirely identical. Iqbal actually attempted to create a bridge between the Islamists to the right of the political spectrum and Jinnah's secular vision to the far left. It was this clash between two poles that began, and continues, the push and pull between the liberally democratic vision of Jinnah and the traditionalist ideology of the Islamists.

In no uncertain terms, Mawdūdi stated that a Pakistan led by Jinnah was destined to be a profane nation:

> Pakistan as envisaged by the Muslim League and Jinnah would be a pagan state and its rulers would not be Islamic but Pharaohs and Nimrods. To call Pakistan an Islamic state would be as misleading as to call an institution

> of ignorance (presumably the Muslim University at Aligarh) a Muslim university, or a bank in the new state an Islamic bank while Islam forbids interest and therefore the very institution of banking, or to call its society modeled on paganism (presumably of the west) an Islamic society, or its forbidden creations in music, painting, and sculpture Islamic arts, or its "atheism and heresy" and "Islamic philosophy."[78]

Mawdūdi founded the Jammāt Islāmi around 1940.[79] It became a political movement against the "Western-based ideals" of Sir Syed Aḥmed Khān,[80] Jinnah, and Iqbal. Mawdūdi stated that,

> Not a single leader of the Muslim League from Jinnah himself to the rank and file has an Islamic mentality or Islamic habits of thought, or looks at political and social problems from an Islamic viewpoint . . . Their ignoble role is to safeguard the material interests of Indian Muslims by every possible manoeuvre or trickery.[81]

Such was the scale of Mawdūdi's appeal to Muslims that his message was spreading, and after the partition of India and Pakistan the Jammāt Islami was divided into Jammāt Islami Pakistan and Jammāt Islami India. In a 1979 festschrift in honor of Mawdūdi, Khurshid Ahmad and Zafar Ishaq Ansari praised the reach of his ideas:

> That influence transcends the boundaries of parties and organisations, and even goes far beyond the Indo-Pakistan subcontinent. Mawdūdi has by now become very much like a father figure for Muslims all over the world. As a scholar and writer, he is the most widely read Muslim writer of our time. His books have been translated into most of the major languages of the world—Arabic, English, Turkish, Persian, Hindi, French, German, Swahili, Tamil, Bengali, etc.—and are now increasingly becoming available in many more Asian, African and European languages.[82]

Mawdūdi, as the leader of a political party and a recognized religious scholar, used his position to preach his religious message across the Muslim world, not just through his writing but also by his numerous international lectures and study tours in Cairo, Damascus, Amman, Makka, Medina, Jeddah, Kuwait, Rabat, Istanbul, London, New York, and Toronto among other locales.[83] Mawdūdi was also one of the founding directors of the Islamic University in Medina, Saudi Arabia.[84] The core tenets of political Islamist ideology easily adapt to different countries of the world.

Despite the broad appeal of his ideas, in Mawdūdi's worldview, there could be no grey areas, and to that end he enacted control over whose say mattered, even within his essentially like-minded movement:

> Mawdūdi was not interested in the emergence of any independent intellectual poles within the Jammāt, nor was he willing to relinquish any of his religious authority by acknowledging the intellectual worth of those around him. . . . Mawdūdi deliberately erased areas of compromise, dividing issues into right and wrong, Islamic and un-Islamic. By putting everything in black and white, he brought moral pressure to bear on his audience, manipulating the psychological impulse that is inherent in a consequential choice between such diametric opposites as truth and falsehood, salvation and perdition.[85]

Mawdūdi declared openly that his understanding and preaching of Islam would make people "good" Muslims—but until that Jammāt-style "goodness" was widely achieved, the only people in real power would be individuals already deemed Muslim enough.[86] For this reason, Mawdūdi was not willing to allow any opposition to his views.

Family as a theocratic political mechanism

Mawdūdi's vision was one of absolutes. According to him, Islam presented clear ideas on all issues, and he advocated marriage and family precisely because of their tight parameters:

> It is in the best interests of the survival growth of social life that indiscriminate indulgence in sexual liaisons should be absolutely prohibited in society. There should be left only one way of satisfying the sex desire, *viz.*, through marriage. To permit individuals to indulge in illicit relationships is tantamount to committing a crime against society; it is rather an attempt to annihilate society.[87]

Mawdūdi's construction of marriage is inclined more towards law and responsibility than towards love. He writes of marriage as a moral bastion:

> It urges both sexes of humanity to subject their relationship to a code of law which protects the morality of man against indecency and immodesty and guards civilisation against chaos. That is why the marriage tie has been termed "fortification" by the Qur'ān, "Hisn" is a fort in Arabic and "Ihsan"

> means fortification. A person who married gets fortified. In other words he builds a fort for himself. The women he married is called "the fortified one." Marriage has provided her with a fort built for the satisfaction of her sexual hunger and the protection of her morals.[88]

Note that the personal moral protections extend, on a macro scale, to civilization as a whole. The threat of extracultural incursions is sometimes explicit in Mawdūdi's work, but it seems always to be at least hovering over his discussions of marriage and the family unit. He politicized marriage by attaching it with his anti-Western sentiments; here he highlights his opposition to marriage between a Muslim and a non-Muslim:

> Muslims, both men and women, are forbidden to have marital relations with non-Muslims who are not believers in the Scriptures. The simple reason is that their religion, their thinking, their civilisation, and culture and their way of life are so different from those of the Muslims that it is impossible for a true Muslim to develop soul-deep love and all-weather harmony in his relations with them. If despite differences, the two of them are tied together, by the marriage bond, the relationship will be only carnal.[89]

A true Muslim is made so distinct by the culture that he or she cannot be bound to someone from outside—this is another way of saying that Islamic culture's integrity is dependent on the life choices its members make.

In order to strengthen his argument against Western notions of marriage, he presented "the feelings of the average American girl" on the issue of marriage as expressed to a judge:

> "Married!," she said derisively, "Why Judge, out of ten girls in my set who have gotten married in the last two years more than half are divorced or separated from their husbands . . . We believe we have a natural right to a companionship and an intimacy which we instinctively crave; we have a knowledge of contraception which precludes the likelihood that unwanted babies will complicate the situation; we don't admit that such a course on our part imperils the safety of human society; and we believe that this effort to replace tradition with what we think is common sense will do good rather than harm."[90]

While the liberally minded twenty-first century reader might find that statement reasonable, even commendable, Mawdūdi presented this actual

American woman's response to an American judge as a way of dismissing the West as an immoral civilization where women have no love or compassion for unborn children. Perhaps Mawdūdi did see some humanity in Western women: "one thing that can bring shameless women with such ideas round to marriage is the sentiment of love." He quickly goes on to write, "But more often than not, this sentiment is only skin deep, the result of momentary attraction. As soon as desires have been satisfied, the man and wife are hardly left with any attraction for each other."[91] The critique of marriage based on anything but Islamic law is total.

Marriage was so integral to his cultural politics because Mawdūdi preached that Islamic civilization would survive only through the strengthening of the family. Much was at stake:

> All the machinery that is required to run the great factory of civilisation is produced in the small workshop of the family. As soon as boys and girls attain puberty, administrators of the workshop become anxious to pair them off as suitably as possible, so that their union may bring forth the best possible generation.[92]

It was for this reason that he opposed men and women from leading single lives, calling the willfully unmarried "disloyal to the community, its parasite and robber." Those who enjoyed the trappings of marriage (presumably sexual and otherwise) without the attendant constraints and obligations are, according to this logic, deviants, who were too "liberated":

> When, therefore, he is busy squandering his sexual energy aimlessly for temporary pleasure in a secret place, he is in fact sowing the seeds of anarchy and disruption in society, depriving it of its rights and harming it morally, materially and socially. In his selfishness he is striking at the root of all those social institutions by which he benefited as a member of society, but has refused to support their maintenance and survival.[93]

Mawdūdi cast single men and women as "disloyal and deceitful to the community." He continues: "If the community had sense it would regard this culprit, this black sheep of society as it regards thieves and robbers and forgers, and not as gentleman or a respectable lady."[94]

Family and married life were excellent means for Mawdūdi's argument for social control in that they were central factors in his construction of the Islamic "gentleman" and "lady." He wrote extensively on issues relating to marriage as a means to preserve the "family" and believed that social relationships between men and women were the cornerstone of faith and society:

> The first and foremost problem of man's community life on whose fair and rational solution depends his real advancement and well-being is the proper adjustment of the mutual relationships between the husband and wife. For it is these relationships which provide the real basis for man's social life and on their strength and stability depends his future well being.[95]

The artifice of family has played an essential role in policing and promoting very specific gender roles. It's worth mentioning that no matter how egalitarian the relationship between a man and woman may be before entering into a marriage, their specific roles after marriage are not so easily challenged. On some level, Mawdūdi must have known this: he repeatedly defined the roles of men and women in a family and used the issue of morality and faith to confirm that gendered schema.

Mawdūdi's own central relationship was not strictly traditional. He married Mahmudah Begum in 1937. She was from a wealthy family that was hereditary Imam of the Delhi Mosque—perhaps that status bought her some flexibility in terms of gender norms. She certainly was not, from the start of their courtship, a picture of the ideal Muslim woman that Mawdūdi would later paint. Middle East expert Seyyed Vali Reza Nasr reports that "she rode a bicycle around Delhi and did not observe purdah (the veil)." Recall that *purdah* was to be the very title of Mawdūdi's magnum opus on Muslim women:

> Mawdūdi clearly loved his strong willed, liberal, and independent-minded wife, however, and allowed her greater latitude than he did Muslims in general. The standards that prevailed in his household were very different from the standards he required of others, including Jama'at members.[96]

Mawdūdi did not use his wife as a role model for Muslim women, as the ideal he constructed was very different. Despite those outward nonconformities, Mahmudah Begum may have satisfied some of Mawdūdi's other criteria for the upstanding Muslim woman, which included "managing the household, training and bringing up children in the best possible way, and providing her husband and children with the greatest possible comfort and contentment."[97] Men, on the other hand, have the "responsibility for earning and providing the

gender role explanation / def

necessities of life for his wife and children and for protecting them from all the vicissitudes of life."[98]

In its ability to cement social relationships, the "family" unit was the most powerful mechanism for upholding Mawdūdi's political Islamist thought on gender and sex. His vision was to have absolute conformity among men and among women, and he utilized the existing patriarchal structure of family and marriage to support his views. The single Muslim man was then understood to be less of a man than his married counterparts. He was incomplete and of less use to his community—that is how Mawdūdi marshaled the power of social pressure to enforce his vision at the expense of masculine diversity (not to mention feminine agency). To this community aspect of prescribed gender roles, Mawdūdi added scriptural support as he consistently and constantly used the Qur'ān and Islamic law as buzzwords in every statement in order to cement his power.

He used the Qur'ānic verse "All things We made in pairs"[99] to base his ideas of Islamic masculinity and femininity on the dualism and pairs among human beings: "all the parts of this great machine have been created in pairs, and all that one can see in this world is indeed the result of the mutual interaction of these pairs."[100] Mawdūdi's construction of sex and gender centered on procreation, which he considered fundamental, and he enforced his views by arguing that this was God's argument—not his: "the principle according to which Allah has created this world and the way according to which He is running its great system cannot be unholy or vile."[101] As he called the family a "small workshop," he continued his analogy of "the great factory of civilisation" to explain gender roles, especially with respect to reproduction:

> The existence of both the active and the passive partners is equally important for the purposes of the factory. Neither the "activity" of the active partner is in any way exalted not the "passivity" of the passive partner in any way debased. The excellence of an active partner is that he should possess the ability to act and also (possess) the other masculine qualities, so that he may effectively perform the active part of his duty in the sex-relation. In contrast to this, the excellence of a passive partner is that she possesses the feminine qualities to an extent that she may carry out the passive part of the sex-relation well. As a matter of fact, only a foolish, unskilled person can think of removing even a minor part of an ordinary machine and employing it for a function for which it has not been actually designed.[102]

↑ demand of strict roles

Thus, Mawdūdi made explicit the specific and divine roles for men and women, which he mapped onto dominance and passiveness. He believed that men's superiority over women was indeed their submission to God—the very heart of masculine commitment to Islam.[103]

Beyond simply marshaling scriptural support for his ideas on gender and society, Mawdūdi used sayings of the Prophet Muḥammad—and his legendary life—to back his view that women should remain the "queen of the house" because earning a living for the family was the responsibility of the husband:

> "The woman is the ruler over the house of her husband, and she is answerable for the conduct of her duties." (Al-Bukhari). She has been exempted from all outdoor religious obligations. . . . The woman has not been allowed to go on a journey except in company with *mahram*.[104] In short, Islam has not approved that a woman should move out of her house without a genuine need. The most appropriate place for her, according to the Islamic law, is her home. . . . A woman may have nobody to look after her, or she may have to go out for earning a living on account of the poverty, insufficient income, sickness, infirmity or such other handicaps afflicting the male protector of the family.[105]

The restriction for women outside the bounds of their homes is indicative of political Islamist ideology, and, in the case of Saudi Arabia, became state law. In his *tafsīr* of Qur'ān 4:34,[106] Mawdūdi used an alleged saying of the prophet Muḥammad as explanation: "The best wife is she who, if you look at her, will please you; who, if you bid her to do something, will obey you; and who will safeguard herself and your property in your absence."[107] Mawdūdi made it clear that the Muslim women had to "obey" her male attendants—family members especially—throughout her life, but he claimed "this dependence of her on others does not in any way deprive her of her freedom of action and will."[108] Restriction is not unfreedom, Mawdūdi was keen to insist.

Mawdūdi understood the differences between men and women from a biological point of view, too: "it has been established by biological research that woman is different from man not only in her appearance and external physical organs but also in the protein molecules of tissue cells."[109] Women's physiological "disabilities" helped Mawdūdi dismiss the sameness of men and women. To this end, Mawdūdi listed nine points that render women sick when menstruating as a way of highlighting the deficiency of being a woman.[110] Intellectual feebleness was a chief concern:

Why women can't do
"Men's jobs"

A lady tram conductor, for instance, would issue wrong tickets and get confused while counting small change. A lady motor driver would drive slowly as if under strain, and become nervous at every turning. A lady typist would type wrongly, take a long time to type and omit words in spite of care and effort, and would press wrong keys inadvertently. A lady barrister's power of reasoning would be impaired and her presentation of a case would lack logic and the force of argument. A lady magistrate's comprehension and ability to take decisions would both be adversely affected. A female dentist would find it difficult to locate the required instruments. A female singer would lose the quality of her tone and voice; so much so that a phoneticist specialist would easily detect the fault and its cause also. In short, a women's mental and nervous system becomes lethargic and disorderly during menstruation.[111]

Mawdūdi also argued that pregnancy was even more "terrible" than menstruation for women,

> A pregnant woman cannot undertake any work of mental and physical exertion which she could easily undertake at other times. If a man is made to pass through the rigours of pregnancy, or for that matter a woman when she is not pregnant, he or she will be pronounced a sick person by all standards.[112]

"feminizing"

↑ pregnancy even more

Mawdūdi is setting up the construction of powerful men over weak women who have to go through the rigors of pregnancy, labor, and motherhood. In his own logic he may well have felt quite broad minded in using this as a way of advising husbands to "look after" their wives but at the same time cementing his rigid notions of Islamic masculinity and femininity. Unfortunately for women, the "sickness of motherhood" continues after childbirth, when "the best of her body is turned into milk for the baby." Essentially, the new mother "does not live for herself but for the trust that nature has placed in her care."[113] Mawdūdi made it very clear that he expected mothers to breastfeed their children because "to deprive the child of this natural food is to be inhuman and callous."[114] His early experience with critical, independent study came to bear here because, as he does with menstruation, he cites scientific studies as support. By characterizing these three biological activities of women as enfeebling, Mawdūdi asserted that men and women have different functions: "not only is it unfair to load woman with outdoor duties, but she cannot in fact be expected to perform them with manly vigour."[115] Those duties are to be left to men; womanly deficiencies create a space for masculine competencies.

Still, Mawdūdi acknowledged the power of sexual urges as natural for both men and women. In his chapter titled "Laws of Nature" in his book *Purdah*, Mawdūdi outlined the problem with human beings:

> Man knows no restriction of time and clime and there is no discipline that may control him sexually. Man and woman have a perpetual appeal for each other. They have been endowed with a powerful urge for sexual love, with an unlimited capacity to attract and be attracted sexually. Their physical constitution, its proportions and shape, its complexion, even its contiguity and touch, have a strange spell for the opposite sex.[116]

Mawdūdi acknowledged that the world is full of potentially stimulating elements—for men. Since that is the case, he thought that men should not actively create for themselves sexually exciting situations because that threatens society and men's fitness for it: "in such a case his animal side will soon dominate the human side of his nature, and his animal instinct[117] will eventually suppress both his humanity and civilisation."[118]

Mawdūdi understood sexual freedom among men and women as the main reason that civilizations, especially Western ones, fail—and that this was because they were violating the laws of nature. For this to be rectified, and for Islamic civilizations to grow, limitations were much needed. He argued that human beings needed to be socially controlled, "social life should be so organised that it becomes really difficult for a person to commit a crime, even though he be inclined to commit it."[119] Where some might argue that sexual drives motivated the very artistic endeavours that made for a vibrant society, Mawdūdi writes, "the nude pictures, sexual literature, love romances, nude ballroom dancing, sex-inciting films, all are means of intensifying the same fire which the wrong social system has kindled in every heart. To save their faces, they call it 'art.'"[120] He did "concede that art and aesthetics are valuable things which must be protected and made to flourish, but social life and the collective well-being of man are even more valuable."[121] That was the higher purpose, but he also rants that exciting environments more often than not *prevent* inventive pursuits:

> Obviously, the people who are surrounded by sex stimulants on all sides, who have to face a new temptation and a new spur every moment, who are submerged in an emotionally wrought-up environment, and who perpetually remain in a feverish condition on account of nude pictures, cheap literature,

> exciting songs, emotionally erotic dances, romantic films, highly disturbing scenes of obscenity and ever-present changes of encountering members of the opposite sex, cannot possibly find that peace of mind and tranquillity of heart that is so essential for constructive and creative work. More than that, such an environment that prevails in the Western world today is not at all conducive to that calm and peaceful atmosphere which is essential for the full development of the mental and moral qualities of the coming generations. As soon as the young people attain maturity, animal passions lay complete hold of them with the result that the moral growth of their personalities is almost wholly impeded.[122]

For example, Greek civilization, while full of art and aesthetics that even Rome saw as worth appropriating, was ripe for Mawdūdi's critique. In the section titled "Status of Woman in Different Ages"[123] in his book *Purdah*, he says the Greeks were "overwhelmed by egotism and sexual perversion,"[124] and he believed that the Roman Empire was "overwhelmed by animal passions."[125]

He then leads the discussion to Europe with an overview of the role of Christianity in "curing the west of its moral ailments"[126] and an explanation of how the Christian church had lost sight of the "divine code of life" by being too accepting of societal norms:

> Every notion with passage of time was accepted as an article of faith and any controversy about it even in thought is condemned as heresy. Therefore, every convention that found its way into society attained the position of a commandment and denial of it meant the denial of the Deity and religion itself. All the forms of literature, philosophy, sociology, polity and economics adopted under feudal system were included by the church as "Divine," and any attempt to change it became a crime—nay—heresy.[127]

Essentially, Mawdūdi believed that there were three distinct features of Western society: (1) equality between the male and the female, (2) economic independence of woman, and (3) free intermingling of the sexes.[128] The independent woman was a detriment to man, in Mawdūdi's view, because she undermined the responsibilities delegated to man:

> Why should a woman who wins her own bread, supports herself economically and does not depend on anyone for security and maintenance, remain faithfully attached to one man only for satisfying her sexual desires? Why should she be prepared to subject herself to so many moral and legal curbs to shoulder the responsibilities of family life?[129]

Mawdūdi argued that where there was no religion, there was sin and prostitution, the latter of which led to illegitimate children, abortions, and sometimes the callous discarding of unwanted babies. He takes the example of girl who was prostituted to almost fifty clients a day in earlytwentieth-century eastern France.[130] After this lurid example, he explains—rather unscientifically—how sexual promiscuity weakens the constitution of France as a nation and a culture:

> The French people's sexual indulgence has gradually resulted in the loss of their physical strength. Ever present emotional situations have broken down their power of resistance. Craze for sexual pleasures has left them with little or no forbearance, and the prevalence of venereal diseases has affected their national health fatally.[131]

Extrapolating from France, Mawdūdi called the United States of America the "zenith" of debauched culture,[132] for at least five reasons: sexual crimes committed with minors,[133] sexually active youths (including homosexuality and masturbation),[134] general promiscuity among women,[135] sexually transmitted diseases (he says nine out of ten Americans have them),[136] and a decline in maternal instincts, which is tantamount to "national suicide."[137]

The fantastic idea of extreme Western sexual practice shaped Mawdūdi's own ideals and helped him define an Islam-versus-West divide. Although he in some way held that Westerners were inferior to Muslims, Mawdūdi feared the rise in Western influence on Islamic society, "Western ways of living, western etiquette, even western manners of moving about, were imitated and all-out efforts made to mould the Muslim society after the western patterns. Heresy, atheism and materialism were accepted as fashion."[138] Since all things "Islamic" were so far removed from all things "Western" that two could never be reconciled, Muslims needed to choose one or the other. It was a rhetorical choice, for he says, "now, any intelligent person can see how sadly mistaken are those people who, on the one hand, feel inclined to follow the Western civilisation and, on the other, cite Islamic principles of social life in support of their trends."[139] Mawdūdi made it very clear to "modern Muslims" what was expected of them: to remain Muslim, they were to "give up their hypocritical attitude towards life" after considering Western culture with Qur'ānic commandments and lessons of the Ḥādīth in mind.[140]

Purdah: A modesty proposal not just for women

In his major work *Purdah*, Mawdūdi detailed his very strong opinions on the effectiveness of the veil in Islamic societies. His views on the *Purdah* were based on his belief that free mixing among men and women was something Western that should not be emulated by Muslims. He advocated a complete segregation of the sexes and the necessity of Muslim women to wear the complete veil. Woman's movement in society was severely restricted, and if there was a necessity for her to leave the house, she was expected to have a male chaperone, an immediate family member or her husband only. There was absolutely no reason for such measures to be eased in Mawdūdi's view: "before we ever think of relaxing *Purdah*, we should have mustered enough strength to pluck out those eyes that stare at Muslim woman who has to come out of her house for some genuine piece of business."[141]

He argued his position from a standpoint of modesty, a concept that he dissects in a way he considers novel:

> Though modesty has been regarded as the most noble trait of feminine character, this has nowhere been kept in view in a rational and balanced way. No one has cared to determine exactly how far and to what extent the female body needs to be covered. No attempt has been made to formulate principles for the preservation of modesty in the dress and social etiquette of the men and women. Nothing has been done to set rationally the bounds of nakedness for the human body, which may not be exposed between male and male, female and female, and male and female.[142]

This general lack of clarity on appropriate modesty was not just a Muslim issue. It will by now be no surprise that Mawdūdi begins his discussion on the "veil" by railing against the West:

> One finds a strange admixture of modesty and immodesty in the dress and way of life of different communities, expressing no rational propriety, no uniformity, no adherence to any principle. In the Eastern countries it did not go beyond certain crude forms, but in the West immodesty in the people's clothing habits and way of life has crossed all limits with the result that they have lost all sense of modesty.[143]

He says his concern about modesty in the West goes beyond just dress, and that is the case for his analysis of the veil in Muslim society, too. Traditionally,

Purdah is also a physical barrier between the sexes in society and, to an extent, the isolation of women from men's space. He writes, "women's sphere of activity should be segregated from that of man's. They should be entrusted with separate responsibilities in the social life according to their respective natures and mental and physical abilities."[144] Even during Mughal times it was customary for the sexes to be physically segregated. This cultural reality that was, and continues to be, extolled as a symbol of piety and beauty was politicized to the extent that in the hands of Mawdūdi became a weapon of power and control. However, the segregation that Mawdūdi advocated was of a much stricter nature and clearly in reaction to the West. Based on his understanding that all men and women were like animals, he created much stricter commands for this segregation because he saw the prevalence of many concerning trends in society: nonphysical adultery caused by lusting after someone other than one's spouse;[145] a feminine obsession with looks;[146] conversation between individuals of different genders in which the participants comport themselves to be more attractive;[147] the use of perfume, which subtly communicates immorality;[148] and nudity, which Mawdūdi contended was better understood in Islam than in "most civilized nations in the world today," where people "do not feel any hesitation to uncover any part of their bodies."[149]

In highlighting these seven social phenomena, Mawdūdi clearly aims to highlight the reasons why the veil is important—primarily for the prevention of sexual "sin." However, the basis of Mawdūdi's understanding of sin was the West. In Mawdūdi's preamble of his main sections of his book on the veil, he outlined in clear terms the "ills" of Western society, and such ills are infused into all his preventative measures. Take, for instance, how he presents his views on the "punishment of fornication":

> Islamic law differs radically from the western law. The western law does not hold fornication by itself a crime; it becomes a crime only when it is committed forcibly, or with a married woman. . . . Islamic law looks upon fornication by itself as a crime, and regards rape or the act of encroachment as additional crimes.[150]

He believed that anyone not adhering to his form of social system should be disciplined, and it is here that Mawdūdi expresses his view of lashings as a punishment for all forms of fornication: "the western people abhor the infliction of a hundred lashes. This is not because they dislike the idea of physical torture. It is because their moral sense has not yet fully developed. At first they regarded fornication as something indecent; now they look upon it as fun, as a pastime, which amuses two persons for a little while."[151] In order to define the segregation of the sexes further Mawdūdi presented "preventative measures,"[152] such as clear boundaries around the areas of the body that are not to be exposed (*satar*)—for men, the area between the naval and the knee; for women, everything but hands and the face.[153] Men of a household should also announce their arrival so that any women can cover up in advance.[154] Mawdūdi also forbade physical contact and privacy between men and women who are not married to each other.[155]

In making these points, Mawdūdi highlighted the distinction between males' *mahram* (nonmarriageable kin) and non-*mahram* relationships with women: "the Qur'ān and Ḥādīth clearly point out the limits of freedom and intimacy of relationship that can be had with the *mahram* males only, but not with the non-*mahram* males in any case."[156] Mawdūdi's argument for women to wear the veil was initially based on his reading of Islamic history, since "a person who considers carefully the words of the Qur'ānic verse, their well known and generally accepted meaning and the practice during the time of the holy prophet, cannot dare deny the fact that the Islamic law enjoins on the woman to hide her face from the other people, and this has been the practice of Muslim women ever since the time of the holy prophet himself."[157] Mawdūdi interpreted passages of the Qur'ān[158] to state that a, "sense of modesty is a part of human nature. Man by nature wants to cover and conceal some parts of his body. This urge has impelled him from the earliest times to adopt one or the other sort of dress."[159] The Qur'ānic exegesis in favor of covering can only be made more solid by positioning the veil as reviled by the West as a sign of savagery.[160] Mawdūdi believed that "reformers" heavily influenced by the West were fundamentally in favor of veiling but lacked the fortitude to stand up for it. He says that "when modestly dressed veiled women were dubbed 'moving tents and shrouded funerals' these so-called reformers felt shamed into disgrace. Obviously, they could not put up with this disgrace and humiliation for a long time. They were, therefore, impelled to wash off this shameful blot from the face of their social life as soon as possible."[161] Where Western models had clearly failed to uphold modesty—this value intrinsic to humanity—Mawdūdi's notion of "social system in Islam"[162] would succeed.

The family, from Mawdūdi's standpoint, upheld men's superiority over women. In addition to Qur'ānic support (4:34 reads, "Men are the maintainers of women"), basic sociology, he says, dictates this: "For the smooth running of the household affairs, one of the partners has, in any case, to be the manager or the executive head."[163] The one who "is naturally fit for the job" is man. Such a position in the family gave men specific duties to uphold in the family: (1) Dowry is "the price of the marital rights he has on [his wife]."[164] The role of family manager is by all rights the man's but the dowry solidifies his ability to assume that position of power. (2) Since his wife's job is to stay at home, the husband shoulders the living expenses for his family.[165] (3) A husband was not to be cruel to his wife, even though he was fundamentally superior.[166] However, Mawdūdi advocated a "stiff" approach to disobedient wives: men were to address any disobedience first with guidance, then, if needed more severe intervention, which could escalate to a "light beating, so that she sees reason to obey him."[167] Mawdūdi was also supportive of polygamy if it was a means to morality. He wrote, "the most important objective of the Islamic marital law is the preservation of morals and chastity. If a man is disgusted with one wife, he can marry another one, and thus save himself from evil ways and evil glances."[168] In his commentary on the Qur'ānic passage relating to multiple wives,[169] Mawdūdi rebutted those who thought Islam "confined itself to placing restrictions" on polygamy because the practice was so rampant that abolishing it altogether was impractical: "Such arguments only show the mental slavery to which these people have succumbed," Mawdūdi thought.[170]

The family provides a man with responsibilities and authority. The husband has to be the chief administrator of the household in the same way that "a school has a head master"—he is there to keep the family "disciplined." The head of the family has a duty to do all the work outside the household. The wife has been freed from doing anything outside the home, as Islam does not want to "tax them doubly" by looking after the home and any outside work. Mawdūdi then goes on to say that this does not mean that women are not allowed to leave the house but should do so only when "necessary"—the law, he thought, had specified that the home is her "special field of work."[171] Mawdūdi believed that a man taking the superior role in society (and home) was a privilege for any woman and that this was something to be appreciated and cherished, as opposed to the competition he saw between women and men in the West. However, what is questionable is the extent to which this privilege of separate, hierarchical roles is in reality thrust upon both genders. It is through his opposition to the independent Muslim women that Mawdūdi empowers the domination of an idealized Islamic masculinity. Whereas "hundreds of thousands of young women in ever Western country like to live unmarried lives, which they are bound to pass in immoral, promiscuous and sinful ways,"[172] a fully Islamic society frees both genders from the immorality that comes of "the free intermingling of the sexes."[173]

Although Mawdūdi writes in ways that have circumscribed female roles—and received due feminist attention as a result—his rhetoric constructs (even depends on) a somewhat stable and predetermined kind of masculinity, too. Consider this passage, where deficiencies distinguish the roles of men and women:

> This explains why she has been endowed with tender feelings of love, sympathy, compassion, clemency, pity and sensitiveness in an unusual measure. And since in the sexual life man has been made active and woman passive, she has been endowed with those very qualities alone which help and prepare her for the passive role in life only. That is why she is tender and plastic instead of rough and rigid. That is why she is soft and pliable, submissive and impressionable, yielding and timid by nature. With these qualities she cannot be expected to function successfully in the spheres of life which demand firmness and authority, resistance and cold-temperedness and which require the exercise of unbiased, objective judgment and strong will power. To drag woman into these fields of activity, therefore, is to abuse her as well as the fields of activity themselves.[174]

This brand of Islamic masculinity was stronger in all senses than the weaker women, and Mawdūdi dismissed equal engagement of men and women in all activities, including intellectual ones:

> The modern man wants the poor woman to compete with him in those fields where she is weaker by nature. This will inevitably keep the woman suppressed and generally inferior to man. Try however hard he may, it is impossible that geniuses favourably comparable to Aristotle, Ibn-i-Sina, Kant, Hegel, Khayyam, Shakespeare, Alexander, Napoleon, Salah-ud-Din, Nizam-ul-Mulk, Tusi and Bismarck will ever come forth from among women. Similarly, all men of the world together—however hard they try—cannot produce from among their sex even a most ordinary mother.[175]

He considered that competition, which he felt was the reason why women and men would always be unsuccessful when outside their gendered domains. In this way Mawdūdi reserved all leadership roles for men, "good generals, good statesmen, and good administrators are as necessary as good mothers, good wives and good housekeepers. To ignore or discard any of these aspects is tantamount to harming and corrupting man's social life itself."[176] Since men had to be stronger than women, men were expected to take part in the physical Jihād found in his commentary on Qur'ān 4:97.[177]

Leveraging God, precedents, and cultural enemies

Mawdūdi's vision of Islam was based on the political Islamist impulse to return back to an "Islamic" utopia. His sentiments emerged in a region where British rule was coming to an end and an emergence of a country to be known as Pakistan for Indian Muslims. Mawdūdi feared that the power of the West would continue through the leadership of Muḥammad Ali Jinnah and Muḥammad Iqbal, whom he accused of being un-Islamic. In reaction to their brand of liberal democracy, Mawdūdi established the Jammāt Islami party, which he believed would be the bastion of Islam in Pakistan. In order to strengthen the party's position, Mawdūdi wrote a commentary of the Qur'ān and numerous other publications highlighting what he saw as the true Islamic position on matters.

For those Muslims who followed the teachings of Mawdūdi, the path was clear, but those who were not comfortable with his clear-cut definitions of gender and sex had the choice of either being forced to consider themselves "outside" the realms of Islam and lead a life through the liberty of the west (Jinnah's approach could be categorized as such) or attempting a mixture of the two poles that almost often emerged as a crisis of identity in the individual (Iqbal could be considered as an example of this). The danger of not appreciating Jinnah and Iqbal's historical overlap and intertwinement with the Jammāt Islami movement is that Mawdūdi could otherwise be seen as representative of a broad place and time. He is indeed archetypal for a certain kind of Islamism born out of cultural frustration; his plan for Islam responds to serious, important anxieties that perdure to this day.

Mawdūdi believed that God should control all aspects of a believer's life. He outlined strict conformance to a narrow interpretation to Islamic law as the only way to be an obedient Muslim. In this way Mawdūdi made effective use of God throughout his career as a way of promoting his message—to argue against him was arguing against God, something that is not uncommon within right-wing religious rhetoric. The basis of most arguments in the case of Mawdūdi, and also common among other political Islamist movements, was a hatred of the West. It is evident from all of his publications that his arguments were most often led by stating the most negative examples of Western society and then presenting his Islamic understanding that inevitably strengthened the dichotomy of Islam versus the West. As stated by Mawdūdi,

> The biggest impediment in this regard is that the modern man has developed the disease of taking a jaundiced view of things. Especially the westernised people of the east have been attacked by a more dangerous form of this disease which I would call the 'white jaundice'.[178]

Mawdūdi's image of Islamic masculinities must be included within any consideration of the topic. One wonders whether his opposition to being "submissive" to a "dominant" West drove Mawdūdi to his brand of Islamism. Perhaps the outright political element in his Islamic thought re-mapped the power of obedience and submissiveness from the human relationship with God onto a cultural battle between the East and the West.

Mawdūdi argued that social relationships were tantamount to the creation of an Islamic society, and the institution of marriage was at the core of this. He used extreme Western examples of pornography, divorce, venereal diseases, and single men and women as a way of advocating that institution of marriage was divine. Through his insistence on family and marriage, he outlined specific roles and duties that both men and women had to carry out. Mawdūdi preached that men were superior to women and should take on the duty of leading and feeding the family. Women were expected to remain within their homes as their biological deficiencies proved that they were lesser than men. This was again a result of a comparison with Western social norms, where there are relatively few prohibitions against men and women taking on the same roles and duties. This does not equate to liberation, according to Mawdūdi, for "whatever rights the woman has been granted in the west have been granted not for her own sake but as if she was a man. The woman is still inferior in the western eyes as she was in the past ages of ignorance. In the west a real genuine woman has yet to have respect as the queen of a home, the wife of a husband, the matron of children."[179] Islam gives women—and men—the fulfillment that comes through responsibilities and limitations.

In developing and asserting this strong nexus of gender, the family, and Islamic society, Mawdūdi borrowed authority from the scriptures he exegeted, the history he interpreted, and the traditions he explicated. He used the prophet Muḥammad's example as a way of exemplifying his notions of masculinity and femininity: "The prophet of Islam was not only the ideal Muslim or hallowed subject of religious devotion, but the first and foremost Muslim political leader and, hence, a source of emulation in political matters."[180] Apparently, the Prophet's gender was not incidental, since Mawdūdi also opposed female leadership in an Islamic state and believed that such an instatement was the reason why civilizations collapse:

> Some nations have given woman the position of governor over man. But no instance is found of a nation that raised its womanhood to such a status and then attained any high position on the ladder of progress and civilization. History does not present the record of any nation which made the woman the ruler of its affairs, and won honor and glory, or performed a work of distinction.[181]

The ferocity with which Benazir Bhutto, the first Muslim prime minister of an Islamic nation, fought against the religious leaders for her political power in Pakistan was necessary in part because of Mawdūdi's opinion on female leadership.

Mawdūdi's thought supported the gender stereotype of women as coy and fragile and man as macho and strong. It was then Mawdūdi's belief that a truly "Islamic" piety for men was in their being superior and dominant to the truly "Islamic" piety of women, which was in submission to men and God. This is exemplified in his view that the physical Jihād was obligatory for men. There remain serious implications of Mawdūdi's political Islamist thought on such a construction of Islamic masculinity among diaspora communities in the west from a Pakistani background. Although beyond the scope of this thesis,[182] the concoction of an Islam-versus-West divide and upholding of a hegemonic Islamic masculinity in political Islamist thought has the potential of engineering catastrophic events. Some may argue that such events have already taken place, especially when we consider the bombing of the twin towers in New York and the London bombings a few years later.

Mawdūdi spoke and wrote much about the place of women and about the ideal Muslim. It may seem as though his thoughts on masculinity were underdeveloped, but he indirectly puts together a rather clear paragon of Muslim men. His roundabout construction of Islamic masculinity happens in his skillful deployment of God talk, his freighted exegetical exercises, his castigation of Western ways, and his circumscription of femininity. These all act as foils in a sense—they are the things Mawdūdi talks about when he talks about masculinity. To get at the epitome of a Mawdūdi man, we have to read against the grain to see, for instance, that the restrictions he prescribes for women leave a lacuna for men to fill. We have to see that he positions gender roles as a foundation for strong families, which in turn are crucial for a robust Islamic society, which means that humanity is in its right relationship to God. But the inverse progression may be the more pertinent to our line of questioning: Mawdūdi speaks on behalf of God in order to influence humans to create a society worthy of his brand of Islam, which is manufactured through the "small workshop" of the family and dependent entirely on the acceptance of discrete gender roles. Does Mawdūdi's Islam mould gender to fit God's plan, or does it position God to radically restrict gender expression? The rest of this book investigates Muslim men who do not fit Mawdūdi's mould. Their examples predate and outlive Mawdūdi, but no one, since Mawdūdi, can challenge the bounds of Islamic masculinity without contending with gestalt he created from pronouncements about textual precedents, women, and God himself.

- presents mostly Mawdudi's view vs Islamist
- Also middleground + far left (western)
- No secularism, family as core, west as opposite + enemy + bad example

2

Feminists' Nonothering Hermeneutics

If men could see us as we really are, they would be a little amazed; but the cleverest, the acutest men are often under an illusion about women: they do not read them in a true light: they misapprehend them, both for good and evil: their good woman is a queer thing, half doll, half angel; their bad woman almost always a fiend.[1]

Charlotte Brontë, *Shirley*

Muslim women have been a hot topic of late. There are many reasons for this, but largely the interest is linked to the widespread understanding that they are uniquely oppressed. Though attracting somewhat less media attention, certainly in the United States, Muslim feminist scholars have been responding to the structures of Mawdūdi-style Islamism for some time. Completely decentered and marginalized by his social program, feminist Islamicists—as opposed to the *Islamists* in Mawdūdi's camp—challenge the textual and historical grounds of his thinking. They reconfigure the constellation of man, God, woman, and cultural embattledness in ways that depend less on othering and more on recognition of what makes all Muslims Muslim. In doing so, Muslim feminists present an image of femininity that is interconnected with Islamic masculinity because patriarchy and misogyny are exactly what they feel charged to address. If they are undoing Mawdūdi's position that gender is constructed through a series of interactions with the gendered other, then a feminist analysis reckons Islamic masculinity as much as femininity. In fact, Mawdūdi's rhetoric intertwines dichotomies so well that dismantling any element threatens to undermine other aspects of theology and society.

The Muslim women feminists whose work appears in this chapter have to tread carefully in order to demonstrate that they can be both pro-family and in support of women's agency, both critical of masculinity and submissive to God. The exact moment when Muslim feminism began to be identified as such is a difficult one, especially given that the term *feminism* has its own history linked with the West. However, this chapter focuses on the ideas and constructions of Islamic feminism that emerge around the late nineteenth century. The writers and thinkers of Islamic feminism in this chapter vary in terms of the regions of the world they call their own, but there has been a special attempt to include those Muslim women with links, in some way or another, to India and Pakistan. This will allow a much broader comparison and context for locating their ideas and critiques of Islamic masculinity.

Globally recognized feminist Muslim scholar Amina Wadud[2] states, "to disagree with the idea that men are superior can be projected as anti-Islam! This is why theological theories behind gender reform also need elaboration."[3] The contours of the feminist challenge to the "theological theory" of Islamic masculinity are at the center of this chapter. There seems to be a debate among feminist writers about identifying as "Muslim feminist"—as Wadud clarified, "that is why I still describe my position as pro-faith, pro-feminist. Despite how others may categorize me, my work is certainly feminist, but I still refuse to self-designate as feminist, even with 'Muslim' put in front of it, because my emphasis on faith and the sacred prioritize my motivation in feminist methodologies."[4] Pro-feminist Muslim scholars such as Wadud link their work directly with faith, which they believe is essential in distinguishing them from those who may have an anti-faith or anti-Islam agenda when dealing with the position of women in Islam. It may also be the case that such a self-identification is for the purposes of locating the debate within Muslim communities to prompt change. Muslim women feminists—a designation I am using to include pro-feminists—have constructed and challenged mainstream masculinity in Islamic societies and traditions, although to an extent the definition of feminism seems to vary from scholar to scholar.[5] What are the aims of Islamic feminism? Is Muslim feminism a movement towards "equality" with men? Or is it simply expressing a female voice? How do these voices deal with the question of Islamic masculinity and masculinities?

Muslim feminists have been mounting a challenge to patriarchy through two key methods. First, they reflect on their own experiences and offer a critical engagement with their distinct individual circumstances. Secondly, they grapple with religious texts, especially the Qur'ān, to understand the traditions that have become Islamic society and culture. These two methods will be explored in this chapter. As far as possible the voices of those Muslim feminists connected to India and Pakistan have been used, but as the focus of this chapter is twofold, it has been necessary to include the voices of those Muslim feminists who are not connected with the geographical region but are essential in the discourse. It must also be stated at the outset that the Muslim feminist writers on which this chapter focuses do not present their argument on feminism by using specific Pakistani and Indian examples—such a narrative might be found in sociological and anthropological works—but use the term *Muslim women* in its more generalized and global form.

It is important to highlight that Muslim feminist debates are largely limited to forms of Islamic masculinity that are heterosexual. Furthermore, the Muslim feminists who have been highlighted throughout this chapter, all assume a heterosexual context for their critiques. The main reason for this is because it is from the heterosexual Islamic models that Muslim women have suffered the most. However, other forms of Islamic masculinity (e.g. homosexual) or Muslim femininity (e.g. lesbian) linked to sexual preference which are virtually absent from the Muslim feminist debate are also marginalized communities who are battling against the heteronormative mainstream in Islamic societies and traditions. The term *Muslim feminist* used throughout this chapter will deal specifically with *female* Muslim feminists, although men can of course also be understood as feminists too.[6]

Patriarchy[7] is generally understood as a system in which men hold the power, whether in society, politics, family structures, or other contexts. The patriarch construct that most Muslim feminists are interrogating is specifically a heterosexual, virile, brave, and powerful man. Asma Barlas, one of the foremost Muslim feminist commentators on the Qur'ān,[8] primarily queries patriarchy on the assumption that

> God is understood as "father/male" or that the Qur'ān teaches that God has a special relationship with males or that males embody divine attributes and that women are by nature weak, unclean, or sinful. Further, does it teach that

> rule by the father/husband is divinely ordained and an earthly continuation of God's rule, as religious and traditional patriarchies claim? Alternatively, does the Qur'ān advocate gender differentiation, dualisms, or inequality on the basis of sexual (biological) differences between women and men?[9]

Barlas has argued that some Qur'ānic passages have been read in isolation from other parts of scripture and this can be corrected by "recognizing the Qur'ān's textual and thematic holism, and thus the hermeneutic connections between seemingly disparate themes, is absolutely integral to recovering its antipatriarchal epistemology."[10]

As Muslim feminists seek various ways to end patriarchy, they turn to some of the turf on which Mawdūdi waged his social war: scriptures. Admittedly, "a Qur'ānic hermeneutic cannot by itself put an end to patriarchal, authoritarian, and undemocratic regimes and practices," but, Barlas avers, "there is a relationship between what we read texts to be saying and how we think about and treat real women."[11] This relationship between patriarchy, text, and society is seen most fervently upheld in the family. But interpretations, even feminist ones, that equate the heterosexual family to patriarchy will only ever be able to see Islam as also patriarchal, according to Barlas, who wants to trouble essentialism in all its forms.[12]

An early pioneer of second-wave US feminism, Betty Friedan argued in her famous 1963 book *The Feminine Mystique* that stereotypical gender roles within the family and outside it could not be used to identify "women."[13] But gender roles do emerge from a system of relationships, and the family has been identified as a key location for patriarchy in Islamic societies and traditions. The prophet Muḥammad's many wives and large family are used as impetus to advocate the "divine" nature of family—certain kinds of family, at any rate. Muslim feminists have not used these examples to call for the dismissal of the kinship unit; they have argued that the family can be whatever its members want it to be. Problematically, the family structure in Islamic societies becomes one of the key structures supporting patriarchy because it positions the father and husband as "God's surrogate on earth" and the "woman/wife as (his) property/child."[14] The family, with its patriarchal head, is then an issue that Muslim feminist raise yet believe is difficult to challenge: "No Muslim culture that I have ever visited or read about constructs their families around the notions of equality. Neither do non-Muslim cultures either, despite various small experiments."[15]

Amina Wadud argues that even the most progressive Muslim men are comfortable in their situation. The male reformers she alludes to do not envision domestic situations changing; they are "at best liberal" when it comes to their own family structures.[16] Beyond the fact that this keeps women's status low, Wadud also grieves that progressive reformists undermine their own movements when they do not turn their critical lenses onto everyday relationships and kinship norms. Not wanting to upset a convenient *status quo* is a characteristic hardly unique to Islamic reformers, but as Moroccan sociologist Fatema Mernissi explains, it renders them unable to counter radical, Mawdūdi-style Islamism: "The secret of Islam's sweeping resurgence today is that it gives men at birth an inherited right to claim world hegemony as a horizon and a guiding dream."[17]

But what do Muslim feminists—and they are not a monolithic bunch—want? To date there has not been a dramatic movement to remove all distinctions between Islamic masculinity and femininity because, as Barlas has stated, "treating women and men identically does not always mean treating them equally."[18] To what extent, if any is the notion of "separate but equal" an Islamic concept? Furthermore, we know that Mawdūdi wanted theological to fuse with politics, but how do Muslim feminists understand the difference between, or the overlap of social constructions of gender equality and theological constructs?

A self-reflexive exegetical foundation

A heightened appreciation of lived reality sets Muslim feminist approaches even further afield from the precedent-based Islamist approach: gender does not conform to ideals; it is an *ad hoc* phenomenon. Legal anthropologist Ziba Mir-Hosseini is one who takes this view:

> My own initial premise is that gender roles and relations, and women's rights, are not fixed, not given, not absolute. They are negotiated on changing cultural constructs, produced in response to lived realities, through debates that are now going on all over the Muslim world, through the voices of women and men who want either to retain or to change the present situation.[19]

Muslim feminists' personalized scholarship is meant to be valued as a kind of hermeneutic for understanding and shaping Islamic tradition. The South

African Muslim feminist Sad'iyyah Shaikh writes that "lived experiences constitute a mode of *tafsīrs*"—the Arabic word for interpretation.[20] Such an exegetical mode could be an extension of the legal method of Ijtihād. As Wadud states, the discourse must be moved to a place inhabited by women's experiences:

> When women's stories are brought into the centre, they do not recast the centre story. There is no substantive change, since the marginality in which women live is still unreformed. This position of women's lives *in the margins* must be redeemed from where they continue to experience it. No mere performances in the centre will reconstruct status as legitimate for female agency. Instead, the whole of the community must enter the margins with women to affirm the place where women's lives are experienced.[21]

Given the history and power of this heuristic method, then, a bit of familiarity with the backgrounds of some of the most prominent Muslim feminists sets the stage for our understanding of their agenda and strategies.

Theologian Riffat Hassan was born in Lahore, Pakistan, in 1943 into an upper-class family: she says, "my father and mother came from among the oldest and most distinguished families in the city and were both 'good' parents in that they took care to provide us with a high quality of life."[22] Hassan recalls a difficult relationship with her mother and father and comments on the difficulty being torn between a mother who always expected too much from her—who told her, "I do not love you, I love your qualities"—to a father whose "traditionalism" she "hated" because he believed that girls should be married at sixteen years of age.[23] The distance grew between Hassan and her father, whom Hassan could not see as the honest and kind man that he was in society.[24] Her father wanted her to enroll in an all-girls school, something she resisted but her mother received the brunt of her father's wrath. He accused Hassan's mother of "spoiling and misguiding" the young girl.[25] Hassan enjoyed writing poetry at an early age and found it a way to escape from the world that confounded her:

> This humble work of mine do bless my God,
> My fervent message to the world proclaim,
>
> I do not covet wealth or power or fame,
> I just want satisfaction for reward.

> I felt it was Your Will that I should write
> Of Beauty, Love and Joy, Eternal Peace,
>
> Of Sorrow, Struggle that a Death does cease,
> Of Hope, its sweet illuminating light.[26]

As she grew older, Hassan became considerably worried about her imminent arranged marriage; in order to avoid it, she moved to Durham, UK, to study. It was there that she spent 7 years, first completing a degree in English and philosophy and then a Ph.D. which focused on the work of Iqbal in 1968, who we will recall was the national poet-philosopher of Pakistan.[27] After returning to Pakistan, Hassan married a man named Dawar, who "seemed to need me intensely."[28] There may have been an intellectual gap between Hassan and her husband, who was not as highly educated as she. Needless to say, this marriage did not last:

> Dawar was a typical product—victim—of the patriarchal society and had a compelling need to be "head" of the family. He found it impossible to fulfil this need being married to a woman who was a super achiever, while he regarded himself as a loser. He was attracted by my strength but resented it at the same time.[29]

Hassan was left with a daughter named Mona. She did embark on a second marriage with Mahmoud, an Egyptian Arab Muslim who was more than 30 years older than her, but the happiness and love that he promised was also short lived:

> I came near to total destruction, physically and mentally, at the hands of a man who was not only a male chauvinist par excellence but also a fanatic who could invoke the holy name of God in perpetrating acts of incredible cruelty and callousness upon other human beings.[30]

When she wrote these accounts, Hassan's experience of men was not a pleasant one. The three men that she recalled, her father and her two husbands, all present a form of Muslim masculinity that can easily be identified in Islamic traditions, societies, and cultures, especially India and Pakistan. These men pushed her to conform to the roles which they understood to be becoming of women, yet she challenged all three of them and has sought alternatives in her life and formal work.

Asra Nomani is another Muslim feminist whose life experience highlights the way in which Islamic traditions and gender understandings are not easily challenged. Nomani is an Indian-American feminist journalist who has written two books.[31] Her struggle, similar to Hassan's, came in the form of strict family values:

> Over the years my mother had warned me: "if you marry an American, your father will have a heart attack." Muslim guilt set in. Within weeks I left an American Lutheran boyfriend who loved me fully, said he was willing to convert to Islam, and was ready to learn Urdu. I got engaged, sold the condo I had bought off Chicago's Lake Shore Drive, and moved to Washington to prepare for a wedding in Islamabad, Pakistan. The deeper voices of my religion were speaking to me: the ban on Muslim women marrying non-Muslim men, the disapproval toward sex before marriage. I was looking for a reunion between my two selves.[32]

Honor can be used to police the way in which Muslim women are expected to uphold the ideals of Islamic masculinity. Nomani's mother used family honor to dissuade Nomani from her path of love in order to support her own husband, and Nomani's father, something of an archetypal patriarchal man. Nomani's statement that the deeper voices detracting her from her path were of "religion" highlights the way in which gender and sex also become matters of religious rights and wrongs.

Nomani's arranged marriage did not last, but by honoring her parent's wish she strengthened her father's role by agreeing and in turn failed to reach that sacred union that she set out to achieve. Nomani once again embarked on finding that perfect man, and it was in Pakistan on a working visit that she felt she found him. But this relationship also imploded. The man with whom she fell in love had made her pregnant but left her as soon as he found out about the child:

> Throughout my pregnancy I tried to make peace with my boyfriend so that we could marry and make the nuclear family that so many people in my religion and culture expected. But my baby's father broke promise after promise, leaving me empty and depressed.[33]

Nomani tried to live up to the expectations of being a wife and a mother while desperately seeking that perfect husband and father. She believed that a fully

Islamic woman would be incomplete without the man. Patriarchy provides a deep tension in Nomani's world, and a trip to Mecca with her parents, son, niece, and nephew identified its significance in Islamic societies. When her father was at one point absent, her nephew wanted to go to Kentucky Fried Chicken, but with strict Saudi laws forbidding women from traveling alone without male chaperones, this was looking like a difficult task:

> In the Mecca Sheraton, my mother wasn't about to let her grandson stay hungry. She gathered up her resources and pulled her hijāb over her head. "Okay, let's go," she said. As they crossed the street in their stealthily KFC run, Samir looked both ways for any religious police ready to swoop down on them. He urged my mother to move more quickly. "Hurry, Dādī! (Gran) You might get arrested!" In front of the counter at KFC, Samir felt scared. "Are people going to say, 'You can't come here'"? They ordered carryout.[34]

Strict Islamic societies have made it difficult for women even to buy food from shops on their own, forcing them to have men around them at all times. Initially, fathers or brothers take this role, but ultimately women are expected to have husbands "chaperoning" them.

Islamic societies tend not to have a high degree of egalitarianism, and the indoctrination begins when individuals are very young:

> Male dominant civilization discriminates between male and female children. The male child is taught from the very beginning how to project his personality and how to prepare for a man's life involving strength, responsibility, authority and a positive attitude in the face of difficulties. A girl, on the other hand, is trained and educated right from the start to shrink into a corner, to withdraw and to hide her real self because she is a female and is being prepared for the life of a woman, a life where she must be passive and weak, and must surrender to the domination of the man and be dependent on him.[35]

A former prime minister's daughter, Pakistani stateswoman Benazir Bhutto found herself wrestling with the very same predicament: Figure 2.1

> It was in America, over milk and cookies at night in my dormitory, that we would discuss how we wanted more out of life than the traditional roles of wife and mother. We believed that women should have the right to choose whether they want to live life as homemakers or seek careers.[36]

Figure 2.1 Pakistan's slain prime minister recites the Qur'ān at the grave of her father, Zulfikar Bhutto in 1998

During Bhutto's childhood especially, many Pakistani Muslim women were conditioned to accept their role as homemakers, while careers were left for men to pursue. In seeking a way out of the home, she aspired to the example of her father. As a Pakistani man, he had adopted roles inside and outside of the family home, and Bhutto firmly believed that her path was not in contradiction to Islam:

> And when the time came to pick up my father's mantle and legacy and lead the Pakistan Peoples Party, I, as his eldest *child* present in Pakistan, led the struggle for democracy. No one among my father's followers opposed this on the ground of gender. This was the gender equality in Islam under which I was brought up. It is the gender equality that has been passed on to my son and two daughters. And I know it to be the gender equality that is specifically provided for and endorsed by Islam.[37]

However, it must be acknowledged that Bhutto's experience was far from the accepted norm in Pakistani society, a reality she acknowledged:

> In our male-dominated culture, boys had always been favored over girls and were not only more often given an education, but in extreme instances were given food first while the mother and daughters waited. In our family, however, there was no discrimination at all. If anything, I received the most attention.[38]

Bhutto's experience raises the question of whether a successful Pakistani Muslim woman is expected to remodel her femininity and female roles into "masculine" ones.

Positions of leadership may only increase the pressure to conform, but they also come with the responsibility to challenge monolithic gender norms. In Wadud's words,

> The voice of a woman must also include something about herself, particularly as a woman, and this must then be incorporated into what it means to be human in the world. If she only offers herself in the public role like a man, what is the advantage? A single model of normative Islamic leadership persists, whether in male or female form. This single model of what it means to be human has consequences within ambiguities of the lives of Muslims today. When the boundaries of identity are no longer so clear, we can benefit from new stories and new centres of attention actually located in the margins.[39]

The normative Islamic leadership to which Wadud is alluding could be defined, in the case of Bhutto, as that of her father's "iron mantle." And so even though it was a breakthrough for a Muslim woman to occupy the highest office in a Muslim state, she negotiated her position into that seat by locating herself within the sphere of Pakistani men. To assert that to be female is not a disadvantage in leadership Wadud appeals to the Qur'ānic example of the Queen of Sheba, Bilqis:

> The Qur'ān shows that her judgment was better than the norm, and that she independently demonstrated that better judgment. If her politics were feminine, then her faith was feminine, which, by implication would indicate that masculinity is a disadvantage. Her faith and her politics may be specific to females, but they both were better.[40]

Wadud's piercing attack is directed at a particular form of masculinity that disallows women into the sphere of politics but is clearly contested in the Qur'ān through the story of the Queen of Sheba.

The few biographies presented here highlight the difficulty in defining and understanding the parameters of Islamic feminism; every life brings with it an alternative story with its own battles. However, what does emerge definitively is that each Muslim feminist's voice expresses opposition to the prevalent, generalized Islamic masculinity that is oppressive and dominant. Muslim feminists seek to challenge this understanding in the first instance but most of all want to see this challenge materialize into change.

From Hassan's perspective, lived experiences produce a sense of conviction and even obligation to act:

> The more I saw the justice and compassion of God reflected in the Qur'anic teachings regarding women, the more anguished and angry I became, seeing the injustice and inhumanity to which Muslim women, in general, are subjected in actual life. I began to feel strongly that it was my duty—as part of the microscopic minority of educated Muslim women—to do as much consciousness-raising regarding the situation of Muslim women as I could.[41]

If patriarchy is embedded in men as they grow up and is strengthened through the gender roles in Muslim families, it also involves patriarchal readings of the Qur'ān—something Mawdūdi's approach took to an extreme. Muslim feminists are rereading the Qur'ān from their perspectives in order to challenge Islamic masculinity because they believe that the Qur'ān as a text can be read in a variety of different ways and it is from within the Qur'ānic world that such readings gain legitimacy and hope for a more egalitarian reading and practice in Islamic traditions, societies, and cultures.

Hermeneutics without hegemony

Barlas begins the interpretive process by re-asking fundamental questions before making generalized assumptions about the Qur'ān's contents, especially its supposed misogyny:

> Does Islam's scripture, the Qur'ān, teach or condone sexual inequality or oppression? Is it, as critics allege, a patriarchal and even sexist and misogynistic text? Intimately related to that question is the second: Does the Qur'ān permit and encourage liberation for women?[42]

The broad strokes are clear: beyond the prescribed and somewhat authoritative roles of father, husband, son, and the like, Islamic masculinity has been strengthened by the notion that God is male and addressed as "He" in the Qur'ān. All the prophets mentioned in the Qur'ān are also men, a fact which men have used to cement their position over women.

Muslim feminists are also aware of the problematic nature of reading the Qur'ān with a philosophical or rational method, and in this they can plot themselves as continuing a long tradition of prioritizing "unmediated religious experiences and intuition." This was the position of eleventh-century theologian Abū Ḥāmid Muḥammad ibn Muḥammad al-Ghazālī, whose influence on Islam then and since is difficult to overstate.[43] Feminists like Barlas are careful to place themselves *within* Islamic traditions, not outside the religion.[44] Barlas's book *Believing Women in Islam: Unreading Patriarchal Interpretations of the Qur'ān* aims to reread the text and without undermining her convicted faith. She thus attributes the patriarchal elements of Qur'ānic discourse to the culture surrounding its reception:

> The central question I have posed... whether or not the Qur'ān is a patriarchal text, is perhaps not a meaningful one from the Qur'ān's perspective since its teachings are not framed in terms of the claims made by either traditional or modern patriarchies. However, since the Qur'ān was revealed in/to an existing patriarchy and has been interpreted by adherents of patriarchies ever since, Muslim women have a stake in challenging its patriarchal exegesis.[45]

That search for an alternative reading is crucial because accepting "misreadings of Islam not only makes one complicit in the continued abuse of Islam and the abuse of women in the name of Islam, but it also means losing the battle over meaning without even fighting it."[46] It would be safe to assume that the misreading group to which Barlas alludes is most likely men since it has been the business of men in past and present to comment on the Qur'ān.[47] Barlas understands that preconceived ideas stunt interpretive diversity because, whether they mean to or not, readers only read as deeply as they need to in order to find support for the ideas they already hold: "the perspective of the individual exegete is superimposed on to the Qur'ān itself."[48]

One method for neutralizing misogynist preconceptions is Muslim feminists' process of ungendering Islamic obligations and undoing the assumption that general commands are aimed only at men. Bhutto modeled this approach when she argued,

> Throughout the Holy Qur'ān, there is example after example of respect for women as leaders and acknowledgement of women as equals. Again, the first word of the Holy Book is "Read." It does not say, "Men Read"; it says, "Read." It is a command to all believers, not just to men. For in the religion of Islam in which I was brought up, there is only equality.[49]

Barlas hopes that an ungendering method like Bhutto's will help women establish their right to read the text through their own eyes, "I also read to uncover what I believe already is there in the Qur'ān; that is, I hold that certain meanings are intrinsic to the text such that anyone can retrieve them if they employ the right method and ask the right questions."[50]

In large part, Muslim feminists are battling a form of Islamic masculinity that they feel has denied them the appropriate recognition of their status. As we have seen, many Muslim feminists speak out against the men who oppress them, and they write about those experiences.[51] In this complementary tactic of approaching the Qur'ān, Muslim women challenge male-centric interpretation of Islamic traditions, which Barlas says have effectively been sacralized. For Barlas the critique of the Qur'ān cannot be equated to the Qur'ān itself,

> In the end, of course, a reading of the Qur'ān is just a reading of the Qur'ān, no matter how good; it does not approximate the Qur'ān itself, which may be why the Qur'ān distinguishes between itself and its exegesis. Thus, it

condemns those "who write The Book with their own hands, And then say: 'This is from God'" (Qur'ān 2:79)[52]

Elevating "male-authored exegesis" to essentially scriptural status threatens to undermine the authority of the Qur'ān as uniquely divine revelation, "thus violating the cardinal tenets of God's absolute Sovereignty, or *Tawḥīd*."[53]

These are serious allegations stemming from serious questions which are leveled with the recognition that interpreters always bring their own experiences to their readings.[54] Barlas reminds us that "even the single phrase *bismillāh ar-raḥmān ar-raḥīm* that occurs at the beginning of every Sura except one has been rendered in six different ways by exegetes."[55] However, Muslim feminists also argue that their rereading is not something new. This is especially the case with Barlas, whose "work remains traditional in its view of the Qur'ān as an egalitarian text, a view I share with some Muslim exegetes of the classical period and certainly with many Muslims today."[56]

Following from the fundamentally egalitarian precept that is so well evidenced in Islamic history, we find the conviction that a variety of interpretations is the means to promote the Qur'ān's core message. Wadud raises a rhetorical question in support of this stance: "Whose perspective and definition are we to apply if we are to determine if these teachings are ethical and egalitarian—those of the Qur'ān itself or of (Muslim and Western) patriarchies, feminists, or some combination?"[57] Muslim feminists use their interpretative skills to bring forward a renewed legitimacy because "more female-inclusive interpretations raise legitimacy of women's claims to authority within the intellectual tradition and bear upon the practical implementation of that tradition."[58]

Barlas argues that opposing the normative patriarchal readings of the Qur'ān requires men and women to be diverse in their questions[59] yet not seek a "dual-gendered" text with both male and female voices in it.[60] She seeks a rereading of the Qur'ān that will bridge the moral and the social realm, since that divide is so often used to justify gender oppression: "They concede that the Qur'ān treats women and men similarly, hence equally, in the moral realm (conceived as the realm of worship, or *Ibadah*), but they argue that the Qur'ān treats women and men differently, hence unequally, in the social realms by giving them different kinds of rights in marriage, divorce and so on."[61]

Hassan's approach rests on the idea that there are three theological assumptions on which the inequality of men and women is erected in Islam—and these three bases also indicate the way in which Hassan defines Islamic masculinity for her purposes. First she argues that man, not woman, is supposedly God's primary creation since women are believed to have been created from Adam's rib. This has led to men's understanding that they are closer to God or even loved more by God. Secondly, she identifies the conception that the woman and not man was the primary agent of the "fall" of Adam and expulsion from heaven to earth, which makes her a figure to be despised. Such an assumption could be understood to mean that men are not capable of making mistakes and that it was the woman—here generalized to all women—who brought man down from a heavenly abode. Thirdly, it is commonly understood that woman was not only created *from* man but *for* him, which makes her merely instrumental and not important in a fundamental sense.[62] This is probably the most dangerous of the three notions because it reduces women to mere objects whose purpose is to glorify the position of the Muslim man. This could also fuel an understanding that women are to be used by men "for" the purposes of sex and procreation.

The creation story has played a disproportionate part in the way gender is practised and understood in Islamic tradition and society, which makes it a both interesting and important vantage point from which to examine Muslim feminists hermeneutics. In what way do Muslim feminists understand creation to challenge dominant, oppressive forms of Islamic masculinity? These scholars do not begin the debate from the basis that men and women are created the same, because that idea is so slippery, says Wadud: "Sameness is extremely illusive and difficult to achieve. Sameness cannot be sustained with regard to any two people for more than an instant in the course of a single day—let alone in the course of a whole lifetime."[63] Barlas also critiques the pursuit of "sameness," which she says is understandably a first step in feminist thought and women's movements but not ultimately helpful when trying to eradicate patriarchy:

> It is not only the notion of *sexual difference* (the two-sex model) that is phallocentric, but also of sexual *sameness* (the one-sex model), in that both view man as a Subject and woman as the Other. And elements of both persist in modern patriarchal discourses in which woman is re-presented not only as the opposite of man but also as a "lesser man."[64]

Both Wadud and Barlas may disdain women being "compared" and "contrasted" with men, but they still hold that men and women have certain differences. Those differences intrinsically link them; they were created by the same divine force and sexually differentiated in order to, as Barlas writes, "create closeness, not opposition, between them."[65]

Similarly, Wadud considers men and women "two categories of the human species given the same or equal consideration and endowed with the same or equal potential."[66] However, Wadud also highlights the idea of necessary pairs:

> I am interested in the Qur'ānic use of *zawj* as one in a necessary or contingent "pair" essential to the Qur'ānic accounts of creation: everything in creation is paired. "And of all things We have created (*zawjayn*) pairs, perhaps you [will all] reflect [on this fact]." (Qur'ān 51:49). Dualism becomes a necessary characteristic of created things.[67]

Has this necessary dualism,[68] which is surely found in the form of the family structure, created the patriarchy that Muslim feminists seek to challenge? Is this dualism restricted to heterosexual, childbearing couples? These kinds of questions that seem to probe the issue of gendered norms in Muslim feminist thought could take us far afield, however, from what Wadud actually means. She does not accept that God creates masculine and feminine ideals, which are products of *culture* that "have figured very strongly in interpretation of the Qur'ān without explicit Qur'ānic substantiation of their implications."[69] The women who appear in the Qur'ān fall into three types of roles, categorized by Wadud: roles that faithfully reflect particular historical contexts; roles that seem universally feminine, such as nurturers; and roles that are universally human, not specifically feminine.[70]

Beyond women characters, the Qur'ān also uses ambiguous metaphors for women:

> Your wives are your tilth; go, then, unto your tilth as you may desire, but first provide something for your souls, and remain conscious of God, and know that you are destined to meet Him. And give glad tidings unto those who believe.[71]

The Arabic term used for tilth is *harth*, which is generally understood by Muslim feminists as cultivation, or land, soil. A literal understanding of this would give Muslim men free reign to "cultivate" women in whatever way they desire, but there is an added injunction which compels the Muslim man to remain conscious of God. Hassan's interpretation stresses that the passage can be understood on many levels, and Muslims are likely to accept the most facile reading:

> The likening of a wife to life-containing soil has a profound meaning but the average Muslim is not sensitive to the subtleties of the comparison or to the implications of the Qur'ān's reminder to the husband that he should act righteously. Since wives are described as a 'tilth' and permission has been given to the husbands to approach them "when or how you will," the average Muslim man believes not only that husbands have the right to have sexual intercourse with their wives whenever they choose, but also the right to impregnate them at will in order that they might yield a harvest.[72]

Hassan further argues that women always seem to be given a secondary position to men when the Qur'ān is read in a hegemonically expedient way:

> The Qur'ānic regulations over the matters most important to women: marriage, divorce, child custody, unquestionably discriminate against women, when taken at face value. In essence, they permit men a sexual license completely forbidden to women: the right to marry up to four wives, to have an unlimited number of concubines, and to divorce with extraordinary ease.[73]

Those issues relating to sexuality and family—as organized around gender and produced from sexuality—are the most contested because men and women must read them at very different levels if they are to maximize their own genders' agency. Narrow interpretations of the Qur'ān have upheld narrow understandings of Islamic masculinity, which have then been read into existing social relationships, most importantly in the family, to support the notion of "same but different." The parity between social and moral realms that Barlas has highlighted would require a radical shift in gender relationships in society and most importantly a challenge to the "family" and the family roles that have become the key and central feature of Islamic society and Islamic masculinity.

Honoring the family, dismantling hierarchy

Masculinity is constructed around the tenets of power, and the powerful needs a power base. In the lives of most Muslim men this locus has become the heterosexual family. Muslim feminists have argued that this family structure has now become a part of Islamic culture, and it is difficult to establish that family and marriage in Islam are nonpatriarchal and nonoppressive. The patriarchal husband has then become a part of the tradition and culture of Muslim families, meaning that "women are oppressed *by those who love them*: their fathers, brothers, husbands, and sons who enjoy the fruits of their labor without acknowledging the full extent of that labor" in terms of its moral and social dimensions.[74]

The Muslim man as the maintainer (or breadwinner) of the family and the Muslim woman as the homemaker have become synonymous with Islamic societies and cultures. It is often understood that such roles are God given because passages of the Qur'ān—controversial as they are—have become a basis for the creation of such roles,

> Men shall take full care of women with the bounties which God has bestowed more abundantly on the former than on the latter, and with what they may spend out of their possessions. And the righteous women are the truly devout ones, who guard the intimacy, which God has [ordained to be guarded]. And as for those women whose ill-will you have reason to fear, admonish them [first]; then leave them alone in bed, then beat them; and if thereupon they pay you heed, do not seek to harm them. Behold, God is indeed most high, great![75]

"Care" here could mean many things, but in its most extreme sense it is understood as the maintenance of women by men. This Qur'ānic passage explicitly gives an understanding that men have a superior power over women and are charged with maintaining them, to the extent that if they are to fault then the man has a right to admonish her. Muslim feminists have argued against this exegetically and philologically:

> The key word in the first sentence of this verse is "qawwamun." This word has been translated variously as "protectors and maintainers (of women)," "in charge (of women)," "having pre-eminence (above women)," and "sovereigns or masters (over women)." Linguistically, the word "qawwamun" means breadwinners or "those who provide a means of support or livelihood." A point of logic that must be made here is that the first sentence is not a descriptive one stating that all men as a matter of fact are providing for women, since obviously there are at least some men who do not provide for women. What

> the sentence is stating, rather, is that men ought to have the capability to provide (since "ought" implies "can"). In other words, this statement, which almost all Muslim societies have taken to be an actual description of all men, is in fact a normative statement pertaining to the Islamic concept of division of labor in an ideal family or community structure. The fact that men are "qawwamun" does not mean that women cannot or should not provide for themselves, but simply that in view of the heavy burden that most women shoulder in child-bearing and rearing, they should not have the additional obligation of providing the means of living at the same time.[76]

Although Hassan is here arguing against the superiority of men over women she still believes that men should be the breadwinners. Barlas agrees, "however, even though the Qur'ān charges the husband with being the breadwinner, it does not designate him head of household, especially as the term has been understood in Western feudal cultures."[77]

These give-and-take hermeneutics ("yes, the man is the breadwinner, but . . .") negotiate the position of the Muslim man in a powerful way, giving him duties but not status that trumps that of his female counterpart. They leave intact the distinctions between men and women but redirect the implications of those distinctions. Hassan considers gendered division of labor within the family as "necessary for maintaining balance in every society."[78] Men, who cannot bear children in a physiological sense, are assigned the maintenance, or breadwinning role almost by default—it is therefore not superior to women's imperative, which is to carry, deliver, and raise children. Ghada Karmi, the Palestinian medical physician, author and academic, rejected the understanding of this same passage (Qur'ān 4:34) as superiority in general but sees as a superiority in financing the home pertinent to a certain historical context: "Indeed, the verse in question occurs in the midst of several verses concerned with financial details. It is not unreasonable, therefore, to see it only as a part of an economic arrangement suited to the time when it was written."[79]

Muslim feminists have also argued against the idea that men are the maintainers of women based on their physical strength (Qur'ān 4:34), even though this particular passage could be read in ways that creater a power struggle between the sexes. Whether this means all men are superior to all women is up for debate, but Hassan has said that she reads the passage as saying "that some men are more blessed with the means to be better providers than are other men."[80] In her commentary, Hassan moves towards accepting different forms of masculinity—since men are logically not all the same in terms of physical strength—but by using the phrase "more blessed" for the providers, she gives the impression that being provider is a role far superior to not providing at all. The role of providing and strength seems to be something that Muslim feminists accept as long as it does not allow men to become superior. Islamic legal scholar Raga El-Nimr sees no need for feminism because physical differences make for efficient family units:

> [Men] are protectors because of their physical strength and capacity for strenuous work. Moreover, it is necessary for the functioning of the family that there should be a head who settles things among the members of the family and ensures their compliance. It is for this reason that the wife is asked to obey her husband and she should not obey him if what he asks is against Allah's injunctions.[81]

El-Nimr's view is one that many Muslim women quite possibly agree with that men "naturally" have a superior position than them. There are many Muslim women who thrive under patriarchy and believe this is Islamic, especially at a practical and pragmatic level of family functioning, but in opposition to this are Muslim women who oppose such structures and believe that their opposition is their Islamic.

The Qur'ān contains passages that support the notion that men are the maintainers of women and are charged with reprimanding women with a beating if they disobey. It has been a difficult task for Muslim feminists to dismiss the passage (Qur'ān 4:34) about domestic violence without being seen to reject the Qur'ān, as has been the case with Wadud, who wrote:

> There is no getting around this one, even though I have tried through different methods for two decades. I simply do not and cannot condone permission for a man to "scourge" or apply *any kind* of strike to a woman. . . . This leads me to clarify how I have finally come to say "no" outright to the literal implementation of this passage. This also has implications in implementing the *hudud* (penal code) ordinances. This verse, and the literal implementation of *hudud*, both imply an ethical standard of human actions that are archaic and barbarian at this time in history. They are unjust in the ways that human beings have come to experience and understand justice, and hence unacceptable to universal notions of human dignity.[82]

However, feminists do use the example of the prophet Muḥammad to highlight that he did not use his masculinity as a means of exerting power over or beating his wives.[83] Hassan makes sense of the passage about domestic violence thus:

> The three injunctions in the second part of the verse were given to the Islamic Ummah in order to meet a rather extraordinary possibility: a mass rebellion on the part of women against their role as child bearers, the function assigned to them by God. If all or most of the women in a Muslim society refused to bear children without just cause as a sign of organized defiance or revolt, this would mean the end of the Muslim ummah. This situation must, therefore, be dealt with decisively.[84]

Hassan aims to place the particular Qur'ānic passage into its historical context but its contemporary significance has created much tension and controversy in the lives of Muslim men and women.

The prophet Muḥammad's taking of many wives has also shaped this identity of ideal "Muslim husband." Most Muslim feminist authors express a reading similar to Barlas'; she writes that the Qur'ān allows a man to take up to four wives according to the strength of his sexual needs. Thereafter, a man must be—as each of his wives must always have been—modest, faithful, and restrained. These ideals are shared by men and women, as "the Qur'ān does not stress a high, civilized level for women while leaving men to interact with others at the basest level. Otherwise, the mutual responsibility of *khilāfah* (trusteeship) would be left to one half of humanity while the other half remains near the animal state."[85] Regardless of how many wives are involved, everyone in a marriage is charged with upholding Muslim social values.

But Muslim feminists point out that this egalitarian aspect of marriage goes unchampioned while polygamy and the practice of marrying young girls flourish. The prophet's role was strengthened by having so many wives in a context where having more than one wife was a sign of a strong man physically, socially, and politically—all areas of concern for the prophet, certainly:

> Yet, it is usually not these egalitarian aspects of the Prophet's *Sunnah* that many Muslim men want to emulate today; rather, they place a great deal more emphasis on the fact of his multiple marriages, as also on the age of one of his wives, Aysha, which they use to legitimise marriages to little girls.[86]

The idea behind the Qur'ānic injunction about multiple wives is rightly read, feminists say, as a challenge for men to marry only women whom they can honor and support fully. It may be that the passage was an exercise in reductio ad absurdum—pointing out the virtual impossibility of treating so many wives equally. So polygamy in Islam teaches more than what men learn from it:

> Contrary to what patriarchies and many feminists claim, its provisions on polygamy are not meant to pander to male sexual needs or lusts. Indeed, the Qur'ān counsels chastity both outside of marriage and within it, and extends its notion of chastity—associated with "the feminine"—to men as well.[87]

Because it can devalue women while at the same time inflating men's sense of self, polygamy can become another means of supporting the power base of Islamic masculinity. Mernissi informs us of the intimate nature of this gender disparity:

> Polygamy is a way for the man to humiliate the woman as a sexual being; it expresses her inability to satisfy him. For Moroccan folk wisdom, this function of polygamy as a device to humiliate the woman is evident: "Debase a woman by bringing in to [the house] another one."[88]

But polygamy is also a way of domesticating male behavior. Sex and sexual desire were most likely the bane of medieval Islamic scholars who had to work with an Islamic ethos of sex positivity yet needed to find ways of curbing, controlling, and policing such passion to strengthen the particular models of Islamic masculinity and femininity that would support their views on Islam. To drive the Muslim man towards family life, modes of intercourse are classified as legitimate or *zina* (illicit): "*Zina* was one of the practices the Muslim recruits were required to renounce. . . . A sexually frustrated member of the community is considered dangerous."[89] It then becomes necessary to regulate Muslim society by curbing sexual fulfillment, but could this police the independence of both the male and the female in society, thereby posing a serious challenge to the patriarchal structure of family life? We are beginning to see how Muslim feminist scholars reinforce the idea of equal constraints on men and women, leveraging this idea to argue for essential gender equality. Of course, this umbrella of equal responsibilities alters the picture of Islamic masculinity at the same time that it attempts to put an end to patriarchal traditions.

As much as they want to put men and women into mutual, coequal relationship, Muslim feminists have argued that women have for far too long been understood and identified through a comparison to Islamic masculinity.

Where women are shaped in relation to Islamic masculinity, they are expected to conform and obey. For this reason Muslim feminists use the role of motherhood to highlight the uniqueness of femininity. Wadud considers this aspect of her life essential even to her professional success:

> When I submit my resume for jobs, grants, or creating short bios in other public roles, the twenty-plus pages is impressive to some, but if a short biographical sketch is composed I always request they include that I am a mother of five children as the most important achievement.[90]

Barlas' exegesis explains that motherhood is not just a social act but also a divine one,

> In Arabic, "the word for womb (*rahim*) derives from the same root as the words mercy (*rahma*) and All-merciful (*rahman*)," which are attributes the Qur'ān scribes to God; all Surahs, barring one, begin by describing God as *Rahman* and *Rahim*. Etymologically, then, divine attributes and the womb are related and signify benevolence and compassion. . . . By using the words *taqwā* and *rahma*, the Qur'ān not only brings mothers into the same sphere of symbolic signification as that reserved for God, but, in so doing, it also privileges them over fathers, to whom it never extends the concept of *taqwā*. Clearly, *taqwā* for God and for mothers cannot be of the same nature; however, the fact that the Qur'ān extends it only to mothers shows it privileges them in a way that it never privileges fathers. (The Qur'ān also gives mothers the same share in inheritance as fathers and, if the deceased has no son, double the father's share.)[91]

By this reckoning, **motherhood is a key characteristic that shapes femininity and cannot be reduced to a secondary position by men**. Motherhood is also not just for women who procreate. Barlas reminds her readers that the Prophet's youngest wife Aisha did not have children, 'but that neither diminished her importance in his life nor her appeal as a role model for women.'[92]

Given Hagar's prominent role in the Muslim origin narrative—tradition holds Ishmael, her son with Abraham, was Muḥammad's forefather—her plight is ripe for feminist interpretation. As her son, a crying baby, lay hungry in the desert, it was Hagar who ran between the two hills of Safa and Marwa to feed him. This has become an integral part of the annual pilgrimage to Mecca that Muslims undertake, but Muslim feminists are unsure if the actions of this frantic mother are appreciated by men as much as they should be. Wadud emphasizes

Hagar's ability to move between public and private spheres when necessary to accomplish all of the "nurturing mother" roles.[93] Hagar's outdoors act—helping Ishmael in the wilderness—relocates women from the confines of the home to the outside. However, even though the story is based in the desert, Wadud does not feel that her new rendering of Hagar's story will be accommodated in contemporary society: "Islamic personal law is built upon a notion of family that does not include a woman (Hagar) thrown into the desert, forced to construct a healthy, happy life for her child and to fend for herself."[94] But in the end Wadud still contemplates the position of men in the motherhood process:

> The childbearing responsibility is of grave importance: human existence depends upon it. This responsibility requires a great deal of physical strength, stamina, intelligence, and deep personal commitment. Yet, while this responsibility is so obvious and important, what is the responsibility of the male in this family and society at large? For simple balance and justice in creation, and to avoid oppression, his responsibility must be equally significant to the continuation of the human race. The Qur'ān establishes his responsibility as *qiwamah*: seeing to it that the woman is not burdened with additional responsibilities which jeopardize that primary demanding responsibility that only she can fulfill.[95]

Men's *de facto* "maintaining" role is one that women biologically could fill; the reverse is not the case. Mothering, that absolutely essential process, is reserved for women.

Law and radical submission

But an obsession with women's biological and physiological attributes is also something in which patriarchy engages. Other than the patriarchal image, there also seems to be the view among Muslim feminists that men are predatory and intrusive;[96] this is how many of them frame the issue of veiling, which in Western media is often portrayed as a degradation of *women*. Muslim women's dress has been a central identifying feature of Islam,[97] but does the issue of the veil explain more about the Muslim woman or about Islamic masculinity? The key Qur'ānic passage that is used to ground assertions about dress states:

> Tell the believing men to lower their gaze and to be mindful of their chastity: this will be most conducive to their purity—[and,] verily, God is aware of

> all that they do. And tell the believing women to lower their gaze and to be mindful of their chastity, and not to display their charms [in public] beyond what may [decently] be apparent thereof; hence, let them draw their head-coverings over their bosoms. And let them not display [more of] their charms to any but their husbands, or their fathers, or their husbands' fathers, or their sons, or their husbands' sons, or their brothers, or their brothers' sons, or their sisters' sons, or their womenfolk, or those whom they rightfully posses, or such male attendants as are beyond all sexual desire, or children that are as yet unaware of women's nakedness; and let them not swing their legs [in walking] so as to draw attention to their hidden charms.[98]

It is evident that emphasis is placed more on female dress and chastity than on men's. It elaborates on women's "charms" yet fails to talk about the charms of men.

The operative verse in the Qur'ān is based on the assumption that women's bodies are sex objects that need to be covered from men: "if a man respected a woman as an equal human being and not as an object as his sexual fantasies, then even a naked woman should be safe from male abuse."[99] The onus to uphold the Qur'ānic injunction, then, should be on men, but, as Barlas criticizes, the law constrains women to various degrees:

> Conservatives read these *Ayat* as giving Muslim males the right to force women to don everything from the *hijāb* (a head veil that leaves the face uncovered) to the *burqa* (a head-to-toe shroud that hides even the feet; some models even mandate wearing gloves so as to hide the hands). They justify such forms of veiling on the grounds that women's bodies are pudendal, hence sexually corrupting to those who see them; it thus is necessary to shield Muslim men from viewing women's bodies by concealing them.[100]

Such notions have led to segregation of the sexes because "the intrusion of women into men's territory leads to disruption, if not the destruction, of the fundamental order of things."[101] Covering the complete body, even a woman's face, essentially accomplishes that separation when actual separation is not practical.

Thus the veil and segregation of women from male spaces become a means to locate the Muslim man as the centre point of the social world. In fact so much can be seen to revolve around this "wariness of heterosexual involvement," Mernissi says, that "the entire Muslim social structure can be seen as an attack on, and a defense against, the disruptive power of female sexuality."[102] However, many Muslim feminists have read the Qur'ānic passage as equal to both men and women. This is Barlas's exegesis:

> Even though, as this Ayah makes clear, the real veil is in the eyes/gaze, the Qur'ān is concerned also with the dress/body. In this context, it is important to note, first, that it requires both men and woman to dress modestly. . . . Second, the Qur'ān describes modesty of dress rather sparingly as the covering of private parts. . . . Third, that the function of the *khumar* (shawl) is to cover the bosom, not the face; this is evident not only from the nature of the garment itself, but also from the Ayah which, in so many words, refers to the bosom and to private parts.[103]

She is contesting the veiling policies themselves, saying that they need not be so restrictive and that they should not be disproportionately constraining to women. Bhutto appealed to this logic, too: "There is a famous saying of the Holy Prophet that 'the best veil is the veil in the eyes.' That means that men should be God-fearing and look at women with respect."[104]

Wadud challenges the use of the veil as some form of ethical scale of piety: "If you think that the difference between heaven and hell is 45 inches of material, boy will you be surprised. This is my *hijāb* mantra."[105] Observing a women who veils confers very little information about that woman:

> While the *hijāb* can give some semblance of a woman's affiliation with "Islam," it offers no guarantee of respect or protection. . . . In reality, the *hijāb* of coercion and the *hijāb* of liberation look the same. The *hijāb* of deception and the *hijāb* of integrity look the same. You can no more tell the extent of a Muslim woman's sense of personal bodily integrity or piety from 45 inches of cloth than you can spot a fly on the wall at two thousand feet.[106]

In fact, Islamic traditions, societies, and cultures have adopted and rejected women's veiling for a variety of reasons. Muslim feminists have argued that Islamic traditions, societies, and cultures have placed "a veil" between men and women because of the threat of sexual distraction, especially for men from women. Even as veiling is commonly construed as a women's issue, the feminists open up a line of questioning for those of us who wish to interrogate Muslim masculinity, for separation policies unveil as much or more about the men who enact and enforce them.

From the very first, Islam has intervened in social order to the *benefit* of women and girls. During the medieval period, female infanticide was relatively commonplace in the Prophet's part of the world. Muslim revelation forbade the practice, so it is often said that Islam gave women their rights many centuries ago. There was a concentrated effort by the prophet to see that such actions be stopped and, although they are now widely condemned in Islamic traditions, societies and cultures, has this practice been redefined and women's subjugation transformed into other, still acceptable misogynist practices? Hassan argues that the killing of baby girls may have stopped but they are still not regarded highly by parents:

> However, it needs to be added here that though Muslims do not kill their baby daughters, they do not, in general, treat them equally with boys. Generally speaking, the birth of a daughter is met with resignation and even sadness. A woman who only produces daughters is likely to be the target of harsh and abusive behavior and threatened with divorce. It will be interesting to see what change, if any, takes place in Muslim culture when the fact becomes widely known that it is not the mother but the father who determines the sex of the child!

Thus, the amount of social progress that Islam has ushered in with respect to gender is difficult to calculate. But Muslim feminists do argue that this early statement against female infanticide makes an important *theological* point. The Prophet's commandment against disposing of unwanted girl babies establishes a welcome separation of men from God, feminists argue:

> Had the Qur'ān given fathers powers of life and death over children, or designated girls their parents property, it could not have held them to account for murdering or abusing their daughters; nor would it have enjoined on the children the duty of disobeying parents in matters of faith. Thus, Muslims who view children, or wives, as the father's or husbands property fail to consider that the Qur'ān delineates relationships between parents and children, husbands and wives, and even masters and slaves, in terms that rule out the idea of ownership altogether.[107]

This undermines the linkage between the God's total agentic control and the domineering position of the Muslim husband and father.

In fact, understanding God as "father" has been a topic of debate within faiths throughout history, especially Islam and Christianity. Muslim feminists join many critics in highlighting the way in which the assumed analogy between men and God has helped to construct a specific form of Islamic masculinity. The deductions that feminist question begin with God being understood as a father who created human beings and that same God being represented in the Qur'ān by the masculine pronoun *he*. "God's sacralization as Father" may be unwarranted, for, as Barlas writes, "If God is not Father in heaven in either a literal or a symbolic sense, how can fathers represent their rule on earth as replicating the model of divine patriarchy?"[108] The whole of patriarchy is undercut by dissociating the male gender from any special connection with the divine.

Even though the Qur'ān promotes a separation of God from all that God creates, God has still been understood as a male. Human logic and patriarchal examples have constructed a masculinized God rather than promoting the gender-ambiguous nature of God revealed in the Qur'ān.[109] In order for there to be a solution to the real, lived predicament in which Muslim women find themselves, there has to be a shift of power in gender construction. This could be resolved by understanding the role of submission to God—the ultimate power—as a uniting factor for men and women. Their experience and ideal of submission is common, but differences in men's and women's acts and practices could still be tolerated. This would allow Muslim feminists such as Wadud to advocate core differences between, and among, men and women without creating a gendered power struggle. Such a theological model of gender challenges the significance and centrality of the nuclear family, something that Wadud believes should be unequivocally egalitarian.

The concept of human beings constituting a single humanity has been a central understanding in Islamic traditions, but Muslim feminists are also skeptical of the term *submission*, as promising as it is. The very act of submission, or surrender, has united creation as *powerless*. Wadud prefers the phrase *engaged surrender*, where surrender is a choice, not a forced stance. She argues that submission cannot be the operative force because Muslim history is full of deviations from God's ideal: "Muslims disobey Allah's will obviously because they *can* exercise choice."[110] Wadud's rejection of submission is based on the most negative understandings of the word—being "involuntary," "coerced," "limited," and following "required duties." The Qur'ānic model of submission may not be as narrow as Wadud's: Both Adam and Eve were reprimanded for seeking power from something that was created by God, Satan. It was the "choice" that allowed Adam and Eve to take from the tree, on the invitation of Satan, but they were reprimanded for shifting power from God to another form of creation.

Engaged surrender entails retaining some form of power—power as God consciousness (*Taqwā*). This again is related to Ijtihād, that intellectual creativity and scrutiny, and Barlas contends that the "Qur'ān is rare among Scriptures in teaching that women and men are able equally to acquire *taqwā* (moral personality)."[111] In order to retain this power in her model of engaged surrender, Wadud formulates a "*Tawḥīdic* paradigm:"

> As an ethical term, *tawḥīd* relates to relationships and developments within the social and political realm, emphasizing the unity of all human creatures beneath one Creator. If experienced as a reality in everyday Islamic terms, humanity would be a single global community without distinction for reasons of race, class, gender, religious tradition, national origin, sexual orientation or other arbitrary, voluntary, and involuntary aspects of human distinction. Their only distinction would be on the basis on *taqwā*. (Qur'ān 49:13)[112]

Barlas has also used the sovereignty of God to challenge patriarchy, saying,

> In its simplest form, Tawḥīd symbolizes the idea of God's indivisibility, hence also the indivisibility of God's sovereignty; thus, no theory of male (or popular) sovereignty that pretends to be an extension of God's Rule/Sovereignty, or comes into conflict with it, can be considered compatible with the doctrine of Tawḥīd.[113]

We recognize *Tawḥīd* as one of the pillars of Mawdūdi's thought, and Wadud connects it to another of the forces that also motivated Mawdūdi's social program: *Khilāfa*. She writes, "*taqwā* is a volitional function of our *khilāfa* or agency. If consciousness of Allah is absent, it is possible to think of others on the vertical plane of inequity and transgression, leading to oppression, abuse, and transgression."[114] Where Mawdūdi politicized the idea and notion of *Khilāfa*, Wadud is clearly bringing the notion back to its root, submission to God.

In their attempt to raise the position of women in Islamic traditions and society, Muslim feminists have rejected the idea that men constitute the standard by which equality is measured. Instead, they tend to favor locating all of creation into the oneness of God. While many classical philosophers position man as the standard bearer,[115] there are many examples in the Qur'ān itself which specifically distance all of human creation from God. Because attributing ultimate power to God, and not to men as God's miniatures on earth, can shake the core of patriarchy, disempowering all of God's creation, including men, could be the basis of a better balance of power for harmony between and among God's creation.

For the disempowerment exclusively of the Muslim *woman* to take place, the Muslim man has needed significant tools to empower his own status. In his most powerful method, man has equated himself with God as ruler of *the rest of* creation. Barlas dismisses that idea out of hand, saying:

> To the extent that theories of male rule over women and children amount to asserting sovereignty over both and also misrepresent males as intermediaries between women and God, they do come into conflict with the essential tenets of the doctrine of *Tawḥīd* and must be rejected as theologically unsound.[116]

This collapsing of man with God becomes concretized in textual interpretation, which comes to stand for tradition and morality. Hassan's concern about most Muslims reading the text at face value is made more serious when we consider Wadud's point that these dominant interpretations become indistinguishable from God's word itself:

> I wrestle the hegemony of male privilege in Islamic interpretation ("master's tools") as patriarchal interpretation, which continually leaves a mark on Islamic praxis and thought. Too many of the world's Muslims cannot perceive a distinction between this interpretation and the divine will, leading to the truncated notion of divine intent as well as of the divine nature and essence limited to the maelstrom perspective, hence violating the actual transcendent nature of Allah.[117]

This limited understanding conflicts greatly with the ultimate role of submission to which both men and women are expected to adhere.

Sovereignty and rule are also associated with the male because of the widespread understanding that God is male, and returning to scripture itself is a strong feminist strategy in the face of intervening centuries of patriarchal tradition:

> The Qur'ān's tireless and emphatic rejections of God's sexualisation/engenderment—as Father (male)—confirm that God is not male, or like

> one. However, if God is not male or like one, there also is no reason to hold that God has any special affinity with males (thus positing of such an affinity allows men to claim God as their own and thus to project onto God sexual partisanship).[118]

Muslim feminists have challenged this by highlighting the notion that all human beings, men, and women, have been created by God and they are intrinsic to the unicity of God, *Tawḥīd*. Wadud has argued for an "engaged surrender" as opposed to "submission" to God. However, if men and women are to be understood equally, bridging the moral and social realms together, then there is a necessity to understand and practice submission to God without an essential need for each other, which in turn would create a disempowered condition leading to a much more productive gender parity. It would also allow for Muslim men and women to have more flexibility as spiritual individuals in their own unique quests.

But, as we have seen, Qur'ānic passages have been *interpreted* to support an Islamic masculinity that advocates men as maintainers of women and, in turn, the breadwinners. The dominant role of maintainer has been upheld through the gender roles to which the Muslim man is exposed during his early life at home and then expected to uphold in his own family. Even though the term *maintenance* has been understood by some Muslim feminists to mean the division of financial income between men and women, there has been little challenge to the underlying foundation of men "maintaining" women. Those who have challenged this, such as Wadud does in her rejection of men "beating" their wives to conform to this maintenance, have found their views being described as un-Islamic. The best example of this is the general views of women and men as presented by the likes of Mawdūdi.

Hassan understands that men and women are ideal partners because, "in the context of human creation, the Qur'ān describes man and woman as each other's *zauj*, or 'mate'." But that does not make a husband some kind of ultimate patriarch who can lead family life to the exclusion of women's agency:

> The term "zauj" is generally used to refer to one of two in a pair when reference is made, for instance to "a pair of shoes" or "night and day." Not only are both parts necessary to complete a pair but also the proper functioning of each requires the presence of the other.[119]

While she makes no attempt to challenge this "pairing," Hassan later quotes the Ḥadīth in which the Prophet had stated that, had it been permitted for a human being to bow down to anyone except God, it would be to the husband "when he enters into her,"

> A faith rigidly monotheistic as Islam cannot conceivably permit any human being to worship anyone but God, therefore the hypothetical statement "If it were permitted . . ." in the above cited ḥadīth, is, *ipso facto*, an impossibility. But the way this ḥadīth is related makes it appear that if not God's, at least it was the Prophet's will or wish to make the wife prostrate herself before her husband. Each word, act or exhortation attributed to the prophet is held to be sacred by most of the Muslims in the world and so this ḥadīth (which, in my judgment seeks to legitimize *shirk*: associating anyone with God—an unforgivable sin according to the Qur'ān) becomes binding on the Muslim woman.[120]

The Muslim wife is religiously taught to be obedient and subservient to husbands as a way of serving God, since

> most *aḥadīth* (traditions attributed to the Prophet Muḥammad) dealing with the subject of married women describe a virtuous woman as one who pleases and obeys her husband at all times. Pleasing the husband can, in fact, become more important than pleasing God. Putting it differently, one can say that most Muslims believe that a woman cannot please God except through pleasing her husband.[121]

Hassan points out the hypocrisy of Muslims deriding Hinduism for the value it places on husband worship (*patipuja*) since Indian and Pakistani women take "almost as an article of faith that her husband is her *majazi khuda* (God in earthly form). Undoubtedly, this description constitutes 'shirk' (idolatry, blasphemy)."[122]

Clearly the construction of family is one that cannot be "done away with" in order to eradicate patriarchy, which leaves Muslim feminists with the difficult question of how to challenge gender-based hierarchy without undermining the social unit. Muslim feminists have exemplified from their own lived experiences that the family is not absolutely essential in strengthening a relationship with God. The very fact that Nomani's spirituality remained throughout the difficult times she had, for example, indicates that the institution of "marriage" and "family" bears significance only at a societal level and matters little in terms of piety and submission to God, something that is supported even within the Qur'ān.

Muslim feminists have also grappled with notions that the prophetic example is entirely an image and empowerment of men. The prophet Muḥammad's life is understood as an idealized form of Islamic masculinity, but Muslim feminists argue that his example contradicts patriarchal constructions of manhood: "the Prophet was unconventional by the hyper-masculinist standards not only of traditional Arab culture, but also by modern ones, that disparage tenderness, gentleness, and humility in men."[123] Mernissi has argued that the Prophet's heroic qualities all derive from his human vulnerabilities, which inspired his contemporaries and Muslims to this day.[124] The prophet Muḥammad's mission was set in a deeply patriarchal society, raising further the stakes of the Prophet's masculinity because "no society in the seventh century was egalitarian since no society at that time recognised women as full human beings, or as moral agents, or as independent legal persons."[125]

Muslim feminists challenge the way that God and the prophet Muḥammad's life are used to strengthen and uphold an Islamic masculinity. When men equate themselves to God and prophet, they elevate their position, and this tactic is used by men far more progressive than Mawdūdi: "It is in this way that some progressives and conservatives actually embrace the same paradigm: to be fully human, a moral agent, and a public leader, one must be male."[126] Maleness becomes a means to power, but Muslim feminists believe that this power is not complete:

> It is time for men to be *empowered with* and not exert power over female identity and contributions. It is time for women and men to accept the full humanity of women by removing the veils put over women being female. . . . Those "manly" traits, which perhaps once helped the whole human race to move out of subjectivity to the vicissitude of nature's unpredictability, have long outstripped their merits.[127]

Muslim feminists also encourage Muslim men to reject their entitlements "unless they are also granted to women."[128] Muslim men must then realize that they yield equal power in relation to women and no power in relation to submission to God.

Still, the interpretations justifying men's authority over women—and women's need to revere the men in their lives in a manner similar to divine worship—continue. And where Qur'ānic interpretations become legal policies (as in an Islamist theocracy), the debatable theological ideas become practice.[129] Generating policies directly from theological, ethical, and moral precepts has been a part of Islamic tradition for as long as we can tell. The Prophet advocated a family structure that was so radical that "he had to codify its regulations in detail," and that meant some very clear stances toward sexual relationships:

> Sex is one of the instincts whose satisfaction was regulated at length by religious law during the first years of Islam. The link in the Muslim mind between sexuality and the *shar'ia* has shaped the legal and ideological history of the Muslim family structure and consequently of relations between the sexes. One of the most enduring characteristics of this history is that the family structure is assumed to be unchangeable, for it is considered divine.[130]

Gender construction is then policed, shaped, and enforced in Islamic societies, especially on issues relating to family law. While the Prophet personally transitioning from moral concepts to ethical codes is powerful, Islamic legal tradition is not alone in extrapolating a social worldview onto society—that is essentially law's function. But this does make radical Qur'ānic exegesis more difficult, since the theological points are so closely tied to prescriptions for enacting them in society. It is crucial, then, for Muslim feminists to understand that *shar'ia's* "'essence' is its religion but its 'expression' is a response to the formal exigencies of juristic style in language, logic and structure."[131]

To understand Islamic gendering, we must follow the Muslim feminists in appreciating that Islamic law becomes another means of social construction,[132] except in this case it carries a lot more weight than just an "interpretation" would. For that reason, however, starting by encouraging a multiplicity of interpretations may call into question the shaky scriptural foundations of entrenched Islamic notions of gender—whether they are as extreme as Mawdūdi's or not. If Qur'ānic interpretation were a personal practice, perhaps one engaged with the creative moral thinking of Ijtihād, then the concept of an Islamic masculinity (or femininity) could be appreciated as unique to each individual Muslim. Shaikh's argument that tafsīr of praxis is based on lived experience certainly supports the idea that religious text is of use to Muslim men and women in their uniqueness.

We have seen in this exploration of Muslim feminist scholarship that Mawdūdi's worldview consisting of diametrical opposites can be reconfigured. The constructs of "man," "God," "woman," and "West" need not depend on othering. In fact, reorienting Muslim life around submission, or surrender—the very definition of the word *Islam*—at once appreciates the all-encompassing human condition that equalizes genders and activates the intrinsic value of multiplicity in interpretation. Tracing major feminist critiques of the Qur'ān opens up a discussion of the Islamic masculinity/ies because that's precisely what feminist have to address. Family is the nexus of patriarchy, text, and society. Because feminists do not want to abolish family, text becomes the preferred site for resistance. They draw on experience as well. If all are to be submissive to God, then that holds the possibility of egalitarianism. Muslim feminist scholars are *not* necessarily committed to breaking down all gender distinctions, so there is not a totally fluid masculinity or femininity there. But openness to diverse interpretations will create the possibility of gender diversity. The next chapter takes on the Muslim feminist challenge of destabilizing dominant readings by analyzing directly the images of masculinity that do exist in the Qur'ān. That they vary will not surprise us, but the powerful possibilities that such variance opens up will cast Islamic masculinity afresh.

- Feminists from lived Tafsir
- Prophet's non-alpha-male example
- Verse 4:34 + interpretations/explanations
- well-known feminist academics
- Hegemonic reading issue
- Don't want to abolish family
  — nexus of patriarchy
- Childbearing v. Maintenance

3

The Failed Search for a Single Qur'ānic Masculinity

Are thou not aware that God sends down water from the skies,
whereby We bring forth fruits of many hues—
just as in the mountains there are streaks of
white and red of various shades,
as well as [others] raven-black,
and [as] there are in men, and in crawling beasts,
and in cattle, too, many hues?
Of all His servants, only such as are endowed with [innate]
knowledge stand [truly] in awe of God: [for they alone comprehend that,]
verily, God is almighty, much-forgiving.[1]

In Islam, all of the prophets are paragons of faithfulness, but their situations differ widely precisely in the aspects of life that Mawdūdi wanted to regulate: family situation, sexual morality, performance of male power, and expression of submission. The prophets are, however, all men. And they all illustrate subservience to God, a point that we saw feminists make much of. To understand the picture of Islamic masculinity painted by the prophets as recorded in the Qur'ān, we have to disentangle their vocation from their circumstances and their personal identities. The lives of four prophets, Adam, Joseph, Muḥammad, and Jesus will be discussed in this chapter as key examples of Qur'ānic—which is in some senses different from Islamic—masculinities. This chapter cannot do justice to every facet of their representation in the Qur'ān, so I focus on those qualities that speak to the extreme-Islamist framework we have been working with and against thus far.

The Qur'ān was revealed to the Prophet Muḥammad in the seventh century CE, and it contains statements and stories that lead to discussions on ethics, morality, and most importantly theology, the understanding of God. It is through the Qur'ān that Muslims are made aware of the images of prophets, which they try to emulate in social relationships and actions, including gender construction. The Qur'ān is revered as revelation by Muslims, and here that reverence will be respected but the material will be presented as literature, not history. Medieval scholarship[2] which elaborates on the lives of the prophets is used extensively as it offers a thorough narrative into the lives of these prophets.

Prophets have been defined as those "extraordinary men" who "receive divine revelation and their collective vocation."[3] The prophetic role is to convey a message from God to humankind through a twofold method: first through revelation and secondly through their agency as human beings on earth.

> All mankind was once one single community; [then they began to differ] whereupon God raised up the prophets as heralds of glad tidings and as warners and through them bestowed revelation from on high, setting forth the truth, so that it might decide between people with regard to all on which they had come to hold divergent views. (Qur'ān 2:213)

This Qur'ānic verse clearly stipulates the key concerns of a prophet, which are "announcing of good news, the giving of warning, and the custody of the book."[4] God created prophets for the central purpose of upholding morality and goodness, and there's a sense of nostalgia in it: "God started sending prophets after humankind became separated, when the initial state of righteousness was replaced by moral corruptness" (Qur'ān 2:213). The good qualities of the prophets, such as righteousness and truthfulness, are mentioned in numerous passages of the Qur'ān (3:39, 19:41, 19:56, 19:54) where the emphasis is on their virtues and morality as shaped by God's will: "the guided and divinely chosen prophets possess moral virtues that render them immune to sin and misbehavior" (Qur'ān 3:161). As God created human beings who would live on earth, the message of good needed to be one which would suit the prevailing conditions. In this way the prophets serve this purpose through their human agency.

Prophets are described in the Qur'ān as human, but because of their prophetic mission from God they are not entirely equal with other human

(margin note, handwritten) a what prophets are/do

beings. Here the Qur'ān has God speak of the special status of this elite cadre of individuals:

> And we bestowed upon him Isaac and Jacob; and We guided each of them as We had guided Noah a foretime. And out of his offspring, [We bestowed prophet hood upon] David, and Solomon, and Job, and Joseph, and Moses, and Aaron: for thus do we reward the doers of good; and upon Zacharia, and John, and Jesus, and Elijah: every one of them was the righteous; and [upon] Ishmael, and Elisha, and Jonah, and Lot. And every one of them did We favor above other people. (Qur'ān 6:85)

Prophets hold no divine position, yet they are divinely guided. They are human beings who had to function and live in the world just as every other human being does. This in turn creates a conflicted identity: both elevated above human beings and kept at a fair distance from God's supremacy.

The prophetic mission inextricably binds the prophet to God's command, and the term *rasul Allah*[5] (prophet of God) emphasizes this link. It is God who remains the prophet's most loyal companion, since prophets are "most often rejected by their people."[6] Human acceptance is not what motivates prophets; acceptance and selection by God do. The lives of the chosen prophets are reflections of God's will, and the Qur'ān highlights the fact that God has generated everything for a reason, since "God in His wisdom creates nothing without setting a worthy end for the object created."[7] Thus, the nature and nurture of the prophets are controlled by God, and the subservient nature of the prophet in relation to God must be understood as essential for the task of prophecy.[8] The prophet has the capability of communicating with God but must accept God's superiority; if not, he is constantly reminded in his life of his limitations in relation to God's infinite power over him.

What is the essential factor making one a prophet—is it one's identity or one's vocation? The prophets' role can only function in the context in which they find themselves, so in order for this to be strengthened, God had to make sure that in any given context their "selves" and "mission" were equally positioned. The link between being and vocation is an important one when the question of female prophecy is raised, since certain driven and pivotal female Qur'ānic characters are not considered prophets. Classical and contemporary scholars have discussed at length the issue of male-only prophethood. Ibn Kathir's famous work "Stories of the Prophets" highlights only male prophets without any mention of the possibility of female prophets. The *Zahirite* (literalist) scholar, Ibn Ḥazm, who lived in the eleventh century CE in Muslim Spain (Andalucia), mentioned in one of his writings[9] that a clear distinction needed to be made between prophethood (*nubbuwa*) and messengerhood (*risala*) and although he believed both men and women could be prophets he believed messengerhood was restricted to men alone. If the sex of the prophet takes precedence over the act of message bearing, then we must ask why the Islamic God has chosen the male over the female to be a prophet. Is the exclusion theological or a matter of societal custom?

> The woman's role as mother and housekeeper has made it difficult for the general body of exegetes to accept that women could be prophets. Since such office would mean interaction with society at large, an image seemingly at odds with Arab tribal concept. The Qur'ān does not even hint at female prophets, and many use Qur'ān 21:7 to insist on maleness as a prerequisite for prophethood, since the verse states, "We did not send before you but men to whom we revealed."[10]

As we have seen, contemporary Muslim feminists excavate the gender-neutral message of God's oneness. But obedience only to God has become gendered through the interpretation of classical scholars who uphold the division of roles.

The Qur'ān itself, however, depicts God as leaving many issues ambiguous:

> And they say, too, "Why was not this Qur'ān bestowed from on high on some great man (*rijāl*) of the two cities?" But is it they who distribute thy sustainer's grace? [Nay, as] it is We who distribute their means of livelihood among them in the life of this world, and raise some of them by degrees above others. (Qur'ān 43:31–32)

On the issue of prophetic gender, there are thus tensions between (a) the ultimate message of God, so far as it can be ascertained or argued; (b) the Qur'ānic text, and (c) commentators. The prophetic role of conveying a message includes no task which could only be carried out by men, but does the Qur'ānic male-only tradition justify excluding women from prophecy? These are matters for other research projects to take up; here we are concerned with the observable fact that prophecy has traditionally been reserved for certain special male agents.

As we investigate the functioning of gender in the Qur'ān, we will be brought again to the topic of family and its ways of sorting individuals into functions according to gender. Many stories in the Qur'ān give us a clear impression of a shared value system between members of the same family and humanity. The Qur'ān has many passages that uphold the relationship and roles within families and goes into great detail concerning how to conduct the affairs of a family. Sura al-Nisā is one such chapter of the Qur'ān which outlines clear guidelines for men, women, and children. The chapter opens with

> O Mankind! Be conscious of your sustainer, who has created you out of one living entity, and out of it created its mate, and out of the two spread abroad a multitude of men and women. And remain conscious of God, in whose name you demand your rights from one another, and of these ties of kinship. Verily, God is ever watchful over you! (Qur'ān 4:1)

There are numerous prophetic and Qur'ānic traditions which elaborate on the rights of parents and children and the respect expected between them, for example:

> we have enjoined upon man goodness towards his parents: his mother bore him bearing strain upon strain, and his utter dependence on her lasted two years: [hence, O man,] be grateful towards Me and towards thy parents, [and remember that] with Me all journeys end. (Qur'ān 31:14)

However, the lives of the prophets do not always reflect idealized families. The lives of Adam, Joseph, Muḥammad, and Jesus, as presented in the Qur'ān, reveal the prophetic vocation's relationship to family, the locus of most gendered roles. What emerges is not one ideal Islamic masculinity but a tableau of exemplary men found in situations far from textbook.

Adam: Archetypical Islamic man

The Qur'ān recounts the initial act of creation through the story of Adam and Eve, the first humans. Their tale strengthens the link between human beings and the essential process of procreation that promotes a wider understanding of the concept of "family"—with one initial father and mother. In Sura al-Baqarah the creation story is recalled: "And Lo! Thy sustainer said unto the angels: 'Behold, I am about to establish upon earth one who shall inherit it'"

(Qur'ān 2:30). The name of the first created man as God called him is Adam, which comes from the Arabic "*adim al'ard*," meaning from the "surface of the earth."[11] His name is mentioned 18 times in the Qur'ān, and "sons of Adam," meaning humankind, is used seven times.[12] Ibn Kathir highlighted the diversity of humankind in God's creation,

> Imam Ahmad has narrated from Abu Musa, who said that the Prophet said,
>
> Allah has created Adam from a handful (soil) which He had gathered from all over the earth. That is how the children of Adam came according to the (color and nature of the) earth. There are white among them, as well as red and black, and cross colors. There are those among them who are of bad nature and good nature, soft as well as harsh and in between.[13]

The essence of God's creation is linked to the environment in which it is to dwell. God created the angels with "wings" Qur'ān 35:1 and *Jinn* from fire; Qur'ān 15:27, God chose to create Adam from "dust"[14] or "clay."[15] The human body, in all its diversity, is then best suited for the earth, with the ultimate task of submitting to God, who is not dependent on anything.

Adam is an individual prophet and the progenitor of difference among humans. There is a kind of tension in that position, as we will explore.

Prior to the creation of Adam, it was the angels who were God's most obedient creations. God's decision to create a something new shocked the angels, who question God on this new creation,

> "Wilt thou place on it such as will spread corruption thereon and shed blood—whereas it is we who extol thy limitless glory, and praise Thee, and hallow Thy name?" God answered: "Verily, I know that which you do not know." (Qur'ān 2:30)[16]

Angels, as God's most submitted creatures, carry out actions to uphold goodness over evil,

> O You who have attained to faith! Ward off from yourselves and those who are close to you that fire [of the hereafter] whose fuel is human beings and stones: [lording] over it are angelic powers awesome [and] severe, who do not disobey God in whatever He has commanded them, but [always] do what they are bidden to do. (Qur'ān 66:6)

According to Abdullah bin Umar, angels were sent by God to exile the violent Jinn, who predated humans by approximately 2,000 years, "to remote islands."[17] Unlike Jinn, angels are referred to in the most honorable way in the Qur'ān,[18]

> Say [O Prophet]: "Whosoever is an enemy of Gabriel"—who, verily, by God's leave, has brought down upon thy heart this [divine writ] which confirms the truth of whatever there still remains [of earlier revelations], and is a guidance and a glad tiding for the believers:—"whosoever is an enemy of God and His angels and His message bearers, including Gabriel and Michael, [should know that,] verily, God is the enemy of all who deny the truth." (Qur'ān 2:97–98)

The distinct form in which God created angels is highlighted in a Ḥadīth of the prophet, in which he has a dialogue with Gabriel:

> It is related that the prophet said to Gabriel one day, "Gabriel, I should like to see you in the most magnificent form that God created you." "Beloved of God," said Gabriel, "I have such an awesome form that neither you nor anyone else could bear to see it without falling down in a swoon." "But I want to gaze upon you in your greatest form," insisted the prophet. "Where then do you want to see me?" asked Gabriel. "Outside Mecca, the valley." "Beloved of God," said Gabriel, "the valley is not big enough." "Then on Mount Arafat." As the prophet was headed for Arafat, suddenly there came a great rustle and clashing, and a face was blocking out the horizons. When the prophet looked, he fell down in a swoon. Gabriel resumed his former shape and came to the prophet, embraced and kissed him, and said, "Fear not, beloved of God, for I am your brother Gabriel." "You spoke the truth Gabriel," said the prophet. "I did not suspect that any of God's creatures had such a form!" Then Gabriel said, "O beloved of God, if you were to see Israfael, you would think *my* form but small and insignificant!"[19]

This prophetic dialogue with Gabriel highlights that all God's creations are as one family, united in their ultimate role of obedience and submission to God. Ka'ab al-Ahbar stated that the angels never cease to glorify and praise God, be they "standing, sitting, kneeling, or prostrate."[20] Still, their form is far from similar to human beings, as mentioned earlier: "All praise is due to God, originator of the heavens and the earth, who causes the angels to be [His] message-bearers, endowed with wings, two, or three, or four" (Qur'ān 35:1).

Gabriel's comparison to Muḥammad and Israfael alludes to angels' ability to take various forms, perhaps as humans comport themselves as masculine and feminine. One cannot be sure whether angels have genders, even though Gabriel is referred to by masculine pronouns throughout. It is also not clear whether he procreates, and whether he would do so in the same way that Adam was expected to. Gabriel's use of the fraternal address of "brother" to the Prophet highlights that regardless of how powerful God creates his creation, they all remain equally disempowered in relation to God. The Qur'ān clarifies that those who convey God's messages are selected from within their own created community in order to strengthen the divine message in its given context: "Say: 'If angels were walking about on earth as their natural abode, We would indeed have sent down unto them an angel out of heaven as Our apostle'" (Qur'ān 17:95).

Before Adam became the first prophet, one angel was set apart—for ability and, later, for arrogance. Iblīs (Satan) was given knowledge by God and had been known for this attribute: "Iblīs used to be called 'Azazil and was one of the most zealous and knowledgeable of the angels. This led him to pride."[21] Al-Tabari states,

> Iblīs was sent by God to judge among the Jinn on the earth. He did so truthfully for 1,000 years and was eventually called the "Arbiter" by God. Because of this, Iblīs considered himself great and became arrogant, and among those to whom God had sent him as an arbiter, Iblīs caused affliction, enmity and hate. These creatures fought among themselves on earth for 2,000 years, causing so much bloodshed that their horses waded in their blood.[22]

In an attempt to isolate Iblīs and undermine his powers, God gives Adam knowledge.[23]

In Qur'ānic exegesis, Iblis is seen as being replaced by God's new creation:

> In the days of the rule of Iblīs, God created Adam, our father, the father of humanity. The reason for this is that the other angels did not know about Iblīs being arrogant, so God wanted to expose this matter to them, to show them what had gone wrong with Iblīs and why his authority and kingship came to an end.[24]

Iblīs' arrogance is not conducive to submission, the purpose to which all of God's creations are put. Al-Tabari stated, "God created Adam with his own hands so that God could say to Iblīs (Satan) that he was exalting himself over that which God formed with his own hands. So God created Adam as a human and his body was from clay."[25]

Iblīs attempts to undermine Adam's formation:

> The angels used to pass by him (Adam) and kick him because they were frightened, the most frightened being Iblīs. Iblīs told the other angels not to be afraid because whereas God is solid, Adam is hollow. Iblīs entered Adam's mouth then out of his anus, then in the anus and out the mouth. Iblīs said: 'You are not an instrument for making sounds, so why were you created? If I am given authority over you, I will ruin you and if you are given authority over me, I shall destroy you.'[26]

Iblīs' statement that God is *solid* and Adam is *hollow* distinguishes God's superiority and position in comparison to the rest of creation. It is also an indication of Iblīs' respect for God in that although he shows arrogance to other creations he still positions God as superior to them all. However, Iblīs' fault lay precisely in arrogance toward God's other creations, especially Adam, and his belief that God had created superiority and inferiority through the different forms of creations.

Even though Adam, angels, and Iblīs are seen to assert their own roles and positions with respect to each other, God once again highlights their equal, disempowered submitted position and function when he presented Adam to them all. In an episode that demonstrates the different roles but ultimate submission of the creations present early on, the angels are asked about some matter that had been imparted to Adam: "Limitless art thou in Thy glory! No knowledge have we save that which Thou hast imparted unto us. Verily, Thou alone art all-knowing, truly wise" (Qur'ān 2:32). The immediate response from God is, "O Adam, convey unto them the names of these (things)" (Qur'ān 2:33). Adam is then able to present his knowledge by conveying what he had been commanded. Such knowledge could be understood as a means to empower an Islamic masculinity, yet the power of the knowledge was with God, who responds, "Verily, I alone know the hidden reality of the heavens and the earth, and know all that you bring into the open and all that you would conceal" (Qur'ān 2:33). The angels accept God's decision to create a human being with more knowledge than they have, and they highlight God's knowledge of all things and concede that God has the power to bestow as much or as little of his knowledge upon his creation.

All the angels are commanded to bow before Adam, but it is Iblīs who refuses to do so: he "gloried in his arrogance: and thus he became one of those who deny truth" (Qur'ān 2:34).[27] Iblīs answered, "I am better than he: Thou hast created me out of fire, whereas him Thou hast created out of clay" (Qur'ān 7:12). God strips Iblīs of his grace, primarily due to the arrogance he was showing, and shuns him from heaven, "for it is not meant for thee to show arrogance here! Go forth, then: verily, among the humiliated shalt thou be!" (Qur'ān 7:13). Iblīs quite correctly draws the distinction between himself and Adam, but the important point of this event is less about creation than about obedience and submission to God, the top of the hierarchy.[28]

Iblīs has some reason to be angry at the love that God is showing Adam over him. Al-Tabari and Ibn Abbas state that God creates Iblīs beautiful, makes him the keeper of paradise, and gives him authority over the earthly heavens and earth. After his revolt, Iblīs vows to divert the attention of human beings who were "righteous on the straight path" Qur'ān 7:16 to the path of evil. God promises a punishment for those who follow Iblīs "as for such of them as follows thee—I will most certainly fill hell with you all!" Qur'ān 7:18. As Barbara Stowasser states, "Satan is shown to have started his career together with Adam, as Adam's coeval; thus his role is essentially linked with man, his nature is brought out by antagonism against man, he is an 'anti-man' force."[29] It is then for no other reason but disobedience to God that Iblīs was shunned, and it was his fixation with other details apart from submission to God that drew him the wrath of God.

The story of creation is then essentially a story about God's submitted creatures and the lessons to be learnt from the way in which God's creation turn to anger and dispute between each other. Each of the created—Adam, angels, and Satan—vie for the love and attention of God, the creator. The angels remain obedient to God's commands, Adam is established as the new creation on earth, and Satan is the rejected one who promises God that he will succeed in creating chaos on earth. As all of creation remains submitted to God's power, such a dynamic disempowers any form of hierarchy among them, especially among and between men and women.

The Qur'ān uses the term "*zawjaha*" to mean companionship between a male and female: "and among his wonders is this: He creates for you mates out of your own kind, so that you might incline towards them, and he engenders love and tenderness between you: in this, behold, there are messages indeed for people who think" (Qur'ān 30:21). John Penrice, one of the foremost translators of Arabic, stated that the root verb is "zā ja" which he translated as "to stir strife up"[30] and then translated the Qur'ānic word "Zawj" illustratively as

> A companion, mate, spouse, husband or wife, and individual when consorting with another; that in which individuals are united, as a kind, species, class, or sex, also a pair, a couple; Examples, "And we have caused (vegetables) to spring up in it of every generous species."[31]

However, legal scholars have used the term to mean "marriage" between a man and woman in order to create laws relating to this.[32] Marriage between a man and women has become a part of Islamic tradition for the purpose of legitimizing, in some way, procreation: "and God has given you mates (*azwajun*) of your own kind and has given you, through your mates, children and children's children, and has provided for you sustenance out of the good things in life" (Qur'ān 16:72). The historical Islamic legal schools wrote extensively on marriage and divorce law, even calling the unions obligatory (wājib) for some people.[33] The ḥadīth traditions also speak extensively on the issue of marriage: "It is narrated by Anas that the messenger of God said, 'When a man marries, he has fulfilled half of his religion, so let him fear God regarding the remaining half.'"[34] Marriage traditions between men and women have also helped to regulate gender roles, since "Men shall take full care of women with the bounties which God has bestowed more abundantly on the former than on the latter. And the righteous women are the truly devout ones, who guard the intimacy which God has ordained to be guarded" (Qur'ān 4:34). This passage has been discussed and rejected by the feminist scholars whose work is the focus of the previous chapter, but the point to note here is that it has shaped the expectations of husbands and wives. Adam and Eve are understood as a central story for understanding the concept of marriage, procreation, and gender.

The creation of Eve from Adam is not mentioned in the Qur'ān; however, al-Tabari, the Persian scholar, historian, and exegete of the tenth century, quoted a ḥadīth which names Adam's wife as "Hawwa."[35] This prophetic tradition states that Adam dwells in paradise alone and falls asleep. When he awakes, he sees a woman sitting beside him. Ibn Ishaq said that God takes a rib from Adam's left side and fashions it to become a woman so that Adam could live with her. When

Adam awakes he said, "My flesh and my blood, and my spouse." According to Ka'ab al-Ahbar, a prominent seventh-century Islamic authority,

> Adam saw her in a dream. When he awoke he said, "O Lord, who is this who was so kind to me when she drew near?" "This is my handmaiden," said God, "and thou art my servant, O Adam. I have not created anyone nobler in my sight than you two, for you have obeyed me and worshipped me. I have created for you an abode and called it Paradise: whosoever enters therein shall be my friend in truth, and whosoever enters not therein shall be my enemy in truth." Adam grew alarmed and said, "O Lord, dost thou have enemies? Thou art the Lord of the heavens and the earth." "Had I willed all of creation to be my friends I should have done so," said God, "but I do what I will and I decree what I desire!" "O Lord," said Adam, "this thy maid Eve, for whom hast thou created her?" "O Adam," said God, "I created her for thee that thou be content with her and that thou not be alone in paradise." "Lord," said Adam, "marry her to me." "O Adam," said God, "I will marry thee to her on one condition: that thou teach her the precepts of my religion and be thankful to me for her." And Adam accepted.[36]

The central characteristic of Eve, as with all other creations, is her ability to worship and submit to God's command. God clarifies here to Adam that the central significance is for the created to worship him; their enjoyment of one another is secondary to their primary submitted function. God allows them both to dwell in paradise as companions, or mates, to each other. The only command Adam and Eve are to observe was the prohibition of eating from the forbidden tree, "lest you become wrongdoers" (Qur'ān 2:35). Wahb Bin Munabbih, the eighth-century scholar of Jewish and Islamic traditions, stated that the "tree's branches were intertwined and it bore fruit which the angels ate to live forever, and it was this fruit that God prohibited to Adam and Eve. The tree is the most excellent in paradise, and on earth, the acacia (*talh*) and the lotus tree (*sidr*)."[37] Ibn Kathir narrated a ḥadīth of the Prophet Muḥammad in which he said, "In paradise is a tree in the shade of which the stars course 100 years without cutting it: the tree of immortality."[38] This beautiful, superlative tree is used as a symbol of ultimate submission to God and his commands. If Adam and Eve obey the instruction, then no one (Iblīs or the tree) could extend or shorten their lives. The tree is then a symbol of and (a temptation to) curiosity and ambiguity as it is up to Adam and Eve to show the strength of their faith and submission to God.

It does not take long for Iblīs to begin his campaign of sabotaging Adam and Eve; he whispers to them, suggesting that they eat from the tree (Qur'ān 2:36 and Qur'ān 7:20).[39] Iblīs attempts to gain the trust of Adam and Eve and successfully "led them on with deluding thoughts" (Qur'ān 7:22). It is here that both Adam and Eve eat the forbidden fruit from the tree and as result of their wrongdoing become conscious of their nakedness. The Prophet Muḥammad said,

> your father Adam was like a tall palm, 60 cubits in height, with a lot of hair, his nakedness covered. When he sinned in paradise, his private parts were revealed to him and he left paradise. A tree caught him and took him by his forelock and his Lord called to him: "Are you running from me, Adam?" He said: "No, I am ashamed for that which I have done."[40]

It could be that nakedness is used as a symbol of disobedience to God. Adam and Eve covers themselves with leaves, which symbolizes not only their embarrassment but also their discontent.[41]

God then calls them, "Did I not forbid that tree unto you and tell you, Verily, Satan is your open foe?"[42] Adam and Eve are then sent down to earth[43] where they are to spend their lives, awaiting their resurrection back to God. It is only after the event that God states,

> Say, "Who is there to forbid the beauty which God has brought forth for his creatures, and the good things from among the means of sustenance? Verily, my sustainer has forbidden only shameful deeds, be they open or secret, and (every kind of) sinning, and unjustified envy, and the ascribing of divinity to aught beside Him." (Qur'ān 7:32–33)

God's reprimand to Adam and Eve is based on their failure to submit fully only to him.

The companionship, or marriage, with which God blesses Adam and Eve was subordinate to their ultimate role of submission: indeed, the addition of Eve could then be understood to support God's divinity. God is the only one who does not require a mate or companion for enjoyment or procreation. It is essentially a biological fact that human beings require an opposite sex to procreate, but there is also no mention of any sexual relations between Adam and Eve in heaven. Intercourse only takes place when they are on earth, and the enjoyment always occurs in contrast with God's mode of creation, which itself recalls the painful memory of paradise lost.[44]

The story of Adam and Eve challenges the very roles on which families construct themselves. Adam and Eve are given the same command to submit to God but they fail to uphold this. Their gender is not significant in this commandment and Adam is not given the role of "breadwinner" and Eve that of "homemaker." Procreation is then to be understood as a way to highlight God's divinity, as "the One." The lesson being taught is that it is Adam and Eve who need one another in order to create other human beings but God only needs to say "may it be" and it is.

It is on earth that we are introduced to Adam and Eve's children, Cain and Abel, who in Muslim scriptures become cautionary tales about right kinship relations and, necessarily then, gender roles. Of early human population, Ibn Kathir stated,

> They were commanded (by God) that every son of them would marry the sister of his brother with whom she was born and every daughter would marry the brother of her sister with whom he was born. No one was allowed to get married with his sister with whom he was born.[45]

Adam asks Cain to marry his twin sister to Abel, but Cain refuses to do this because he wants to marry his sister himself on account of her extreme beauty. This is in direct defiance of the regulation to which Ibn Kathir draws our attention: God commands that twin children cannot marry one another. Upon hearing of Cain's decision, Adam tells his son to offer a sacrifice to God while he goes on pilgrimage to Mecca in hopes of finding a solution to this dispute. Abel offers a lamb, and Cain offers his worst crops. This leads to a horrific fire that destroys Cain's crops but leaves Abel's lamb untouched. This sacrifice scene, which leads to Cain killing Abel, highlights the distinction between the obedient son (Abel) and the disobedient son (Cain). This is also evident in the Ḥadīth of the prophet,

> When Muḥammad passed by Adam on the first heaven (on his night journey to Jerusalem and then to the heavens), he said, "welcome to the pious son and pious prophet." Muḥammad said, On his right side was a huge crowd, and on his left side was a huge crowd. When he looked on his right side, he smiled; and when he looked on his left side he cried. I (Muḥammad) said: "O Gabriel! What is the matter?" He replied: "He is Adam, and they are the souls of his children." When he looked on his right, who were the people of

paradise he smiled and when he looked on his left, who were the people of hell, he cried.[46]

In the same way that all stories related to creation show the way in which good overcomes evil through the ultimate submission to God, Cain and Abel are used to exemplify good and evil—"Be like the better of the two of Adam's sons."[47] Cain and Abel exemplify a typical form of dominant masculinity that aims for power over the other, but from a theological perspective it tacitly acknowledges that multiplicity in gender is a means toward ethics and morality.

We can see why feminists consider the creation narrative a cornerstone of patriarchal reading, but the players might be reoriented once we lay bare the relationships between them. Marked by obligations, Adam's partnership with Eve is what distinguishes him from God, who stands alone. On the other hand, Iblīs is Adam's foil, too, and it is really Adam's overlapping and negotiated relationships among these three others that start to define Islamic masculinity in the creation story. There is an ideal (God), a partner or cohort (Eve), and an antagonist (Satan). We'll see throughout this manuscript that these roles are very layered—with the West sometimes as the antagonist, as it is for Mawdūdi—and they reify narrow masculinity as much as they complicate it. Man finds himself in the center of all these relationships, which are all inflected with submission or its lack (Figure 3.1).

Joseph: Restrained virility

Joseph is one of the few prophets whose life warrants a full chapter in the Qur'ān. Sura Yusuf (Joseph) is a Meccan sura which recounts the life of Joseph, which is very different from that of Adam as there are more human characters within it and sexual ethics are explored in more detail. The story is also based in a family setting and the very fact that Joseph was one of 12 sons born to Jacob, also a prophet, gives dimension to the family roles. Joseph was said to be "the most noble, the most exalted, the greatest" of all the sons of Jacob.[48] The close relationship between Jacob's two sons from his wife Rachel, Joseph, and Benjamin, adversely affected the relationship between the other ten brothers and Jacob: "The close fraternal relationship between Benjamin and Joseph is a leitmotiv in the Qur'ānic story."[49] This then offers an understanding of the

Figure 3.1 Yusuf before Zulaykha, Yusuf, haloed and bearing a ewer on a tray, enters from the left before Zulaykha and her maids who, overwhelmed by his beauty, cut their fingers. A miniature painting from a sixteenth century manuscript of Majalis al- 'Ushshaq ("The Assemblies of the Lovers"). Image taken from Majalis al- 'Ushshaq of Sultan Husayn Mirzā. Originally published/produced in Shiraz, Iran, 1590–1600. (Photo by The British Library/Robana via Getty Images)

roles expected of "brothers." Joseph's distinction is further underscored—or exacerbated, depending on the point of view—when he is given a staff of light which had five branches. On the first branch was written, "Abraham, friend of God;" on the second, "Isaac, sacrifice of God;" on the third, "Ishmael, pure of God;" on the fourth, "Jacob, Israelite of God;" and on the fifth, "Joseph, Righteous of God."[50] This puts him in a somewhat direct line of male succession and identifies him as playing a special role.

The Qur'ānic chapter begins with Joseph recalling a dream to his father, Jacob, indicating God choosing him as a prophet: "O my father! Behold, I saw [in a dream] eleven stars, as well as the sun and the moon: I saw them prostrate themselves before me!" (Qur'ān 12:4). It is widely accepted that this dream took place when Joseph was young, before maturity. The 11 stars signify his 11 brothers; the sun and the moon are his parents.[51] This dream highlights the way in which Joseph is to gain high merit for his actions, causing Jacob to worry that Joseph's brothers may envy him: "O my dear son! Do not relate thy dream to thy brothers lest [out of envy] they devise an evil scheme against thee; verily Satan is man's open foe" (Qur'ān 12:5). Here Joseph is set against the same driving force—envy, perhaps born of arrogance—that altered Adam's existence. God insinuates at the outset in the Qur'ānic story that Joseph's end will be successful, possibly to re-assure before his life was to change.

In the Qur'ānic story, Joseph's envious brothers throw him into a well and sell him to Zulaykha,[52] wife of Potophir (al-Aziz). Joseph is adopted into the house of al-Aziz as a son, and the Qur'ān comments how God gives Joseph a "firm place on earth" Qur'ān 12:21, which gives him the security and comfort for God to "impart unto him some understanding of the inner meaning of happenings" (Qur'ān 12:21). The narration then continues at a later point in Joseph's life: "and when he reached full manhood, we bestowed upon him the ability to judge [between right and wrong], as well as [innate] knowledge: for thus do we reward the doers of good" (Qur'ān 12:21).

As a prophet of God, Joseph's life has to convey the divine message, as is the instruction to all prophets. In the case of Joseph this takes place through his relationship with the wife of al-Aziz, Zulaykha, who tempts him: "And [it so happened that] she in whose house he was living [conceived a passion for him and] sought to make him yield himself unto her; and she bolted the doors and said, 'Come thou unto me!'" (Qur'ān 12:23).[53] Although Joseph seeks salvation from God, he is equally tempted:[54]

> May God preserve me! Behold, goodly has my master made my stay [in this house]! Verily, to no good end come they that do [such] wrong! And, indeed, she desired him, and he desired her; [and he would have succumbed] had he not seen [in this temptation] an evidence of his sustainer's truth: thus [we willed it to be] in order that we might avert from him all evil and all deeds of abomination—for, behold, he was truly one of Our servants. (Qur'ān 12: 23–24)

Joseph and Zulaykha's attraction is mutual. However, Joseph resists his feelings for her only because of God's command and fear, as this exchange illustrates:

> "O Joseph, I love you with all my heart. Lift up your head and look at me in the fullness of my beauty!" "Your master (husband) has more right to that than I do." "Come close to me, Joseph." "But I fear lest my portion of paradise be lost." "I have discretely veiled my affair from the people, so come close to me!" "But who will veil me from God, the Lord of the universe?"[55]

There is tension between Joseph and Zulaykha, between their feelings and social mores, and between mutual desire, on the one hand, and obedience and submission to God, on the other. Joseph is clearly tempted by Zulaykha's beauty and charm, but his concern is with fulfilling his obligation and submission to God in the correct way.

Joseph and Zulaykha love each other deeply, perhaps, but the scriptures make clear that they are both surpassing in physical beauty.[56] The Qur'ān and Ḥadīth elaborate on the connection between beauty and temptation in an attempt to present a moral framework for sexual ethics that hinges on these various axes. As a son in the house of al-Aziz, Joseph cannot have a sexual affair with Zulaykha, the housemaster's wife. Ibn Kathir narrated a Ḥadīth on this matter:

> Allah will provide with refuge under His shelter to seven peoples on the day of judgment when there will be no shelter except His shelter: the just ruler; and to a man who remembered Allah in his solitude that his eyes overflowed with tears; and to a man who is always in the mosque when he goes out from it till he returns from it; and to two people whose friendship was only for the sake of Allah, they came together for this reason and they departed each other for this reason; and to a man who gave in charity secretly that what his

> right hand spent was not known to his left hand; and to a youth who spent his life in Allah's devotion; and to a man who was seduced by a woman of beauty and position but he said fear Allah.[57]

Joseph's experience is echoed in the last of these seven categories, which maps him squarely in God's camp. Though he may have intrinsic personal qualities outside of the ability to resist temptation, it is Joseph's successful navigation of the sexually tempting ordeal that demonstrates his right to be counted among prophets and in that strong male lineage.

Stowasser challenges this interpretation as demeaning to women, since "the concept of *fitna* ('social anarchy,' 'social chaos,' 'temptation') . . . indicates that to be a female is to be sexually aggressive and, hence, dangerous to social stability."[58] Zulaykha's attraction is not understood as woman's love but as an essential "flaw" in female nature.[59] Stowasser argues that according to tradition, "God has instilled an irresistible attraction to women in man's soul, which works through the pleasure he experiences when he looks at her or deals with anything related to her."[60] It is evident from the Qur'ānic narrative that God is chastising not the mutual attraction and love between Zulaykha and Joseph but the associated factors in which they were about to conduct their affair. These issues are highlighted in the gossip that spreads: "the wife of this nobleman is trying to induce her slave-boy to yield himself unto her! Her love for him has pierced her heart; verily, we see that she is undoubtedly suffering from an aberration!"[61] This section of the Qur'ān attempts to show the affection that Zulaykha has for Joseph. Indeed the Qur'ān is not admonishing the attraction that each had for one another but is against the way in which this relationship is taking shape.

The relationship between Joseph and Zulaykha could be understood as an exploration of the way in which God allows love to grow between them but wants to make an example of the two in deceiving and hurting others, especially al-Aziz. It is also a relationship which highlights the way that gender, sex, and submission to God are inextricably bound to morality and ethics. Muslims are expected to be cautious that their physical relationships do not infringe on the rights of others, for this would be contrary to submission to God. Zulaykha is not redeemed in the same way that Joseph is; hence, the *men* who can put their higher duty ahead of their baser urges are considered to be following in the prophet Joseph's footsteps.

Us conclusion abt how men are to resist urges & that it only responsibility sexually

Muḥammad: The ultimate messenger and his context

Muḥammad, as the last and final messenger of God, is often understood as the ideal male in Islam. His life has been documented and commented on intensively throughout history. There are two main concerns when approaching Muḥammad's life as we will see in this chapter: his prophecy and his personhood in relation to his family. Compared to those of the other prophets, Muḥammad's biography is the most detailed, but to what extent can he be accepted as the perfect example of masculinity? I agree with Kecia Ali, who quips, "it is a tricky proposition to accept that the prophet is a model of conduct for all Muslims while simultaneously believing it would be wrong of a Muslim man to follow his example in consummating a marriage with a nine year old."[62] Muḥammad's marriages are one of the most contentious areas of interest. To ascertain the effect that Prophet's own life has had on Islamic masculinity, we have to determine whether his prophethood—that is, his special standing—is coterminous with his life or a separate matter altogether.

Muḥammad is born into a broken family to parents Amina bint Wahb and Abdullah Ibn Mutallib. Abdullah, his father, dies while away on a business trip to Palestine and Syria.[63] When Amina is pregnant, she hears a voice which says, "thou carriest in thy womb the lord of this people; and when he is born say: 'I place him beneath the protection of the One, from the evil of every envier'; then name him Muḥammad."[64] Muḥammad has been denied a father—this biography's first challenge to the ideal, much less nuclear, family system. In patriarchal Arabia, Amina's shock and despair at being told that she will give birth to a boy named Muḥammad are inevitable. Muḥammad is initially adopted by his grandfather, Abdul Muttalib, who tells his own newborn son, Abbas, to kiss Muḥammad as his "brother."[65] Muḥammad is then sent to a wet nurse, Halima, who was to care for him in the open, fresh air of the desert. It is here that Halima experiences something extraordinary. Muḥammad later explains the events from Halima's perspective:

> there came unto me two men, clothed in white, with a gold basin full of snow. Then they lay upon me, and splitting open my breasts they brought forth my heart. This likewise they split open and took from it a black clot which they cast away. Then they washed my heart and my breast with the snow. Satan toucheth every son of Adam the day his mother beareth him, save only Mary and her son.[66]

Halima returns Muḥammad to his mother, Amina, but she also dies while Muḥammad is at a young age. It is clear from the outset that Muḥammad's significance is much broader than the bounds of his biological family. Muḥammad is protected from Satan in order for him to fulfill his duty to God. It is for this reason that Halima decides not to look after Muḥammad any longer—he is so unusual for a young boy, especially compared with her own son.

After the death of his mother, Muḥammad is placed under the full care of Abdul Muttalib, his grandfather. However, this is also short lived: Abdul Muttalib dies, and so his uncle Abu Talib cares for him. It is during a business trip in Bostra with his uncle that Muḥammad meets Bahira the Christian monk, who identifies Muḥammad as a special prophet and tells Abu Talib to look after him. Bahira states, "this (Muḥammad) is the master of all humans. Allah will send him with a message which will be a mercy to all beings."[67]

Muḥammad grows up in the household of his uncle Abu Talib and quickly becomes fond of his cousin Fakhita, whom he asks his uncle for permission to marry.[68] However, this is not to be; she marries her cousin, Hubayrah.[69] Later, Muḥammad meets Khadija, the rich merchant who has been married twice before. Khadija offers him a job, and he goes on a business trip for her in which he is accompanied by Maysarah, a young boy. During this journey, Muḥammad meets another monk, Nestor, who states to Maysarah that Muḥammad is the awaited prophet. On his return, Muḥammad becomes more attractive to Khadija. After consulting with her friend Nufaysah, Muḥammad marries Khadija.[70]

Muḥammad's initial attraction and love towards his cousin Fakhita is something that develops over a long period of time, and had that marriage taken place, Muḥammad's life would have been very different. Fakhita is not as powerful in society as Khadija is, and with what is to become of Muḥammad in later life he most likely needs the support of powerful people, including his wife. Khadija is also 15 years Muḥammad's senior, raising the question of whether marriage was rooted in financial and social status during this time. Finances certainly motivate Fakhita's marriage to Hubayrah, but what role does marriage play in the realm of Islamic *ideals*?

The prophet Muḥammad mentions what was required by men from eligible women for marriage: "A woman is married for four reasons, for her religion, her property, her status, her beauty, so you should choose one with religion."[71] Here he is reflecting society—marriage for property, status, and beauty—against the ideal, which is marriage for faith. A couple of Bukhārī ḥadīth encourage men to marry as a safeguard for morality (presumably sexual) and to fast if they are not able to wed.[72] Through this advice Muḥammad creates two forms of Islamic masculinity as he emphasizes the importance of marriage to some "young men" who are to marry for the sole purpose of "restraining the eyes and immorality," but those unable to do so are urged to fast. This then presents a difference between the advice of Muḥammad to the "potent young man" and the "impotent young man" as the former takes on an active male role within his community through marriage but for the latter, who is expected to fast takes a more submissive role in relieving himself from his sexual frustration through hunger. The physical impact of fasting weakens and slows the body cycle, and it could be understood as a way of castrating sexual urges. Muḥammad's advice gives us a clear image that there are some young men who are capable and best suited to adopt the active potent male role and some who are better suited to a more submissive, impotent role. Is such advice given to restrict sexual liberty of men and emphasize marriage or to remind young men of their ultimate role in submission to God and not be led solely by sexual satisfaction?

Muḥammad himself does not lead a celibate life, and in the year 619 CE his first wife Khadija dies. Muḥammad was married to her for 25 years, during which time they had six children, two boys and four girls. The boys all died in infancy. Muḥammad had received revelation, and people were converting to Islam, Khadija being the first to do so. Lings commented that 619 was the "year of sadness" as it also saw the death of the Prophet's much-loved uncle Abu Talib. Al-Mubarakpuri comments that after the death of Khadija the prophet decided to marry Sawdah, his first wife after Khadija's death, because he is "lonely."[73] The marriage of the prophet to Hafsah, the daughter of Umar, only happens because her first husband, Khunays, had died in the battle of Badr. Hafsah might have lived a widow's life had it been acceptable in Arabian society at the time, but this was clearly not the case. It was for this reason that Umar is frantically trying to find a husband for his daughter. Umar asks Uthman, who had just recently become a widower himself after the death of Ruqayyah, the prophet's daughter. Uthman refuses, arguing that he is not ready for marriage at the time. Umar then asks Abu Bakr, who also refuses only because he has been confided in by the prophet himself who has shown an interest in Hafsah. It is for this reason that the prophet asks Umar for Hafsah's hand and, in doing this, gives his other daughter, Umm Kalthum, to Uthman to marry. On this marriage, Watt stated that the "binding together of the leaders of the emigrants" was "another form of consolidation that was evidence in the year following Badr."[74] The various formulations of marriage during early Islam clearly link the political climate, which was steeped in the emerging new form of monotheism, and the prevalent culture of marriage traditions.

All told, the wives of the prophet are Khadija bint Khuwaylid, Sawda bint Samah, Aisha bint Abu Bakr, Hafsah bint Umar ibn al Khattab, Zaynab bint Khuzayma, Umm Salama Hind bint Abi Ummaya, Zaynab bint Jahsh, Juwayriya bin al-Harith, Ramlah bint Abi Sufyan, Safiyya bint Huyayy, Maymuna bint al-Harith, Mariya al-Qibtiyyah, and Raihana bint Zaid. It is important to note that Safiyya is Jewish from the Nudair tribe, and Mariya is a Christian Copt. There are conflicting historical narratives about whether either of these women converted to Islam.[75] Watt argues that there was a definite purpose to these marriages, "these marriages, like all the marriages Muḥammad contracted himself or arranged for his followers, had thus a definite political purpose, whatever else may have been involved."[76] The Prophet's own life, with respect to his wives, is therefore tricky to label as an Islamic ideal. Context—political, personal, economic—plays a considerable part in the decision to move forward with each of the marriages.

Whether the situation was created for expedience or for higher theological significance, Muḥammad clearly has multiple wives at the same time. The Qur'ānic injunction which allows men to have more than four wives has supported a particular form of Islamic masculinity, too.[77] The Qur'ān states, "marry from among women such as are lawful to you—[even] two, or three or four; but if you have reason to fear that you might not be able to treat them with equal fairness, then only [one]" (Qur'ān 4:3). Some commentators have argued that such divine commandments emerged in the context of the prevailing condition, with Arabia not limiting the number of wives a man could have, nor were there many kinship restrictions—wives could be each others' sisters, and men could marry women who had previously been linked to their own fathers. And men controlled divorce virtually all of the time.[78]

Fazlur Rahman argues that the Qur'ān sought to resolve the situation in small strokes of progress: "the truth seems to be that permission for polygamy was at a legal plane while the sanctions put on it were in the nature of a moral ideal towards which the society was expected to move, since it was not possible to remove polygamy legally at one stroke."[79] On this reading, polygamy is allowed but not necessarily recommended, and the Prophet's life is acceptable in this regard but not an absolute standard for Islamic perfection. In the same vein, Rahman raises the issue: although the Qur'ān "legally accepts the institution of slavery," it also strongly urged the emancipation of slaves.[80] Roald argues that the prophet Muḥammad's multiple marriages arose from the fact that there were many war widows during the time, and in a society where men were the leaders and rulers, women needed the protection of men in order to have any form of social status.[81] However, there are difficulties in understanding the multiple marriages of the prophet Muḥammad as purely an act of support to the women he married and not sexual. As one companion of the prophet, Anas, narrated, "The Prophet used to go round (have sexual relations with) all his wives in one night, and he had nine wives."[82]

The multiple marriages of the prophet Muḥammad are an issue of contentious debate both in terms of his vocation of submitting to God and in terms of their ability to uphold sexual ethics. Returning to the role of the prophet, then, one might understand that Muḥammad's main mission is to serve God and make others do the same. During the prevailing time, this was not diminished by his multiple marriages but in fact strengthened because his focus is on securing a one-to-one relationship with God and not any other human being. This further challenges the concept of marriage and monogamous relationships, which could become a hindrance to submitting fully to just God. This would be supported by the Qur'ānic passage which states, "Never can there be a secret confabulation between three persons without His (God) being the fourth of them, nor between five without His being the sixth of them; and neither between less than that, or more, without His being with them wherever they may be" (Qur'ān 58:7).

Such ideas on marriage could have been the reason for the spread of the concept of *Nikāḥ Mut'ah* (temporary marriage) in the *Shi'a* legal system and the idea of *Nikāḥ Mis'yār* (travelers marriage) in the Sunni legal system, which were fully adopted during the medieval period and remain so in certain parts of the Islamic world today.[83] Hughes argued that some Shi'a accounts state that Muḥammad had as many as 21 wives.[84] The Qur'ānic injunction which supports such temporary marriages reads, "But lawful to you are all [women] beyond these, for you to seek out, offering them of your possessions, taking them in honest wedlock, and not in fornication" (Qur'ān 4:24). In one ḥadīth tradition the prophet had authorized his companions to have temporary marriages.[85]

Commentators can either present the prophet Muḥammad as a pedophile who married for reasons relating to sex or save Muḥammad's honor by saying that these marriages were the outcome of variable difficult social factors for the women married to him. In this sense, the Prophet's actions around sexual ethics play into his way of submitting to God, much as Joseph's behavior does, except that Muḥammad is expected to show submission to God through multiple marriages (and sexual partners) and Joseph is to show it through abstention. So while the sexual expression differs so dramatically—their challenges are almost exact opposites—submission to God remains central. As ends on a continuum of what sexual ethics look like when played out, these male paragons Joseph and Muḥammad are able to illustrate that masculinity can look different in its outworkings—which is permissible so long as the core of one's identity is submission to God. The most significant factor in all of the Prophet's relationships was the demand that his life be an example to humanity of obedience and submission to God.

↳ Joseph + Muh. submitted in very diff ways

Jesus: A nonfamilial prophet

Jesus' life events differ greatly from those of any other prophet. It is for this reason that most writers, Muslim or non-Muslim, seem fixated on comparing and contrasting the position of Jesus in Islam and Christianity.[86] Comparing and contrasting the Muslim and Christian Jesus is also a concern within the Qur'ān. Tarif Khalidi, professor of Arabic and Islamic studies, presented four key concerns of the Qur'ān when narrating the life of Jesus, who is mentioned 25 times in the Qur'ān:[87] his birth and infancy, his miracles, his conversations with God or the Israelites, and any divine pronouncements on his humanity.[88] The life of Jesus, especially his upbringing, is not fully narrated in either biblical or Qur'ānic scripture.[89] There is also no narrative description of Jesus' ministry in the Qur'ān.[90] As it does in stories associated with other prophets, the Qur'ān presents key events for a purpose: "his (Jesus) miracles are not mentioned so much as listed as reminders of the power granted to him by God to cure the sick and raise the dead."[91]

Jesus' life begins and ends in circumstances that defy every social and scientific norm that might support notions of a nuclear family or the roles found within one. Jesus, son of Mary, is born through the process of a virgin birth—this is not Muḥammad's origin. However, Muḥammad and Jesus are similar in the sense that they have no father role models in their lives. Although He devised the system of copulation-based procreation, God also has the power to overrule it. God speaks to Mary, a virgin:

> O Mary! Behold, God sends thee the glad tiding, through a word from him, (of a son) who shall become known as the Christ Jesus son of Mary, of great honor in this world and in the life to come, and (shall be) of those who are drawn near unto God. (Qur'ān 3.46)

Even Mary states to God that it is not possible for her to bear a child because no man has ever touched her, but God states that it was his will. Although Jesus is born as a man, God removes the biological issues leading up to his birth—much as it is with Adam, who was created from a substance. The virgin birth of Jesus has left many in confusion, but these miraculous events breaking all societal and scientific norms constitute a theme by which Islamic traditions glorify God.

Unlike Muḥammad, Jesus' life is difficult to compare with any other human being. Muḥammad is conceived from a male and female, married, has children, grows old and dies. Jesus, on the other hand, does not have such life events. It makes some sense, then, that commentators have attempted to compare the lives of Jesus and Muḥammad in terms of their miracles, although the New Testament provides more details about Jesus' science-defying performances.[92] Although Ridgeon highlighted scriptural comparison on the lives of the prophets, the extent to which a comparison of their personal miracles is more important than their ultimate role as prophets of God and conveying the message of God's oneness is one which the Qur'ān clarifies,

> And We caused Jesus, the son of Mary, to follow in the footsteps of those [earlier prophets], confirming the truth of whatever there still remained of the Torah; and We vouchsafed unto him the Gospel, wherein there was guidance and light, confirming the truth of whatever there still remained

> of the Torah, and as a guidance and admonition unto the God-conscious. (Qur'ān 5:46)

God raises Jesus' agency beyond biology and family matters. However, his ultimate role of submitting to God as a messenger is exactly the same as all other prophets, including Muḥammad, whose family life is more conventional: "like Muḥammad, the Qur'ānic Jesus is called a 'prophet' (*nabi*) a messenger (*rasul*) and a servant (*abd*) of God. Like him too he is said to have been sent as a 'mercy' (*rahma*). He received a revelation called the Gospel just as Muḥammad subsequently received the Qur'ān."[93] Jesus explains his own role:

> And (I have come) to confirm the truth of whatever there still remains of the Torah, and to make lawful unto you some of the things which (aforetime) were forbidden to you. And I have come unto you with a message from your sustainer; remain then, conscious of God, and pay heed unto me. Verily, God is my sustainer as well as your sustainer; so worship Him (alone): this is the straight way. (Qur'ān 3:50–51)

Jesus is also believed to have distanced himself from worldly matters and power—either causing or a function of his devotion to God.[94]

Unlike Adam, Joseph, and Muḥammad, Jesus does not have a female companion in the Qur'ān, which further distinguishes this prophet from the others. It also raises the question of Jesus' masculinity, since it can only be understood outside of sexual ethics. The Qur'ān does mention that Jesus was of the same nature of Adam, "verily, in the sight of God, the nature of Jesus is as the nature of Adam, whom he created out of dust and then said unto him, 'Be'—and he is" (Qur'ān 3:59). Since we know that Adam needs Eve and that Jesus is made of the same substance, then Jesus' lack of wife actually undermines the connection between an essential Islamic masculinity and marriage or sex.

↳ Jesus' singleness undermines

Relational, contextual masculinities

Any consistent ideal of Islamic masculinity would be very difficult to read from the lives of the prophets. Adam was given a female companion for the purpose of companionship and procreation, but there is no mention of Jesus reproducing and having his own family. In the case of Joseph, he is created and nurtured by a biological father but finds himself shunned by his brothers and adopted by a wealthy nobleman before falling in love with his stepmother. It is not clear whether Joseph finds a companion and has a family, but the Qur'ān does go into great depths in narrating the love that Joseph and Zulaykha had for one another. Muḥammad loses his biological father at an early stage, and although his grandfather and uncle take up the role of father, his true vocation is beyond the family.

The lives of the prophets are used as examples to human beings, but God made sure to present prophets and messengers best suited to the environment. Their lives tell us much about ethics and morality but little about a uniform Islamic masculinity. As with any story, there are multiple ways of interpreting them and at times this has led to extrapolating images of an ideal Islamic masculinity—but the Qur'ān itself does not present one. Every major commentator on the lives of the prophets has interpreted the stories to suit and support gender roles, especially through the social construction of "family." The family becomes the means of supporting gender construction, including gender inequality, bias, and dysfunction.

The fact that the Qur'ān is read to only support men having up to four wives but interpreters have traditionally not allowed women the same liberty is one such example of gender inequality. Even if one were to believe that in the context of the seventh century this was beneficial, in the contemporary world this stance does not sit well and attracts many heated debates. All sides extrapolate from the Qur'ānic text; one might even argue for the legitimacy of multiple husbands for women on the premise that the prophet Muḥammad's multiple wives and Joseph's abstention from a sexual affair with Zulaykha were opposite means to ultimate submission. Understanding masculinity in Islam as uniform and monolithic without appreciating the diverse lives of prophets would not allow for such a line of thought. At certain stages of human history the God of the Qur'ān has challenged family roles by creating prophets without biological parents: Adam and Jesus. Could this be another lesson from God to highlight his perfection by placing human beings, including prophets, into dysfunctional families but making clear that such deficiencies are resolved when creation submits to God? A literal reading of the Qur'ān leaves many gaps in the stories of any prophet—could this be in order not to present any prophet as an "ideal man" but to present them all as mere messengers who offer lessons on ultimate submission to God through a variety of different lives?

It is a human tendency to make sense of prophet's lives as contributing to an idealized masculinity, even though that contradicts the very diverse nature of every prophet mentioned in the Qur'ān. This tendency is even encouraged by the scriptures themselves: "the Qur'ān states ideas that all prophets are fundamentally the same, and there is no distinction between them (Qur'ān 2:136). So they can be considered as perfect men who manifest the appropriate attribute at the correct time."[95] When we follow in our hermeneutical forerunners' footsteps of looking for the common denominator among the prophets, we see that the prophetic narrative in the Qur'ān is rooted in the role of submission to God. The events in the lives of the prophets may differ or seem extraordinary, but the message which they present is essentially the same: "words spoken by a prophet or to him by God tend to find echoes, sometimes verbatim repetition among other prophets."[96] The best case to be made is that this message seems to be submission, not some prescriptive familial role based on gender.

Masculinity or masculinities are inextricably bound with the act of submission to God and are not identified as separate notions in understanding men in the Qur'ānic text: there is no textual theme of highlighting what makes the prophets masculine. Our interrogation reads against the grain to reveal that there is no ideal masculinity in Islam. The fact that there are numerous prophets mentioned in the Qur'ān and each one has a different biography is evidence of this fact. The first relationship that man (Adam) has is with God. This is not based on any roles or on procreation but on the main premise that Adam, who represents the whole of human creation, would submit to God as creator. There is no ideal masculinity, but submission is a strong ideal in all its forms.

As an analytical approach, masculinities studies is fully complementary to Qur'ānic studies because the Qur'ān upholds the notion that masculinity and femininity are socially constructed at any given time. The only constant overarching power above men and women is God. *Islamic cultures* and *traditions*, on the other hand, have attempted to embed and impose certain ideals upon every man and women. This has led to strong reactions against such ideals, causing many conflicts in society relating to gender, sex, and traditional roles. However, adding God to these relationships could conceivably relieve men and women from adopting any role or ideal. The God of the Qur'ān only demands his creation obey his command. In this way, piety and submission to God trump conforming to societies' ideals and gender roles, and these supreme values could support a diversity of Islamic masculinities. This is only possible because the other relationalities that political Islamists use to constrain masculinity—women and the West acting as profoundly other—dissolve in the presence of the only hierarchical relationship that is common to all the Qur'ānic prophets.

- Prophets (all men)
  - all essentially same; yet vastly diff. family dynamics (non-family) + "masculinity" presentation
- Submission to God vs god as constant, unchanging power over men + women
- Creation story / Adam + Eve

4

Mirzā Ghālib's Hedonistic Challenge

The ocean of sins was not vast enough; it dried right up
And still my garments hem was barely damp with it

Note too how I regret the sins that I could not commit
O Lord, if you would punish me for these committed sins.
Mirzā Ghālib[1]

As the Qur'ān was revealed at a specific time in history and presented many different stories and parables, it is also a window onto a specific culture's way of shaping—even founding—Islamic masculinity. The Qur'ānic icons and figures are products of the Arab world, with its key locations of Makka, Medina, and Jerusalem. To understand the construction of Islamic masculinity beyond Arabia, this chapter pivots to Mughal India during the nineteenth century and specifically to a figure whose relationship to masculinity was complex at best. Mirzā Asadullāh Khān Ghālib was to become forever associated with the Urdu and Persian language. Understood to be the greatest Muslim Indian poet of the nineteenth century, Ghālib wrote on every aspect of life: "happiness and despair, jolly drinking and solemn praise, surprise and nostalgia, longing for death and eternal restlessness."[2]

An exploration of Ghālib's life and work casts, in rather dramatic relief, his commitment to the tenet of submission to God, which he held in tension with a fairly hedonistic lifestyle. He was far from the law-abiding Muslim that commentators such as Mawdūdi would put forth as a model. He saw himself unable to fulfill his ancestors' militaristic ideas of Muslim manhood, and in addition to a conventional marriage he engaged in arguably illicit romantic relationships and drunkenness. But through his poetry and letters, one sees the way in which his entire existence is organized around a deep spiritual relationship with God. He did not follow a ritualistic Islamic practice, and his inability to lay claim to what he feared was the most upstanding form of the religion plagued his thoughts.[3] Religious practice is linked to understandings of Islamic masculinity or masculinities, and to deem Ghālib's masculinity as Islamic, one needs to appreciate that spirituality takes a multitude of guises,

Figure 4.1 Ghālib's poetry hangs on an old Delhi plaque outside his home. It reads "... it was not in my fate ... that ultimate union with the beloved ... had I lived on ... this waiting ... would still be my only desire" (my own translation)

much as we can appreciate the diversity of the Qur'ānic prophets surveyed in the previous chapter (Figure 4.1).

Ghālib is clearly one of the foremost ghazal writers of Mughal India. Ghazals are a poetic form of rhyming couplets with a refrain and a systematized measure. Ghālib's ghazals were complex, and his effective use of complicated vocabulary meant he was either loved or envied. Apart from his poetic genius, Ghālib enjoyed writing letters, which have since been published in numerous volumes. These letters, written to his friends and students (*shāgird*), offer insight into his personal relationship with others, especially men, upon whom he shaped his own masculinity. Some of Ghālib's companions were important figures in society at the time. His closest friend was Altaf Hussain Hali (1837–1914); he wrote an extensive biography on Ghālib called "Yādgār-i-Ghālib" that, along with Ghālib's autobiographical accounts, serves as this chapter's most substantial source material. Sir Syed Ahmad Khān (1817–98), the Indian modernist who set up the Aligarh movement which later became a university, was another key figure closely associated with Ghālib. His interactions with his contemporaries create the portrait analyzed in this chapter.

An Islamic poet for Mughal India

Ghālib was a product of his context, to be sure, but he was also a singular figure, and an examination of his life and the ways in which he did not fit in reveals much about the surrounding culture. He lived during and within an era that was definitive for his region, and he is representative of the broader intellectual renaissance afoot. The Mughal Empire reigned from the early sixteenth century to the mid-nineteenth century and covered the land of what is today Pakistan, India, Bangladesh, Nepal and parts of Afghanistan. The estimated population of the empire at its peak was between 110 and 130 million inhabitants over a landmass of around a billion acres.

It is during the reign of King Bahadur Shah Zafar (1775–1862) that we find some of the most extraordinary Muslim intellectuals at work.[4] An environment of relative peace is conducive to a healthy output from any society and this was, to a certain extent, the case in Mughal India under the rule of King Bahadur Shah Zafar, who was devoutly Muslim, but there were no sectarian divisions.[5] Indeed the court celebrated in earnest *Raksha Bandan*, a Hindu festival honoring the relationship between a brother and sister; *Dussehra*, a Hindu festival of dance; *Holi*, the spring festival of colors; *Diwali*, a Hindu, Sikh, and Jain festival of lights; *Shivratri*, a festival associated with Lord Shiva; and *Basant Panchami*, celebrating the goddess Saraswati in Hinduism. It is said that Muslim intellectual progress was prosperous during this polyreligious time: Delhi College became a hub for Islamic scholarship, hosting in the middle of the century a "sudden enthusiasm for western knowledge, especially scientific, and the first sign of recognition of and interest in, a new world beyond that of Islam among the Indian Muslims."[6]

It may be that creativity in thought and action is heightened in Muslim societies when the identity of the Muslim is strong enough to be open to cultural and religious differences. At the fall of the Mughal Empire around 1757, direct British rule brought with it another cultural identity and power. This in turn gave the Mughals two options: either they could adopt the new culture and assimilate, or they could reject and react against it. The strength of local sentiment may have been underestimated by the colonial powers, as the political situation caused the Muslims much distress. The economic situation was in disarray if not dire:

> A background of decay and corruption, salatins or imperial descendents lived in squalor living on pensions of Rs. 5 or less a month, spending time in gambling or cockfights or bemoaning their lot and an underworld of vice stimulated by idleness and frustration.[7]

Percival Spears, the renowned English historian, argued that, given the economic hardship, it was no wonder that Ghālib's writing was so introverted and fixated on eternity in another world rather than the hardships that had befallen him on earth.[8] At this time of turmoil and bloodshed, the intellectuals turned to producing work lamenting the demise of the Mughal Empire and times gone by, rousing and rallying the emotions of the Muslims.

Formations familial and professional

Ghālib was born on December 27, 1797 in Agra, India. His name at birth was Asadullāh Baig Khān, and his childhood nickname was Mirzā Nausha, which he also used for a certain time as his *takhallus* (pen name), which he later changed to "Ghālib," which in Urdu means "victor, victorious." For a poet to adopt such a grand pen name suggests a sense of achievement and pride, and his life story is evidence of the fact that he was indeed victorious at a number of levels. Ghālib showed utmost poise and conviction in his work—unless, of course, he was being ironic, a strong trait of the man.

Marriage can be seen as a milestone for Muslim men in many Islamic societies. In Mughal India, marriage was a strategic alliance brokered "to maintain the social status, the purity of lineage and the standards of social and economic security which the families of the boy and girl who are to be married have been accustomed to."[9] Parents arranged marriages early so that their scions would have an outlet for sexual satisfaction.[10] In keeping with Indian Muslim culture, Ghālib was married off at the age of 13 to a wife 11 years old. Ghālib and his wife moved to Delhi after marriage, and, also in keeping with the ambient culture, he left little in the way of description about his family life. We can surmise that it was "no more and no less successful than most in society, but he seems always to have felt that a wife was an encumbrance he could very well have done without."[11] It seems likely that Ghālib was a *ghar ja'mai*, the Urdu name given to a man who comes to live with his in-laws. At such a young age Ghālib would have needed the support of others and in this case his father-in-law.

Ghālib's wife was called Umrao Begum: "an exceedingly pious and sober lady, meticulous in keeping the fasts and in saying her prayers. She was as strict in her religious observance as Ghālib was lax in these matters."[12] Ghālib had seven children but none of them lived more than 15 months. Pavan K. Varma, an Indian historian and member of the Indian foreign service, commented that in Mughal times children were able to span the gulf between the otherwise very separate spheres of husband and wife:

> Men were educated, abreast of the affairs of the world, while women, mostly illiterate, and confined to *purdah*[13] and the home was considered—true to stereotypical definition—narrow in outlook and concerned exclusively with petty gossip and the mundane problems of running a home. Between this divide children were the bridge. Their absence seriously eroded the anchorage and solace a home and marriage could traditionally provide.[14]

Although Ghālib did not have any children of his own, he was able to play the role of father to his adopted nephews. The first, Zain al-Abidin Khān

Arif, was not just an adopted son to Ghālib but also a student. Ghālib educated him as he grew up and guided him on life matters. When Arif died in 1857, both Ghālib and his wife "felt the pangs of separation severely," Hali reported.[15] Arif left behind his wife and two sons, Baqar Ali Khān and Husain Ali Khān—both "true gentlemen of excellent character and were able young poets of some promise."[16] Initially they were looked after by their grandmother, but when she also died Ghālib took charge of them. At the time of Arif's death, Ghālib wrote an elegy to him in which he called upon Arif to explain why he had to die so soon, having not even had time to play with his two sons.[17] Given the tenor of society at the time, which did not encourage public or, certainly, written discussion of family matters, this elegy is a somewhat rare glimpse into the high respect Ghālib had for kinship relationships and roles. In a society that expected a man to have a wife and children, Ghālib tried very hard to conform to the pressure, but that was not to be, and it seemed that he spent his entire life working to perfect the poetry which he was so good at and using the effect of lost ideals and sadness as a muse for his writings.

Ghālib and his wife's marriage may not have been especially happy or successful, but as time went on they had become accustomed to each other and learnt to understand and respect each other. One of the leading Ghālib biographers, Natalia Prigarina, reported that Ghālib fell in love with the songstress at their wedding and later mentioned this courtesan in his letters.[18] In other personal communications, Ghālib himself characterized his marriage as a negative event in his life, "then on the seventh Rajab, 1225 (1810, the year of his marriage), sentence of life imprisonment was passed on me, fetters were put on my feet."[19]

Although Ghālib remained committed to Umrao Begum throughout his life, he was not at ease with the concept of monogamy:

> When I visualise paradise, and dream of the eventuality of being absolved of my sins and being lodged in a palace along with a *houri*[20] where I will have to live till eternity with the same blessed person, the idea sickens me and unbearable anguish oppresses my heart. Good God! That *houri* will become a pain in the neck! And that is but natural. Eternally the same emerald palace and eternally the same branch of the heavenly tree and, God forbid, the same *houri* for all time![21]

Even though Ghālib seemed saddened by the idea of being with the same person throughout his life, he did not separate from or divorce his wife at any time. It must also be considered that his sentiments could well be understood as banter between "lads," which quite often had to do with their wives. In order to strengthen their own masculinity, they might belittle the position of their wives among one another, even though they would dare not utter those words in front of their wives. It is clear from the correspondence between Ghālib and his acquaintances that they could not wholeheartedly understand married life as a matter of love—it is better described a requirement for social acceptance, for respectability, and, most of all, for masculinity.

Marriage brought added pressure on Ghālib as the man and provider of his family. The fact that his seven children all died at an early age did not reduce the financial burden on him, for he felt obligated to help the nephews he adopted:

> Not a penny comes in, and there are twenty mouths to feed. The allowance I get from you know where [Rampur][22] is just enough to keep body and soul together. And I have so much to do that during the twenty-four hours I get practically no time to myself. There is always something to worry about. I am a man; not a giant, and not a ghost. How am I to sustain such a heavy load of care? I am old and feeble.[23]

These words from Ghālib indicate the pressure that he was under in order to provide for his family, something expected from a man in Mughal society. Ghālib's wife, on the other hand, was to remain at home and uphold the role of spouse and mother. Ghālib and Umrao had two separate areas in their marital homes. Hali recalled that there was a *zanana* (female) part of their house where Umrao would welcome women guests.[24] In Islamic cultures there have always been multiple interpretations of what *hijab* (veil, separation) is, and Hali commented that Ghālib spent a fixed amount of time every day in the female quarters of the house with his wife.[25] The Prophet Muḥammad was also known to have allocated time to his numerous wives who lived separately from each other, which allows one to conclude that the physical separation of males and females in the household seems to have become a cultural tradition of sort in Islamic societies.

Ghālib and wife differed in character, and it was Hali who commented that Umrao was the one who came across as more pious and observant in faith, which also led to conflict between them. Umrao decided to separate the pots and pans that Ghālib used from hers, most probably due to the fact that Ghālib drank alcohol copiously, something frowned upon in strict Islamic societies and cultures, but she continued to care for Ghālib.[26] In typical Ghālib style, he sought solace in hell from the quandary of married life:

> True that when you are thrown into hell, on doomsday, they put a lid on the entrance. But in that difficult condition, you would not have the trouble of earning bread, providing clothes and quarrelling with your wife. And in that troubled spot, there would not be the menacing demands of the money-lender either.[27]

The arranged-marriage system in which Ghālib's union was conducted has been said to be the main reason why his poems are soaked in tragedy:

> This is not because the poets select only tragic stories for their themes, but because in the society in which they lived, love was a tragedy. In their day love and marriage were two separate things, and were generally regarded not only as separate but also as mutually opposed. . . . Before marriage the boy was to have no chance to fall in love; after marriage society hopes, he would have no occasion to.[28]

Ghālib's father-in-law, Ilahi Bakhsh Maruf, was a distinguished member of the Delhi aristocracy, a poet and a religious man who would attract students to seek spiritual guidance. On one occasion he attempted to impress Ghālib by asking him to copy the line of his spiritual descent through all the principals of his order. Ghālib was not impressed at all by this and copied the line only with alternate names. Maruf became angry and demanded an explanation from Ghālib, who stated that the ladder is used to climb to a higher level so if there are steps missing then the onus is on the climber to have a spring in their step to achieve a higher level. Maruf then tore up the scroll.

Had Ghālib been one who wanted to emulate the method of Maruf as a poet and spiritual guide, he would have toed the line perfectly.[29] The power dynamic between the two men at various levels displays the tension between masculinity and authority in Ghālib's life. He had to remain respectful to Maruf because he was the father of his wife, and it is also clear from his biographers that, at least in the beginning, Ghālib remained under the financial concern of Maruf to provide for his family, namely his wife. The impact of such a reliance may have been an embarrassment to Ghālib, especially since he was known for his earnesty. Although quick to seek a financial loan, he was always reluctant to receive favors from other men.[30] This may have been a reaction to the financial dependency that Ghālib had to live with from a young age. Consequently, he resented anyone who asserted the intellectual and religious superiority over him, and this caused him to rebel against his father-in-law.

Ghālib came from a family of soldiers of Turkish descent. He had a brother named Yousaf and a sister who was known as *Choti Khānum* (little lady). The family was wealthy and Ghālib grew up with every comfort and received a good education. He was taught Persian, Arabic, logic, philosophy, and medicine among other subjects. Ghālib began writing his poetry at the age of eight or nine, but he is said to have "regretted" that he could not follow in the military footsteps of his direct ancestors.[31] Ghālib's grandfather had served under the Emperor Shah Alam, and his own father had died in battle. On this matter he stated,

> Alas for my fate! Born to be struck down by misfortune and to see the granaries reduced to ashes. I had not the means to ride to war like my ancestors . . . nor the capacity to excel in knowledge and ability like Avicenna and the wise men of old. I said to myself, "Be a dervish and live a life of freedom."[32]

Ghālib's self-reflection is a clear indication of the way in which being a soldier was seen as one of the ideals to which a man should aspire. Even in a general sense, it is difficult to distance Islamic traditions from war and fighting.[33] The physical Jihād which was prevalent during the expansion of the Islamic empire has given rise to the notion that a man battling in war is the ultimate form not only of masculinity but also of masculine spirituality.[34] Through his path a soldier not only is fulfilling societal ideals of masculinity but is also understood to remain submitted to God through his acts in "holy war." It is for this reason that Jihād tends to be associated with its more brutal and bloody form rather than understood as an "inner spiritual struggle" to which Muslims must adhere. Ghālib comes across as being apologetic; being unable to "ride to war" made him feel ashamed that his masculinity had not lived up to the level of his relatives.

In a more figurative understanding of the term, *jihād* could be understood as a struggle to understand and submit to God. Through his writings, one may interpret Ghālib's sacred struggle as carried out through his pen in place of the sword. What is surprising is that Ghālib failed to associate his intellectual genius with his spiritual struggle and in turn his masculinity. Ghālib declared that he had opted to be a "dervish" to live a life of freedom as if to release himself from his imagined masculine ideals. In bemoaning his failings, Ghālib's cry "Alas for my fate!" indicates his religious conviction regarding divine decree and predestination, which are central tenets of Islam. Ghālib seemed intent on giving himself no distinction when he said that he was not like the "wise men of old" such as Avicenna. There has been a longstanding conflict between poets and philosophers, emotion and rationality in the Islamic world, and so this could be an indication of Ghālib's feeling that poets are the inferior sort.

Ghālib's attitude demonstrates an inclination toward an ideal Islamic masculinity, but he desponded at the reality of his life. In the poem "Bayān-e-Musanif" ("The Writers Apology"), he clearly sums up his submission and love for God alone:

My intent is to convey what I truly feel,
And not to show my expertise in the poetic field.

My ancestors, for generations, have been men-at-arms,
I take no special pride in my poetic zeal.

A man of independence will, "love all" is my creed,
No ill-will or malice, for anyone I feel

Is it not a rare privilege to serve Zafar, the king,
What if wealth, state or honour do not form my need!

To join issue with the king's mentor is beyond my thought,
Who has strength or courage or guts, to undertake this feat?

The king's conscience is a mirror reflecting people's hearts,
No vow, no pledge, no evidence does my conduct need.

I, and to write in Urdu, not my preferred task,
The marriage song was composed, my lord and liege to please

It was my duty to submit to his desire,
The prothalamion was meant to serve a special need.[35]

Ghālib was accepted as a poetic genius during his time, and this led many to seek his instruction. In that period, male students would be taught more commonly by male teachers than by female; Ghālib's own teachers were male. Initially, he received his education privately from Shaikh Mu'azzam, who was quite a popular teacher from Agra.[36] There are also numerous stories relating Ghālib to a teacher named Mulla Abdu's-Samad, an Iranian wanderer who came to stay with Ghālib's family for two years and during this time taught him Persian.[37] Ghālib commented on this by saying:

> I never had tuition from any person except the ultimate munificence (God) and Abdus Samad is only a fictitious name. But since people used to taunt me for having had no teacher, to close their mouths I have invented a fictitious teacher.[38]

However, this might not be altogether true, as his friend and biographer Hali mentioned a letter from Abdus Samad to Ghālib in which he mentioned how he constantly remembered Ghālib, "My dear one, what are you?, despite all my freedom and independence you constantly come to mind."[39] It may be that Ghālib had left a lasting mark on his teacher, whose insistence comes across rather as obsession with Ghālib. On the other hand, if a fiction, it is clear that the mentorship was to be an important part of his legendary life.

Hali related that a Mr Thompson, secretary of the Indian government, offered Ghālib a professorship in Persian at Delhi College.[40] Upon arrival for his invited interview, Ghālib waited for Thompson to come out and welcome him. The interviewer did not go out in the first instance but after being made aware of his presence went out and told Ghālib that this type of welcome could only be offered to him when he was a guest at the Governors' Durbar. Ghālib responded, "I contemplated taking a government appointment in the expectation that this would bring me greater honours than I now receive, not a reduction on those already accorded to me." The secretary replied, "I am bound by regulations." "Then I hope that you will excuse me," Ghālib responded and left.[41] At this stage in his life, Ghālib was an established poet, and although he had critics as well as admirers he was still highly regarded in society. His full awareness of his own position is reflected in the way he demanded respect from Thompson. As a future employer of Ghālib, Thompson was clearly in the position of power and could well have shown this by not going outside to welcome Ghālib, but he did and in turn attempted to explain why he did not come out quicker. Ghālib's attitude may clash with his claim of selflessness, but this episode could be an indication of the way he responded to other men in power and to God's ultimate power over him.

Even though Ghālib walked away from the professorship at Delhi College, he was destined to teach and throughout his life remained committed to his students. He was renowned for his poetic expertise, and this attracted all sorts of students. In numerous letters he wrote to his students explaining how he awaited their next communication and also drafts of their new work. This was the case with one of his closest friends, the Hindu Harghopal Tufta, of whom Ghālib wrote, "it is a matter of pride for me that I own one friend in India who is sincere and steadfast."[42] In his royal appointment, Ghālib taught King Bahadur Shah Zafar the art of poetry and in the year 1850, this reaped him the benefit of being conferred the honorific title of "Najmu'd-Daula Dabiru'l-Mulk Nizam Jang," which exalted him as a shining example in the kingdom. He was also asked to write a history of the royal descendants of Timur at an annual salary of six hundred rupees.[43] Ghālib took the heir apparent, Prince Fathu'l-Mulk (nicknamed Mirzā Fakhru), as his poetry student, too. His status as teacher accorded him aura and presence in society—he was not employed by an institution, but the students who he had were paying him private tuition.

Men to think with

Although Ghālib never competed athletically with his peers, he was competing with them intellectually. From an early age he would attempt to outsmart those around him. Ghālib's passion was his poetry and hence he took great pride in his work. The art of poetry and ghazal was one way in which male poets would act and react against the writing of other men in order to show their strength. During his time his contemporary and greatest nemesis was Ibrahim Zauq (d. 1854). Zauq was King Zafar's poet laureate (*Malik ush-Shuara*), an appointment that Ghālib bitterly resented. The rivalry between the two was often intense. On one occasion, Ghālib saw Zauq pass by him on his way to the Royal palace. Unable to contain himself, Ghālib retorted, "But a courtier of the King, he struts about so." This angered Zauq, prompting him to immediately complain to the king, who in turn summoned Ghālib to the palace from the tavern where he was still sitting. Ghālib was not concerned for Zauq but felt that the monarch would take this as a personal attack. Ghālib then immediately altered the statement into a poetic stanza:

> But a courtier of the king
> He struts about so
> Ghālib's prestige in the town
> What else—if not this[44]

Ghālib clearly respected the King but was making a moral attack, so to speak, on the arrogance that he felt was being displayed by Zauq.

Momin Khān was another great poet at the time, although Ghālib did not oppose him as he did Zauq. In fact, Momin was also an "intimate friend" of Ghālib from the time that he arrived in Delhi.[45] Momin died in 1851, which affected Ghālib greatly. Ghālib wrote in a letter,

> Just see, my friend, one after the other people of our own age die; the caravan moves off, and we ourselves are waiting one foot in the stirrup. Momin Khān was of the same age as I, and was a good friend too. We got to know each other forty-three years ago when we were no more than fourteen or fifteen years old . . . And my good sir, you'd be hard put to it to find even an enemy of forty years standing, let alone a friend.[46]

Ghālib was indeed known to be sociable and helpful to those men who wanted to learn poetry. Abdu'r-Ra'uf Uruj has compiled an extensive biographical text in which he introduces the reader to 203 of Ghālib's friends, and Malik Ram introduces the reader to 146 poets who were tutored by Ghālib, including Bahadur Shah Zafar, the last Mughal King.[47] He was committed to writing and responding to letters from his male friends. Schimmel stated that letter writing required fine-tuning, and this was mastered by Ghālib through his ability to compose in a mixture of Persian, Urdu, and Arabic as well as "the religious background of a mystically tinged Islam as it has lived in the hearts of millions of people."[48]

During Ghālib's time, gatherings called "Mushairas" in Urdu were places where poets would assemble to recite their new pieces of work. Hali outlined what he experienced of Ghālib at one such gathering:

> His style of reciting his verse, especially in Mushairas, was most moving and effective. I myself only heard him once at a Mushaira, a few years before the Mutiny, when Mushairas used to be held in the Hall of General Audience.

> His turn came at the very end, so that it was already morning when he rose to recite. "Gentlemen," he said, "I too must sing my lament." Then he recited, first an Urdu *ghazal*, and then one in Persian . . . in a voice so full of feeling that his voice alone seemed to be saying that in this whole assembly he sought in vain for one who knew his worth . . .[49]

These presentations would run very late into the night; on one occasion Ghālib recalls arriving home at midnight after a Mushaira.[50] In one of his letters to Mir Mahdi Majruh, he details the proceedings of an evening Mushaira, going into detail about all the poets—all male—who presented their work.[51] The Mushaira could be understood as a form of battle arena for male poets. Each vied for the accolades of the host, who at times would be the king himself. Every male poet was aiming to outdo the previous one, and this became the impetus to write poetry of the highest caliber. There was always some consternation when it came to Ghālib's turn to recite his poetry, as his poetry was often difficult to comprehend; few poets mixed Persian and Urdu as he did. Prigarina argued that Ghālib may have added Persian to his poetry for a reason: to best Zauq, whose chief mode was poetry in Rehkta, a highly Persianized form of Urdu prevalent during the seventeenth and eighteenth centuries in India. Ghālib may have actually underestimated the value of his Urdu poetry, favoring Persian strategically as he did in the Mushaira.[52]

The poet, biographer, and dear friend of Mirzā Ghālib named Khwaja Altaf Husain at birth, but took Hali as his *takhallus*. He went through a turbulent early life; while he was still a boy, his father died and his mother was deemed insane. So he was brought up by his sister in Panipat, India. Ghālib and Hali's relationship began when the latter was around 17 years old. Prigarina stated that Hali was studying at a Madrasah (traditional school) in Delhi and had a fondness for poetry. He would frequent Ghālib's *Mushairas*, and the two quickly became closely attached. Ghālib would explain difficult *ghazals* to Hali, on one occasion even saying, "I never advise anyone to devote himself to poetry, but as far as you are concerned, I think if you didn't write poetry you would be doing violence to your capabilities."[53]

His friendship with Ghālib had a profound impact on Hali's sense of Islamic ideals and Muslim lifestyles:

> I thought that in all God's creation only the Muslims, and of the seventy-three Muslim sects only the Sunnis, and of the Sunnis only the Hanafis,

> and of the Hanafis only those who performed absolutely meticulously the fasts and prayers and other outward observances, would be found worthy of salvation and forgiveness—as though the scope of God's mercy were more confined and restricted than Queen Victoria's empire, where men of every religion and creed live peacefully together. The greater the love and affection I felt for a man, the more strongly I desired that he should meet his end in the state in which, as I thought, he could attain salvation and forgiveness; and since the love and affection I felt for Ghālib were intense, I always lamented his fallen state, thinking, so to say, that in the garden of *Rizwan* (In Paradise) we should no more be together and that after death we should never see each other again.[54]

By comparing himself, God, Queen Victoria, and then Ghālib, Hali presents the method by which he justifies his love for Ghālib and his desire to enter paradise. It is as though Hali is trying to make sense of his attraction to Ghālib but cannot justify it on any religious terms. Hali then concedes that there is more than one way to lead a life in submission to God—more than one way to lead a life as a Muslim man. He declares his love for Ghālib, and it is through this love that he finds a path to justify how God must also accept Ghālib as His creation. After presenting this circuitous argument, it is as though Hali still remains unsure of Ghālib's ability to access the gardens of paradise and whether the two of them would enjoy the experience together. Essentially, Ghālib challenged Hali to consider, or reconsider, theological issues. Such a dilemma, for Hali, is further credit to Ghālib's poetry in terms of its relationship with the divine. The intensity with which Hali declares his love for Ghālib raises the question of whether there was more than just friendship between the two. However, Shackle and Majeed argue that this could well be related to the fact that Hali saw Ghālib as his mentor, taking the place of the father he lost when he was so young.[55]

Sir Syed Aḥmed Khān (1817–98) was another contemporary and companion of Ghālib. Khān was born into a noble family and worked for the East India Company[56] in 1839 but was also a court worker for the nominal Mughal emperor of Delhi "who had conferred upon him several honorific titles."[57] Khān was known for his Westernized ways, which were strengthened in his interaction with Great Britain. He visited Britain between 1869 and 1870, and during this visit he met many members of the aristocracy, which made him feel at ease with the British lifestyle. It was Khān's dream to establish an educational institution that would promote "liberalisation of ideas, broad humanism, a scientific world view, and a pragmatic approach to politics."[58] Against the will of his critics, he did establish a Muslim academic institution, known as Aligarh. The Dar ul-Ulum schools in Deoband and Lucknow were not Westernized like Khān's Aligarh, but they shared "a sense that Islamic education needed reform in order to be meaningful in the late nineteenth century."[59]

Khān found no difficulty in bridging the West and India in educational ventures:

> Syed Aḥmed's mission was to emphasize the rational, secular, and scientific dimension in Islam and educate Muslims along the modern lines, in order to enable them to comprehend the objective and secular correlates of the religious and spiritual dimension and to incorporate these principles in their society and life.[60]

Such a belief sparked outrage by the political Islamists at the time. His ideas were rejected by the founders of the seminary in Deoband led by Muḥammad Qasim Nanotawi (d. 1879) and his close associate Rashid Ahmad Gangohi (d. 1905), whose efforts gave rise to the Deobandi religious movement. Gongohi stated that Khān might well be a well-wisher of Muslims but regarded his religious ideas as a "deadly poison" for Islam.[61] His belief was based on the understanding that their occupied land needed to be liberated from the British, and they found great power in using the example of the past Islamic empire to rouse a fierce group identity among Muslims. Where Khān wanted Muslim men (and women) to bridge the gap between Islamic and British culture in order to have a prosperous society, Gongohi and Nanotawi wanted a more puritanical form of Islam to take shape. Another fierce opponent of Khān's vision was Jamāl al-dīn al-Afghānī (1839–97), who was also a political Islamist calling for pan-Islamic unity, "as a force to ward off the West."[62]

However, Ghālib did not reject Khān's views, and this was most probably what brought the two men together. Ghālib was not unforgiving in critiquing Khān's work, either. When Khān had just finished editing the work of Abul Fazl, the official state historian of Akbar the Great, who reigned over the Mughal Empire from 1556 to 1605, and asked Ghālib to write an introduction to this edition, he was met with some defiance. Hali narrated the events that followed:

> Prominent men in Delhi had written prose introductions to the work, and Ghālib wrote one in verse. . . . He was very attached to Sir Syed [Khān], and

> was on intimate terms with him and his family. But he was not an admirer of Abul Fazl's style; he thought the system of administration which Ain-i-Akbari describes beneath all comparison with those of modern times; and, as he himself admitted, he felt no interest in history. Hence he regarded the editing of Ain-i-Akbari as a pointless task . . . and could not restrain himself from saying so in his introduction.[63]

Khān did not include this in the publication, and the relationship between Ghālib and Khān was strained for a number of years.[64] Hali recalled the humorous way in which the relationship was once again strengthened: Ghālib visited Khān's residence and brought a bottle of wine with him. Khān removed this and placed it into his storeroom; Ghālib asked where it had gone and insisted upon seeing it. When it was presented to him, he saw that some of the liquor was missing. Ghālib asked Khān who had drunk it, at which Khān only laughed. Ghālib then teased Khān by quoting Hafez, a fourteenth-century Persian poet:

> These preachers show their majesty in mosque and pulpit
> But once at home it is for other things they do.[65]

Thus reconciled, Khān, who held the judicial post of Sadr us Sadur, later helped to secure Ghālib's pension with the British in 1860.[66]

Ghālib and Khān were two very different types of Mughal men. Both had a concern with God but displayed their religiosity in different ways. Ghālib was a poet, and Khān bore credentials as a Muslim modernist with a political edge to his work—he was determined in establishing a link between the British West and Mughal India. In order to do this, he needed to follow the established system, and the changes that he sought had to come in small steps as opposed to the bold, hedonistic statements that Ghālib was writing about.[67] At an intellectual level, both men were trying to find an enlightened future for Indian Muslims, but their approaches were in stark contrast to each other. Whereas Ghālib was open about his vices and thoughts, Khān preferred to hide his half-consumed wine bottles and deny his consumption.

Another significant friend of Ghālib's was Shefta, a Delhi-based man, highly educated in Persian and Arabic. It is said that in his youth he enjoyed the usual pleasures of a young Delhi aristocrat: wine and women. This formed part of the regular pleasure alongside his liaison with the stylish, wealthy, and cultured courtesan named Ramju. However, this did not last, and Shefta decided to turn to religion, give up these pleasures, and set out for pilgrimage in 1839 to Mecca.[68]

It is noted that on one occasion in the cold season, Shefta came to visit Ghālib, who was drinking wine. Ghālib invited him to join in, but Shefta declined and told him he had given up. Ghālib smirked, "Even in winter?"[69] Ghālib was never apologetic about his love for alcohol.[70] He even penned a verse on alcohol and God:

> They offer paradise to make up for our life below
> It needs a stronger wine than this to cure our hangover
> All that they say in praise of paradise is true. I know
> God grant though that it be illuminated by your radiance
> He who drinks wine unceasingly alone with his beloved
> Knows well the worth of *houris* and of streams of paradise[71]

Two contrasting images of masculinity appear in the relationship between Ghālib and Shefta. In the same way that Hali spoke highly of Ghālib, Shefta also felt that his friendship with Ghālib was important. This was further strengthened later when it was Shefta who stood by Ghālib during his imprisonment after a raid on his home for a gambling crime. Shefta visited Ghālib regularly and said of him,

> My deep regard for Ghālib was never based upon his sobriety or his piety, but on his greatness as a poet. Today he is accused of gambling, but that he drinks wine has always been known. Why should it make any difference in my regard for him that he has been charged and sent to prison? His poetic talent is the same today as it ever was.[72]

Shefta attempted to legitimate his concern for Ghālib by basing it upon the greatness of Ghālib's poetic achievement and not his "piety." Such a statement may have guarded against Ghālib's lifestyle reflecting unfavorably on Shefta as a "religious person;" and it may have even helped Shefta to remain friends with Ghālib in the sense that such a juxtaposition highlighted his own virtue. Ghālib may have been used as a foil for Shefta's brand of Islamic masculinity.

Worldly love and poetic culture

Courtesans in Mughal times were used, most often, as entertainment for married men; this was especially true in the case of Ghālib. Courtesans were also seen to lead a life much more independent than those of other women in society, especially married women each restricted to one sexual partner. However, there is a general sense in the history and literature of the time (and just after) that the courtesans all yearned to be released from their lives as entertainers and enter into a life of marriage with a loving husband. Family life was central not just to a respectable Mughal life but also to an idealized Islamic one insofar as that could be extracted from context. As alternative avenues for married men to satisfy their desires in Mughal society, female courtesans played an arguably essential role.[73] Russell states that "courtesans were a normal part of the social scene and many poets experienced some sort of relationship with them."[74] To equate courtesans with prostitutes may be overly simplistic, and that is not exactly how society has remembered them. Two of the most famous Bollywood movies centered on the life of Mughal courtesans reveal that they hold a storied, arguably sympathetic position in Indian history.[75]

Umrao Jaan, first released in 1981 under the direction of Rana Sheikh and then in 2006 under the direction of J. P. Dutta, is the shared title of a pair of movies based on a novel written by Mirzā Hadi Ruswa[76] in 1905. Writing only about 35 years after Ghālib's death, Ruswa stated in his preface the reason why he wrote this story:

> About ten years ago a friend of mine, Munshi Ahmad Husain, who lived somewhere near Delhi paid a visit to Lucknow and rented an upper storey flat in the Chowk. Here a party of friends used to meet in the evenings and pass a few pleasant hours reciting and discussing poetry. The apartment next to Munshi Ahmad Husain's was occupied by a courtesan whose ways were quite different from those of other women of her profession. She was never seen on her balcony not was known to receive any visitors. The windows in her apartment were draped with heavy curtains and the door opening on the main street was always bolted—her servants used the back entrance. . . . One evening, we were as usual reciting ghazals. I recited a couplet, and a soft voice in the neighbouring apartment exclaimed "Wah Wah!" "It is no good applauding a poet in this manner; if you are fond of poetry why not honour us with your presence?" . . . Shortly afterwards, a maid servant came in and

> asked, "Which of you gentlemen is Mirzā Ruswa?" My friends pointed to me. "Will you please oblige my mistress by having a word with her?"[77]

It is then that Ruswa met Umrao Jaan, who told him her life story. The novel and the films tell the story of a girl named Ameerun who is kidnapped and sold to a madam named Khānum Jaan. There Ameerun is given the name Umrao Jaan (beloved). She then meets the noble Nawab Sultan, and they fall in love despite the fact that his parents have already arranged his marriage. Nawab Sultan still proceeds to visit her on numerous occasions at the courtesan's mansion, and she spends time reciting poetry, dancing, and entertaining him. However, this is not to last and he eventually gets married. In a bid to move on with her life, Umrao Jaan is courted by a dashing *dacoit* (bandit) who promises to take her away from a life as a courtesan, but he dies before this can happen. There is further distress in her life as the British attack on Lucknow forces her to flee the city. She ends up in her hometown, where she can finally locate her family. They are embarrassed to hear that their daughter is at this point a renowned courtesan, and they reject her. The story ends with Umrao Jaan left all alone lamenting her past.

Pakeezah,[78] "one of the most extraordinary musical melodramas ever made," brightens the ending of the courtesan tale. Directed by Kemal Amrohi, *Pazeekah* was, like *Umrao Jaan's* first film, released in 1981.[79] Meena Kumari, as the courtesan, and Raaj Kumar, as the Mughal lad from an aristocratic background, played the featured roles. The plot revolves around a mother and daughter, both courtesans. After the mother dies in childbirth, her daughter, Sahib Jaan, follows in her professional footsteps. Sahib Jaan falls in love with a man who, she finds out, is her father's nephew. When she is hired to dance at the arranged, socially acceptable wedding of her lover, her father is also in attendance. He acknowledges his paternity, which enables her to marry—a privilege not granted to her when she was a courtesan.[80]

Umrao Jaan and Sahib Jaan's stories are typical of the way in which Mughal men would treat courtesans. Their relationships with them would start as entertainment and fun but most usually would lead to deep love and affection. Even though courtesans often wanted to marry the men that they fell in love with, Mughal society regarded them as most destitute. The men who frequented the courtesan parlors left with their honor intact; it was the courtesans who were ridiculed because of their profession. Ruswa ends his novel with what seems like Umrao Jaan's plea of guilt, even though it was a profession she chose herself,

> O foolish women never be under the delusion that anyone will ever love you truly. Your lovers who today forswear their lives for you will walk out on you after a while. They will never remain constant because you do not deserve constancy. The rewards of true love are for a women who only see the face of one man. God will never grant the gift of true love to a whore.[81]

Yet courtesans were worth a lot more in Mughal society than their sexual services might suggest. In a recent study, Prigarina argues that courtesans were distinguished because of their "education and culture" and the fact that they had "refined manners" and the ability to "hold agreeable conversation."[82] These courtesans had refined their skills greatly, not least in the sense that "the courtesan was the one who had learnt all the skills in lovemaking as a professional accomplishment and added the cultural attainments which are also necessary to the satisfaction of a cultured man."[83] Through Ruswa, Umrao Jaan described the type of education she had from a Maulvi (an honorific accorded to religious men in Mughal society):

is courtesans were also socially intelligent

> Khānum's girls were not only trained in dancing and singing, there was also a school to teach reading and writing, to which I had to go. The school was under the supervision of Maulvi Sahib . . . After teaching me the alphabet, Maulvi Sahib started me on books of elementary Persian like *Kareema*, *Mamakeema*, and the *Mahmud-Nama*. After going through them quickly he made me memorise the grammatical tables of the *Amad-nama*. After that we took *Saadi's Gulistan* . . . The Maulvi Sahib taught me for nearly eight years. I need hardly add that he fostered my interest in poetry till it developed into a passion.[84]

Even the religious elite frequented courtesans, as Fazle Haqq's example will highlight. Haqq was understood to be one of the most famous and respected Muslim religious leaders in Delhi during the time of Ghālib, and it is clear that his keeping a courtesan as a mistress caused no scandal. Ghālib narrated a time when he met the Maulvi's courtesan, "they had barely sat down when the *Maulvi Sahib's* courtesan [Fazle Haqq] came in from the other room and sat down with them."[85]

Ghālib also fell in love with a courtesan named Mughal Jaan, and he made every attempt to seduce her. A poem that he wrote during this time reads, "what ails thee, my silly heart? What cure for your ache, at last? I adore her, she repels. What a predicament, O Lord."[86] She resisted his temptation for a time, but one day she succumbed and, according to Illahi Bakhsh, entered into a temporary Islamic marriage contract with Ghālib,[87] possibly to safeguard Ghalib's honor by religiously legitimizing his relationship with the courtesan. Ghālib felt at ease in his married life with Umrao Jaan and also in frequenting his beloved courtesan Mughal Jaan. Ghālib followed many of the social norms at the time, and in keeping with a culture of arranged marriage had wedded at a young age. Marriage was seen as a milestone by which boys would become acceptable men in Mughal society. Ghālib, something of a hedonist, was able to find more inner spirituality in the taverns and the courtyard of his courtesan.

On one occasion Ghālib consoled his friend Mihr, whose courtesan lover Chunna Jaan had just died:

> I felt extremely sorry, and deeply grieved . . . Friend, we "Mughal lads" are terrors; we are the death of those for whom we ourselves would die. Once in my life I was the death of a fair, cruel dancing-girl. God grant both of them his forgiveness, and both of us, who bear the wounds of our beloveds' death, His mercy . . . I know what you must be feeling. Be patient, and turn your back on the turmoil of earthly love . . . God is all sufficient: the rest is vanity.[88]

As if to soothe their broken hearts, Ghālib initially raves about the "Mughal lads" who are "terrors" but left heartbroken and wounded by courtesans. In the spirit of comforting the ego of brave masculinity, Ghālib uses the Ṣūfi notion of all earthly love being allegorical and advised Mihr to concentrate on the love of God.

As heady as he was, Ghālib felt at ease with his relative lack of sexual boundaries, and the flexibility was prevalent in Mughal culture of the time. It is on this matter that he said,

> In the days of my lusty youth a man of perfect wisdom counselled me, "Abstinence I do not approve: dissoluteness I do not forbid. Eat, drink and be merry. But remember, that the wise fly settles on the sugar, and not on the honey."[89]

Ghālib characterized his own approach to variety and difference, especially romantically thus: "take a new woman each returning spring, for last year's almanac's a useless thing."[90] He was repulsed by the banalities of life, for Hali says of him:

> This well illustrated his aversion to following the common herd, an aversion which made him go out of his way to be different, not only in his poetry, but also, says Hali, "in his ways, his dress, his diet, and his style." He was a man to whom people quickly felt attracted.[91]

Further, He was apparently juicy

> Delhi people who had seen Ghālib in his youth told me that he was generally regarded as one of the most handsome men in the city, and even in his old age, when I met him for the first time, one could easily see what a handsome man he had been.[92]

If Ghālib was known for his appearance during his younger days, as he was growing older, he knew that his looks were fading, and this he mentioned as a cause for concern to Mirzā Hatim Ali Mihr, someone who shared Ghālib's love of poetry and of Delhi courtesans:

> Your auspicious portrait has gladdened my sight. Do you know what Mirzā Yusuf Ali Khān Aziz meant by what he said to you? I must have said some time in the company of friends, "I should like to see Mirzā Hatim Ali. I hear he's a man of very striking appearance." And, my friend, I had often heard this from Mughal Jan.[93] In the days when she was in Nawwab Hamid Ali Khān's service I used to know her extremely well, and I often used to spend hours together in her company. She also showed me the verse you wrote in praise of her beauty. Anyway, when I saw your portrait and saw how tall you were, I didn't feel jealous because I too am noticeably tall. And I didn't feel jealous of your wheaten complexion, because mine, in the days when I was in the land of the living, used to be even fairer, and people of discrimination used to praise it. Now when I remember what my complexion once was, the memory is simple torture to me. The thing that did make me jealous—and that is no small degree—was that you are clean-shaven. I remember the pleasant days of my youth, and I cannot tell you what I felt. When white hairs began to appear in my beard and moustache, and on the third day they began to look as though ants had laid their white eggs in them—and, worse than that, I broke my two front teeth—there was nothing for it but to . . . let my beard grow long.[94]

Ghālib is highlighting those aspects of Ali that he feels are attractive to women and therefore enviable—he reflected on his own masculinity and what others had said about Ali's good looks to the point that Ghālib requested a portrait of the other man.

Ghālib meticulously compared himself with Ali in details such as his complexion, his height, and his beard and moustache. Clean shaving seems to have been a symbol of youth during Ghālib's time—older men wore facial hair—but it was also a prescription that men had to follow in society. Ghālib stated, "but remember that in this uncouth city everybody wears a sort of uniform. Mullahs, junk-dealers, hookah-menders, washermen, water-carriers, inn keepers, weavers, and greengrocers—all of them wear their hair long and grow a beard."[95] The growing of the beard has long been a sign of maturity and masculinity in Islamic cultures and so it is not surprising that Ghālib would be following this trend, although it is interesting that he felt moved to comment on it. There are also Islamic traditions that talk about the growing of the beard, but it is unclear from Ghālib's comments whether this was the reason why he kept one. It is clear from Ghālib's biographers that his lifestyle was a good deal better than he could afford, so it is unlikely that he would have skipped the barber just for financial reasons.[96] Ghālib must have been meticulous in shaping his personal appearance as a result of those beautiful men surrounding him.

Same-sex love in Ghālib's Mughal India

Ghālib's countless love poems demonstrate that love was a special concern for him.[97] However, his love poetry in the form of ghazals had a special purpose:

> Along with most ghazal poets, Ghālib also uses the common mystic concept of God revealing Herself (or Himself) in the beauty of the universe and therefore equates the worship of beauty with the worship of God, whether it be the beauty of nature or of a beautiful woman or of a handsome boy.[98]

It would be correct to state that Ghālib was a man who enjoyed the pleasures of women, as this is illustrated through his relationship with his wife and Mughal

Jaan, his beloved courtesan. However, it was not uncommon during Mughal times for same-sex love to develop, too:

> Male homosexuality in Muslim culture existed during the Mughal period in India. Under the Muslim rulers homosexuality entered court life. In Islamic Ṣūfī literature homosexual eroticism was used as a metaphorical expression of the spiritual relationship between God and man, and much Persian poetry and fiction used homosexual relationships as examples of moral love. Although the Qur'ān and early religious writings display mildly negative attitudes towards homosexuality, Muslim cultures seemed to treat homosexuality with indifference, if not admiration.[99]

Alternative sexualities were in constant negotiation within Mughal society, and they were not necessarily considered intrinsic characteristics, as orientations are today in Western societies. Sexual identities as such are a more modern invention:

> Michel Foucault, Lillian Faderman, David Halperin, and others have argued that it was only in the late nineteenth century that European and American psychologists and sexologists such as Havelock Ellis, Magnus Hirschfield, and later, Sigmund Freud began to think of people as falling into categories based on their sexual-emotional preferences, thus creating the categories of "heterosexual" and "homosexual" people. These scholars claim (a claim widely accepted today but also challenged by many other scholars) that prior to this period, many people performed homosexual acts but were not identified or categorised according to their sexual inclinations.[100]

However, this is not to say that there were no words used to describe those having same-sex relationships: "in late medieval Urdu poetry, *chapti* (clinging or sticking together) was a word for sex between women as well as for the women who practiced it."[101] The word *amrad parast* (boy lover) was used to identify men inclined toward relationships with boys and young men.[102]

What emerges from the homosexual practices of men in Mughal society is a picture of accommodation, not exclusion:

> Homoerotically inclined men could be conveniently accomodated within the framework of heterosexual patriarchy. As long as a man fulfilled his duties as a householder, he was free to seek emotional involvement anywhere he pleased. Romantic attachments outside the family were not only widespread but considered legitimate.[103]

The relationships that men had with other men were not declared homosexual but were an additional relationship that they pursued at the same time that they upheld their marital relationships. It was common to see such practices kept private as opposed to public. The family structure empowered men in Mughal society for their fertility and, partly in consequence, their masculinity. As Kidwai explained,

> Procreation was considered a social duty, but since procreation did not necessitate erotic commitment, erotic commitments were not seen as threatening to marriage. This is evident in the conventions prevailing among the heterosexually inclined male elites—they were allowed not only multiple wives and concubines but also liasons with ever-present courtesans. Hence it was either courtesans or other males who became the focus of attention.[104]

Russell explains that the gendered segregation in Islamic society at this time actually encouraged same-sex involvement: "association with courtesans [was] virtually the only way in which a man could freely enjoy the company of women."[105] Further, one of the 'beloveds' of the Urdu ghazal is a beautiful boy. The beauty of the boy in some Islamic traditions is connected with the beauty of God, so there is some conflation there. Most Urdu poets must have had at least some emotional experience of homosexual love and this experience was part of the raw material of their poetry.[106] Such practices were flourishing under the premise of a tacit "don't ask, don't tell" policy in Mughal society.[107]

In 1861, Ghālib spoke quite openly about the issue of same-sex and mixed-age love with his friend Ala ud Din Ahmad Khān Alai. Ghālib said, "listen to me, my friend. It's a rule with men who worship beauty that when they fall in love with a youngster they deceive themselves that he's three or four years younger than he really is. They know he's grown up, but they think of him as a child."[108] Beauty is not appreciated just in women but in men, too. In another letter Ghālib rebuked his friend who had let his same-sex, pederastic relationship supplant his marital obligations: "is this any way to go on—to leave his wife for a boy?"[109] Ghālib thus seems conscious of the tricky balance between, on the one hand, fulfilling one's masculine responsibilities in society and for the Mughal family and, on the other hand, pursuing outside relationships with some discretion.

The famous Mir Taqi Mir (real name Mir Muḥammad Taqi, 1723–810) is understood to be the Urdu poet most explicit about same-sex love. Mir was

was born in Agra, lived most of his life in Delhi, died in Lucknow, and has on occasions been compared to Ghālib, who came to prominence later. It was Ghālib who once wrote, "you are not the only master of Urdu Ghālib . . . they say there used to be a Mir in the past."[110] Mir was also married and had children, but his poetry was rooted in pedarastic affection,

> I stood before his horse
> Like weakened prey
> God having given these boys such beautiful faces
> Should have given them a bit of compassion too
> It would be strange if an angel could hold its own
> The fairy-faced boys of Delhi are far ahead of them
> Even though the sprightly one is still at school
> He can teach just about any one a few tricks.
> After I kissed him, I too slipped away
> Say what you will, I care only for myself.[111]

Mir made no secret of his love for the son of a perfumer and the son of a mason.[112] It is also said that Mir had a relationship with a poet senior in age—Mir Muḥammad Yar Khaksar, whom he regarded as his *manzur-i-nazar* (beloved).[113] His contemporary biographer C. M. Naim also uses the term *amrad parasti* in Urdu for the love of a man for a boy,[114] and he questions whether we can label Mir's sexuality in contemporary terms:

> Was Mir a homosexual? There can be no easy answer. . . . Should we then see Mir as a pederast hiding behind a façade of conjugal heterosexuality? Should we say he was a heterosexual, but felt compelled by poetic conventions to write about pretty boys? Or should we posit a bisexual orientation on his part? Obviously, given the paucity of our information concerning Mir himself, any categorical statement would be unsound. All we can assert with some certainty is that Mir had intense emotional/erotic involvement with more than one person outside of conjugal relationships.[115]

The same might be said of Mughal men's sexuality in general: the mores are so distinct from our own, whether Western or not, today. Glimpsing the history of Mughal same-sex love permits an image of Islamic masculinity that has most often been hidden for its failure to conform to politically ideal forms of Islamic masculinity. It was for this reason that alternative forms of sexualities under the Mughal Empire flourished only alongside the more acceptable ones revolving around the family.

A concern supreme

The prototypical ghazal poet "rejects with contempt their doctrine of a conduct of life motivated by hope of reward and fear of punishment in the life to come."[116] Ghālib was no exception; one of his commentators, Ikram, wrote, "Ghālib, you write so well upon these mystic themes of Love Divine. We would have counted you a saint, but that we knew your love of wine."[117] Ghālib had no intention of being a saint, either, and wrote a letter to his friend saying as much:

> They say that to despair of God's help is to be an infidel. Well, I have despaired of Him and am an infidel through and through. Muslims believe that when a man turns infidel, he cannot expect God's forgiveness. So there you are, my friend: I'm lost to this world and the next. But you must do your best to stay a Muslim and not despair of God. Make the text [of the Qur'ān] your watchword: "where there is difficulty, there is ease also." All that befalls the traveler in the path of God, befalls him for his good.[118]

Ghālib's advice contradicts itself as he tells his friend of the reason why he falls out with the bounds of God's mercy and then proceeds to raise hopes of a better future using God's mercy. His relationship with God was unusual but spectacularly strong. The main reason why he was understood to be a "bad" Muslim was because of his free character, love for women, wine, and all things hedonistic. But he upheld what he thought was useful:

> From all the duties of worship and the enjoined practices of Islam he took only two—a belief that God is one and is immanent in all things, and a love for the Prophet and his family. And this alone he considered sufficient for salvation.[119]

He presented his own understanding of Islam as a convoluted affair.

Ghālib found no interest in following the prerequisite Muslim ritual practices and would make no attempt to hide this. On one occasion he wrote,

> What joy unless you tread a path beset with thorns?
> Don't set out for the Kaba if the way is safe
> I am a poet, not a theologian
> And wine-stained clothes are no disgrace to poetry[120]

Hali quoted the time when a man said to Ghālib that the prayers of a drunk would not be answered. Ghālib retorted, "If a man has wine, what else does he *need* to pray for?"[121] Ghālib wrote in another verse,

> Forget tomorrow! Pour the wine today, and do not stint
> Such care reflects on him who pours the wine in paradise
> Today we are abased. Why so? For yesterday You would not brook
> The insolence the angel showed towards our majesty
> The steed of life runs on. None knows where it will stay its course
> The reins have fallen from our hands, the stirrups from our feet.[122]

Hali also highlighted that Ghālib wrote most of his poetry under the influence of alcohol.[123]

Hali recalled a time when, at the end of the Islamic fasting month one year, the Mughal king asked Ghālib, "Mirzā, how many fasts did you keep?" Ghālib replied, "My Lord and Guide, I failed to keep one."[124] On another occasion during the Islamic month of fasting, a religious leader came to see Ghālib. In the middle of the afternoon, he asked his servant to bring some water. The Maulvi was astonished and asked Ghālib if he was not fasting. Ghālib replied in humor that he was a Sunni and that he opened his fast two hours before sunset![125] Ghālib's love of alcohol was most likely the main reason why his Islamic credentials were questioned. On this matter, Ghālib wrote, "I talk of contemplating God but cannot make my point/Unless I speak of wine-cup and intoxicating wine."[126] A certain Maulvi Hamza Khān once asked his student Alai to write to Ghālib urging him to give up drink in his old age. Ghālib responded by saying, "you who have never known the taste of wine, we drink unceasingly."[127]

Ghālib spoke openly about his faith and insisted that it was still intact albeit under the influence of his love of alcohol,

> Hell is for those who deny the oneness of God, who hold that His existence partakes of the order of the eternal and the possible, believe that every Muslim shares with the Prophet the rank of the seal of the prophets, and rank newly-converted Muslims with the father of the Imams. My belief in God's oneness is untainted, and my faith is perfect. My tongue repeats, "There is no god but God," and my heart believes, "Nothing exists but God, and God alone works manifest in all things." All prophets were to be honoured, and submission to each in his own time was the duty of man. Yes, and there is

is thought his faith was enough + more important than practice

> this more to be said, that I hold freethinking and atheism to be abhorrent, and wine drinking to be forbidden, and myself to be a sinner. And if God casts me in into hell, it will not be to burn me, but that I may become added fuel to the flames, making them flare more fiercely to burn those who deny God's oneness and reject the prophet hood of Muḥammad and the Imamate of Ali.[128]

Ghālib's reflection shows a deep commitment to God as he tries to evaluate his own submission to God. Ghālib then had something in common with the courtesans that he frequented; both had understood their lives as "un-Islamic." Ghālib's vices placed him far outside the mainstream in the sense that alcohol is forbidden in Islam, and what courtesans offered—a mixed-gender environment—defied the *Purdah* system.[129]

Ghālib's life at the fringes of the more acceptable, mainstream forms of Muslim life was something that followed him throughout his life:

> He had felt keenly that others had regarded him as inferior to themselves—all the more keenly because he himself had accepted the yardsticks—birth, wealth, profession, rank, and social and political influence—with which he measured him, and knew that he could not compete in these fields.[130]

This outsider identity may have made him all the more critical of God, so Ghālib constantly questioned God in his poetry and writing. On one occasion, he lay in his bed looking up at the distribution of the stars and seeing no real design. Ghālib then questioned God: "Just look at the stars—scattered in complete disorder. No proportion, no system, no sense, no pattern. But their King has absolute power, and no one can breathe a word against Him."[131] Ghālib's constant interrogation (*shikwa*) of God led him to reject the more irksome restrictions that were prevalent at his time.[132]

Ghālib can also not be understood as against God or religion in any absolute sense. As Hali wrote, his relationship to other Muslims, to Muslim ideals, and to the divine was constantly on his mind:

> Although he paid very little regard to the outward observances of Islam, whenever he heard of any misfortune befalling the Muslims it grieved him deeply. One day in my (Hali) presence when he was lamenting some such occurrence, he said, "I have none of the hallmarks of a Muslim; why is it that every humiliation that the Muslims suffer pains and grieves me so much?"[133]

Ghālib's love for drink was almost always directly linked to his spirituality, which raises the question whether this drinking was tantamount to his love for God. On this matter Ghālib stated, "the worship of God means the love of God, and love as all consuming as that between human lovers. Rituals of worship are of no significance as compared with this."[134] (Spiritual intoxication is a particularly Ṣūfī practice, as will be discussed in the next chapter.)

It is evident from Ghālib's life and writing that the hedonism shaping his masculinity was one coupled with a deep spiritual love for God. As a poet he was creative in his thoughts on God and was not interested in the narrow interpretation of God that existed in the Islam that he saw practised around him. Russell has argued that Ghālib was of the understanding that the ritualization of worship—such as prayer, fasting, alms giving, and pilgrimage in Islam—may help one to draw closer to God, but in actual fact those practices are harmful to true religion in the sense that they may lead to the arrogant self-satisfaction that one is not like other people.[135] It was this understanding that gave Ghālib freedom to lead a spiritual yet hedonistic life. He would not have cottoned to Mawdūdi's incessant demonizing of others—women and the West especially. Ghālib's final words were rooted in his spiritual position and relationship with God, "my dying breath is ready to depart, And now, my friends, God, only God, exists."[136]

Ghālib's life presents an image of Mughal masculinity that was totally given over to its hedonistic and spiritual outlook. The intricate way in which Ghālib fused both without blaspheming or moralizing was possible through the liberation that came to Ghālib through ultimate submission to God, not ritualistic Islam, society, or culture. Society had already tried to determine the relationships that Ghālib had—with other men, with women, and God. These ideals were something that Ghālib aspired to live up to even though he failed miserably. Ghālib could not locate himself in any of the Islamic movements that were shaping society at the time, from the more conservative and legalistic movements in the form of Nanotawi's and Gongohi's Deobandi seminary to the more liberal and progressive movements in the form of Khān. This is not altogether dissimilar to the varied approaches to Islam that we saw in the dynamic between Mawdūdi, Jinnah, and Iqbal more recently.

Ghālib found himself under immense pressure to achieve the ideals of Mughal masculinity. Not being able to follow in the military footsteps of his forefathers and unable to father any children of his own had profound impact on his brand of Islamic masculinity. Even as a poet, he felt he was a far cry from the pinnacle of Islamic manhood, and this predicament seemed to haunt him. However, he competed with the male poets of his milieu who wrote in Urdu by presenting poetry that straddled the lines between Persian, Arabic, and Urdu and used this as a tool to strengthen his own image. The physical Jihād, which Ghālib had always aspired to, had become a Jihād of the pen, even though he failed to see its enduring worth. Ghālib's relationship and submission to God played a significant role in his life, even though he remained sceptical of God. The poet concludes,

> When nothing was,
> then God was there,
> had nothing been,
> God would have been,
> my being has defeated me,
> had I not been,
> what would have been?[137]

Ghālib questioned his own fitness as a Muslim man, but he also shared that he thought discipline was detrimental to real spirituality. In this tension, he foreshadowed the Islamic masculinity crisis of today. Organized religion seems constraining to many; Mawdūdi-style Islamism is certainly antithetical to diverse expressions of submission, obligation, and gender. Ghālib did not conceptualize God, women, the West, and himself as a Muslim man in a way that would have jibed with various forms of political Islamism. In their more tortured aspects, this poet's life and work illustrate the danger of letting Islamic masculinity be narrowly defined: brilliant minds and upstanding, pious community members begin to see themselves outside the fold of not just Islam but by extension masculinity too. Strict and constraining definitions of Islamic masculinity like Mawdūdi's encourage defection of pious men who do act consistently with the good of the community but have interests other than war, dominance, xenophobia, and the heteronormative family. Ghālib is an illustrative figure because his devotion to God was so complete and his artistry so singular. Through his eyes, we see the struggle of men who do not "fit"—and glimpse the diversity that has long existed in Islamic masculinity.

5

Ṣūfism's Beloved Subversion

The beauty of each lovely boy
each comely girl
derives from His [God]—
on loan.[1]

While Mirzā Ghālib saw himself as hedonistic because of his search for deep love, the mystical side of Islam takes that quest as its only priority. Ṣūfism, as that branch of the tradition is known, has often detached itself from mainstream legalist movements in Islamic culture and society. However, Ṣūfism is not simple to define, and its expressions vary geographically and personally. The term *mystical* may conjure many different images and call to mind multiple approaches within the tradition. For his part, Ghālib held strongly to many Ṣūfī tenets and ideas but was never acclaimed as a Ṣūfī, nor did he position himself as one. Our consideration of Ghālib leads us to explore Ṣūfī masculinity, with particular focus on the Qalandari Malangs in South Asia, whose single-minded pursuit of the beloved holds out the possibility of fluid gender norms. Whether these theoretical possibilities for egalitarianism can buck, patriarchy itself motivates a dissection of dualist notions in Ṣūfī doctrine.

The basis of the Ṣūfī path is said to be love, which the famous Jalal al-Din Rumi[2] said "is the remedy of our pride and self-conceit, the physician of all our infirmities. Only he whose garment is rent by love becomes entirely unselfish."[3] The love that Rumi talked about is a love that must be shown to God and that which surrounds the believer.[4] It could be argued that pride, self-conceit, and infirmities are human characteristics which have binary opposites, so the love that Rumi alludes to is only known as love because of the existence of hate. Ṣūfī love aims to transgress the boundaries of all things against love and to be a constant reflection of God. If Ṣūfī thought is about servitude and submission to God regardless of gender and sex then all seekers, including men and women, should be submissive without creating a gender hierarchy in the act. But men may be more enabled to pursue that spiritual path.

Ṣūfīs have focused considerable attention on humans' relationship with God—gender, sex, sexuality, masculinity, and femininity play roles in this ultimate relationship. One of the foremost commentators on the Ṣūfī path, Reynold Nicholson (1868–1945) has described Ṣūfīsm as having seven stages. It must be accepted that other scholars on Ṣūfīsm may identify alternatives, but some of the key stages that seem to be generic are encapsulated in the ones that Nicholson highlighted.[5] These are repentance, abstinence, renunciation, poverty, patience, trust in God, and satisfaction.[6] These prerequisites of Ṣūfī practice are centered on a relationship with God. Once a Ṣūfī has gone through all of those stages, he can finally be "permanently raised to the higher planes of consciousness which Ṣūfīs call 'gnosis' (*marifāt*) and 'the truth' (*Haqiqāt*) where the seeker (*Ṭālib*) becomes the 'knower' or the Gnostic (*arif*) and realises that knowledge, knower and known are one."[7] The way of the Ṣūfī has no set path; the other experiences that God grants the Ṣūfī are added obstacles or tests that must be accepted in the hope that they will be overcomed. Hujwiri, the eleventh-century Persian mystic, stated, "in the time of the companions and the ancients—may God have mercy on them!—this name did not exist, but the reality thereof was in everyone; now the name exists, but not the reality."[8] In short, Hujwiri seems to be stating that defining the act of *tasawwuf* (beautifying ones self, an inward process of refining spiritual existence) has led to set definitions of the "ism" known as Ṣūfīsm and is reminiscing about the time when those who practised *tasawwuf* were not led by these definitions and now with the definitions, people still fail to live by them. Martin Lings,[9] the renowned English Ṣūfī convert to Islam, quotes the great work of Ibn Khaldūn[10] on universal history, the *Muqaddimah*: "When worldliness spread and men tended to become more and more bound up with the ties of this life, those who dedicated themselves to the worship of God were distinguished from the rest by the title Ṣūfīs."[11] However, it is difficult to separate human beings from the world, for every human being must live his or her faith in this world. Even those who have attempted to separate their lives from the world are still connected to it. The role of the family is one such example, which has been a highlight throughout this thesis.

According to the Persian mystic Mansur al-Hallaj (d. 922), the creation of the human—specifically of Adam—was motivated by a single divine love:

> The essence of God's essence is love. Before the creation, God loved Himself in absolute unity and through love revealed Himself to Himself alone. Then, desiring to behold that love-in-aloneness, that love without otherness and duality, as an external object, He brought forth from non-existence an image of Himself, endowed with all His attributes and names. This divine image is Adam. In and by whom God is made manifest—divinity objectified in humanity. Hallaj, however, distinguishes the human nature (*nasut*) from the divine (*lahut*). Though mystically united they are not essentially identical and interchangeable.[12]

Al-Hallaj understands Adam as a singular divine image, and he saves no mention for Eve. According to Lings, before she appears as a separate being, Eve is encompassed within Adam, much as "the human nature is contained in the Divine." But just as humanity moved away from God, from truth, so does Eve's move away from Adam signal a breakdown of the single divine truth.[13] So even though Ṣūfī commentators on creation root their spiritual understanding in love, they still use the creation of Eve to signify patriarchy, with Adam somehow more original than her.

If man is more original, and more original is more divine, and divine is more love, then that connects masculinity to the highest priority of Ṣūfīsm. The Andalusian Ṣūfī Ibn al-Arabi used the term "*al-Insān al-kāmil*," the perfect man, in his treatise "*Fusas al-hikam*." Nicholson summarized Ibn al-Arabi's views as such,

> Perhaps we may describe the perfect man as a man who has fully realised his essential oneness with the divine being in whose likeness he is made. This experience, enjoyed by prophets and saints and shadowed forth in symbols to others, is the foundation of the Ṣūfī theosophy.[14]

That oneness may be achieved in Ṣūfīsm by the key task of submitting and engendering dependence;[15] this ideal behavior flows from the Ṣūfī view of creation and hence the human condition:

> The proper relationship between God and the believer is one based on servitude and obedience, indeed, one common term for the Muslim, or

> the believer, is *abd* (slave). The structure of this primary relationship is fundamentally hierarchical and unequal. In this worldview men as well as women must learn to be subordinate and submissive.[16]

Although that idea of common submission seems to offer a basic equality to the sexes in terms of spirituality, at a more practical level this is not easily implemented in Ṣūfism because "the burden placed upon women by marriage, in the form of household responsibilities and childbearing, would leave very little time or energy for lengthy devotional exercises."[17]

The Ṣūfī Jamal Hanswi (d. 1333) stated, "*tālib ad-dunyā mu'annath tālib al-ākhira mukhannath, tālib al-mawlā mudhakkar*: 'The seeker of the world is feminine, the seeker of the otherworld is a hermaphrodite, and the seeker of the Lord is masculine.'"[18] If submission is a Ṣūfī necessity, then why would not the more obedient, subservient gender stereotype not raise the feminine to a status superior to the masculine?

The famous eighth-century Iraqi female mystic Rābi'a al-Adawiyya was a model Ṣūfī regardless of her gender. It was the Ṣūfī poet, Shah Abdul Latif of Bhit in the Indus Valley of the eighteenth century, who associated Rābi'a al-Adawiyya to the saying "*tālib al-maula mudhakkar* ('he who seeks the Lord is male')".[19] The Ṣūfī doctrine of mysticism begins on a basis of ungendered notions such as love, submission, and subservience, yet these have often been gendered through an understanding that men are better suited to carry out such acts.

Islamic mysticism in South Asia

South Asian Ṣūfism brings with it its own unique flavor, which is distinct from that of the Arabian Peninsula and other regions. There must be no surprise to this statement because all religions, including Islam, do not flourish in a vacuum but develop their own distinct settings. When Arabo-centric Islam moved to South Asia, it was faced with an Indian culture and land that was already resplendent in religion, namely Hinduism, Sikhism, and Jainism, among others. How does the Arabo-centric Islamic culture and tradition deal with a context completely other? Were there similarities between the incoming Islamic culture and the prevalent culture of India at the time? South Asian Ṣūfism actually complemented the Hindu Bhakti movement, which challenged not only religious but also gendered boundaries. Although there are histories which recall the differences and conflicts between Muslims and other religions, there is an understanding that Ṣūfis quite happily encompassed Hindu traditions in their own path: "In the words of an early Ṣūfī . . . there was no such thing as absolute opposite or antagonism; everything was conceived in relative terms because in the final analysis all were God's creatures."[20]

Ṣūfis believe that God could be witnessed through any fixed or living object, allowing them to consider alternative cultures and traditions as complementary to their paths. As the most prominent religion in Mughal India, Hinduism certainly came in contact with Islam and Ṣūfism there. A monotheist might consider individual Hindu gods and goddesses, such as Lakshmi, Saraswati, Hunuman, idols that blaspheme the one true God's supreme position. However, they could also be seen as the embodiment or incarnation of the overarching concept of God (or Brahma, in Hinduism), and this layering of meaning can qualify Hinduism as monotheistic, too—or at least common theological ground can be found between India's primary tradition and the Abrahamic religions that have also taken root there. As Hindu gods and goddesses personify various aspects of Brahama, the 99 or so names of Allah in Islamic tradition are also different characteristics of God, although not figuratively depicted. Hindus seek Brahma through gods and goddesses or through the guru (teacher), much as the Ṣūfī seeks God through the "master" or certain mystical paths.[21] The famous Mughal Ṣūfī Mazhar Jān-I Jānān (1699–1781) believed that Hindus should be accepted as "people of the book," which is a category created in the Qurān and usually reserved for Jews and Christians. If God does as Qur'ān 13:7 says and provides guides to all peoples and geographies, then, Jānān reasoned, God would have representatives in India—perhaps Ram and Krishna.[22]

However, mystical paths to God, be they Hindu or Muslim, are subject to political contexts which do not always accept them with open arms. Two Mughal emperors worth mentioning here are Jalaluddin Muḥammad Akbar, who reigned from 1556 to 1605, and Aurungzeb, who reigned from 1658 to 1707. Akbar—"the Great," as he is known—had a vision for pluralistic India.[23] He preserved and enhanced art and architecture during his rule but his most significant contribution was his peace initiative covering Hindus, Sikhs, and other faiths in the land. His bold political step repealed the law demanding that non-Muslims, especially the Hindus, pay the *jizyā* monetary tax. Akbar tried in vain to establish a religious outlook that would encompass all the faiths of the land, known as *Din-i-Ilahi* (Divine Faith)[24] but this never happened. Akbar fused his central Asian heritage with Hindu India to form a distinctively Mughal ethos.[25] Akbar is said to have married a Hindu woman who is popularly known as Jodha, but authorities cannot agree on her facticity or, indeed, her relationship to Islam, so the significance of his possibly interreligious marriage is in its status as legend.[26]

A half century later, Aurungzeb, also known as Alamgir, could be seen as the antithesis of Akbar in that he enforced strict adherence to Islamic law during his reign.[27] He commissioned a new legal code known as "*Fatawa Alamgiri*," Alamgir's Fatawa. Aurungzeb repealed and restricted many of the laws that Akbar had enforced. He reinstated the *jizya* monetary tax and halted the advancement of arts because he was against any form of figural representation and prohibited music. He was also known for his anti-Hindu views and believed that all non-Muslims should convert to Islam. At the fall of the Mughal empire, Aurungzeb's views became the norm; "voices of theological rigidity that were minorities in the Mughal heyday amplified to define the majority belief."[28]

Dualistic relationships, stratified oneness

The relationship of the *Murshid* (master) and *Murid* (disciple) is a hierarchy that plays a significant role in gender construction and Islamic masculinity in Ṣūfism. As with all matters, it is based on the premise of deepening spirituality and striving to the beloved through a fixed being or entity:

> He (the disciple) will take a director, Shaykh, Pir, Murshid i.e. a holy man of ripe experience and profound knowledge, whose least word is absolute law to the disciple. A "seeker" who attempts to traverse the "path" without assistance receives little sympathy. Of such a one it is said that 'his guide is Satan," and he is likened to a tree that for want of gardener's care brings forth 'none or bitter fruit."[29]

The first duty of the Ṣūfī master, as given by classical masters, is "not to perform miracles, but to provide what the disciple needs."[30] There are many examples of great Ṣūfīs in history who were either masters or disciples: Ibn Arabi was the Murshid of Sadr al-Din Qunawi, Shams-e Tabrizi was the Murshid of Rumi, to name a few. It was the task of the disciple to reap the benefit of the master, "Gnostics," says Ibn al-Arabi, "cannot impart their feelings to other men; they can only indicate them symbolically to those who have begun to experience the like."[31]

One may think of mysticism as a solitary path, but it's clear that Ṣūfīs venerate the master-disciple relationship, which is sometimes compared to the bond between husband and wife—where there is also a clear supremacy. Scholar Margaret Malamud makes clear that both relationships are considered to be divinely ordained.[32] The very values that are seen as pious in a disciple—submission, obedience, and the like—are the ones that make women subservient. The relationship was unable to survive without constructing it within the existing gendered examples. The relationship between mother[33] and child also obtains,[34] and it is a safe analogy in that it could be seen as an attempt to stem any illicit interpretations of the relationship. However, the master is understood to be the "creator;" as Malamud has observed, "in Ṣūfī discourse spiritual guides have metaphorical procreative powers and are able to produce their own progeny."[35]

It was Ghazālī who suggested that the rights of the teacher were to be understood as greater than the rights of the parents. He explained that parents are the cause of a children's temporal existence, but teachers are the cause of their immortal existence.[36] The spiritual masters were loved dearly because they helped to provide a path to God that one might traverse with discipline and respect, the practice of which would itself yield spiritual improvement.[37]

This meant that, on occasions, some extraordinary ritual practices would take place: some fasted and performed full ritual cleansings before seeing their masters.[38] The disciple was obligated to follow every command of the master, even if the master might be mistaken or outright wrong.[39] Ghazālī felt this way, and so did al-Razi,[40] who uses the analogy of a good fruit-bearing date palm and the Ṣūfī disciple:

> Al-Razi says, "The date palm resembles the believer in this sense. The female date palm will not yield good dates unless it is given semen, impregnated, and fertilised. It is well known that each year a substance is taken from the spathe of a male tree and grafted onto that of a female tree in order for it to produce good dates. If this is not done, it will not bear fruit properly. Similarly, when it is desired that a believer should yield fruit of sainthood, he is impregnated through the transmission of dhikr by a sheikh."[41]

This metaphor only makes more clear the role of dualism in Ṣūfī spiritual pursuits. At times this love-fueled dualism might appear to undermine the very existence of socially constructed gender ideals and break into new forms of Islamic masculinities. The master-disciple relationship constructs a powerful dynamic and struggle:

> In the fluid and ambiguous state of discipleship, passivity and subordination were practiced without fear of humiliation and loss of manliness, indeed, they were valued behaviours. Power and authority were in the possession of the master, and it was through acts of surrender and subordination that a disciple attained spiritual power and maturity.[42]

The master is in command of the disciple and carries the burden of putting the disciple through a thorough training process in order to achieve a divine aim. None of the participants is considered unmasculine in the exchange. In fact, the master trains the disciple to physically appreciate that the submissive role is the role that every submitted Muslim is expected to refine.

The single-minded Ṣūfī passion for God by no means resolves the matters of sex and marriage. Much as those familiar with mystical strains of other religions will expect, celibacy had something to do with Ṣūfī transcendence because "sex disturbs the pure surrender of the soul."[43] Sulami, a Ṣūfī master, put *haya*—decency, or sexual modesty—at the center of his practice,[44] but anything (not just sex) that derails a Ṣūfī from his spiritual path would be approached with caution.[45] It was through abstinence that Ṣūfīs felt they were achieving a greater path to God. They tried their utmost not be tempted and waver in the path of sex and lust. Al-Hujwiri seconded the opinion of Shihab al-Din Suhrawardi, who said that a celibate life is best for the Ṣūfī: "It is the unanimous opinion of the shaykhs of this sect that the best and most excellent Ṣūfīs are the celibates, if their hearts are uncontaminated and if their natures are not inclined to sins and lust."[46]

And it may come as no surprise that this deep suspicion of sex goes hand in hand with some reservations (if not downright denunciations) of women:

> Since their aim was to be with God alone, without the world and its distractions, one can very well understand their aversion to everything worldly; they were disgusted by the world and had therefore come to hate women, since through woman this world is renewed and continued.[47]

Kazaruni, Shaikh Abu Ishak, Ibrahim, the Persian mystic, (963–1033) wrote that there was no "difference, for him, between a woman and a pillar. He prohibited his disciples from sitting with women and with un-bearded young men, but advised them to get married if they could not restrain their lust."[48] He understood women as not just a hindrance but also unworthy of anything, which is evident in his usage of the word *pillar*, which here should not be read as something supportive.

On the other hand, Ṣūfism certainly heightens the appreciation for humanity as perfectly dualistic, and that dualism has theological implications. The Persian mystic Baba Afdal Kāshāni (d. 1213–4) argued that "the (human) form is the greatest, grandest and most perfect correspondence. For it is 'one of a pair' [*zawj*]. In other words, it made the Being of the Real into two. In the same way, the woman makes the man two through her existence. She turns him into one of a pair."[49] Contemplation or witnessing of God through woman is the most perfect kind of witnessing given to a human being, but this assumption derives from the heteronormative position that every man is necessarily, even divinely, paired with a woman.[50]

In the Arab Andalusian mystic Ibn al-Arabi's (1165–240) view, if the Prophet loved women, then women are a dimension of God—since "he (the prophet) could not have been made to love something other than God, since nothing other than the real is truly worthy of love."[51] Here, Ibn al-Arabi moves toward calling women a form of the divine yet continues to uphold an ideal Islamic masculinity because he places the act of submission in a gendered space, between husband and wife. But the very nature of submission of all created forms is not a relational one except in relation to God. Other mystics uphold the masculinist ideals even more boldly. The most celebrated and renowned Persian Ṣūfī mystic of the eighth century, al-Ghazālī, stated that "wives should devote themselves to their husbands and homes, secluding themselves as much as possible from the outside world" because their purpose is somewhat like that of a devotee, who must "defer, obey, and submit" without challenging others' authority.[52] So Ghazālī and Ibn al-Arabi used the ultimate, transcendent submission experience of mysticism not to knock down gender barriers but to reinforce them.

Ṣūfī practices could push women further from the center of spiritual life: on occasions Ṣūfī male masters were given temporary access to disciples' wives, sisters, and other women family members. And the tradition of calling a saint's death an *urs*—or wedding, in which he is finally made one with God—devalued men's actual marriage involving women.[53] Marriage was permitted for Ṣūfis but it was understood as a means to an end:

> if the Ṣūfī is married, it would be better for him to follow Ali's alleged advice: 'Let not your wife and children be your chief concern.' Did not even Abraham leave Hagar in loneliness, and Moses the daughter of Shu'ayb?[54]

This statement creates many difficulties, as on one side it attempts to return back to a genderless submission to God but on the other does so by dismissing the woman. In delineating a superior act of submission, it upholds the hegemonic position of men. The Ṣūfī's dismissal of the wife could then be used to justify many injustices against women based on the belief that women cannot be the "chief concern" in Islamic masculinity.

Abul Hassan Ali Hujwiri, the Persian Ṣūfī and scholar in the eleventh century, felt that the ideal spiritual state for a husband and wife is one in which the husband and wife feel no sexual attraction to one another, and to illustrate this point he relates an account of Ibrahim al-Khawwas, who was said to have visited a pious old man. When he entered the pious man's house, he saw an old woman who turned out to be the old man's wife, although by their demeanur he had assumed them to be brother and sister. The old man then informed Ibrahim al-Khawwas that they had lived together in a celibate manner for 65 years.[55] Although appearing as a story promoting submission to God without sex, the very fact that they were married, due to societal pressures or not, indicates that marriage has often been central—either as a foil or a tool—to Ṣūfī conceptions of submission.

However, some Ṣūfis cautioned against celibacy and marriage on the spiritual path. Hujwiri makes the most outspoken statement in this respect,

> The evils of celibacy are two: 1) the neglect of an apostolic custom, 2) the fostering of lust in the heart and the danger of falling into the unlawful ways. The evils of marriage are also two: 1) the preoccupation of the mind other than God, 2) the distraction of the body for the sake of sensual pleasure. The root of this matter lies in retirement and companionship. Marriage is proper for those who prefer to associate with mankind, and celibacy is an ornament to those who seek retirement from mankind.[56]

His final sentence makes clear the mistake we would make if we assumed that celibacy better fit Ṣūfīsm than marriage does. On another occasion, Hujwiri asserted, "there is no flame of lust that cannot be extinguished by strenuous efforts because whatever vice proceeds from yourself, you possess the instrument that will remove it."[57]

There have been cases in Ṣūfī communities where women have also taken up vows of celibacy as a vehicle to oneness with God. However, the extent to which societal gender roles can also be abstained from is another issue, since they would have a hard time fully abnegating their household tasks.[58] Still, women have indeed followed the mystic path in Islam—only by transforming their femininity and elevating themselves to a higher "masculine" form. The great Egyptian Ṣūfī of the eighth century, Dhu 'l-Nun al-Misri, is said to have met many such women during his travels, some of whom impressed him with their asceticism (*zuhd*), others with their divine love.[59] An example as such is Rabi'a al-Adawiyya, a freed woman whose asceticism was based on a commitment to depend only on God.[60]

Masculinity and femininity are still constructed in Ṣūfī thought as means to the beloved. Ṣūfī doctrine may well be based on ideas of submission and subservience, but they replicate the patriarchal structures that are prevalent in wider society. Ṣūfī thought becomes so engrossed in seeking love and the beloved (God) that its instruction on marriage and celibacy easily becomes a means to use women as commodities. The concept of *al-Insan al-Kamil* (the perfect man), which Ibn al-Arabi coined, may indeed have been exactly that. The way in which Ṣūfīs present two options of marriage and celibacy is an indication of the way in which masculinity seems greater than femininity. The procreating power remains, as the Ṣūfī man has the power to create, through marriage, or not to create through celibacy. In both marriage and celibacy, a "marriage" takes place—one is with a woman and the other with God. Whether the marriage is for the man to seek the beloved through the female (Ibn al-Arabi) or for the women to seek the beloved through devotion of her husband (Ghazālī), both these models elevate the position of men over women. As Elias stated, "in order to understand his own essence, man, or Adam, can contemplate himself in two aspects: as creator (*khaliq*) from which Eve emanates, or as God's creature (*makhluq*)."[61] Man is therefore elevated to a superior position by understanding man as a creator. This understanding upholds the ideals of masculinity because if man has the power of creation, then he has powers similar to God's. However, this is to the detriment of women, who are expected to emulate the path of Eve, which is understood to be inferior to Adam in Ṣūfī thought. Marriage and procreation then become a means to define and uphold the ideal Islamic masculinity for some Ṣūfīs, but this in turn loses sight of the act of submission to God which is genderless, sexless, and beyond procreating.

Oneness ideals, same-sex practices

For Ṣūfīs, homosexuality has been a challenging form of physical expression as it radically accesses the very foundations of Ṣūfī thought based on "love." Ṣūfī traditions contain numerous examples of episodes describing same-sex love. *Nazar* is the practice of contemplating a young man's beauty as a reflection of God, and "Arabic, Persian, Turkish and Urdu poetry contains many descriptions of love (*ishq*) for the beardless youth (*amrad*)."[62] The fifteenth-century Egyptian mystic Abū al-Muwahib al-Shādhili defends *nazar* as a practice that separates the spiritual from the not—a convenient way of casting as dullards any who oppose the practice:

> The manifestation of beauty in objects varies with the gift of the observer. Thus the common folk do not see other than the appearance of physical beauty while the chosen have unveiled before them the picture of abstract beauty in which is manifested the splendor of His name, the Exalted, that is resplendent in all creation through various phenomena.[63]

One example of same-sex love is found in the life of Fakhruddīn Irāqi, the Persian philosopher and mystic of the thirteenth century, who was said to have been attracted to the spiritual master Shaykh Baha'uddin Zakariyya' Multani, the head of the Suhrwardi Order in Multan (current-day Pakistan). On one occasion Irāqi tried to distance himself from Shaykh Baha'uddin, but events brought them back together. Shaykh Baha'uddin chided Irāqi for fleeing from him. Irāqi's response was as follows:

> My heart will not
> for an instant
> flee from you

for how can the body
    wrench itself
        from the soul?
The nursemaid
    of your kindness
        folded me in its arms;
Even before my mother
    it fed me with
        a hundred kinds of milk[64]

Schimmel argues that "many a Ṣūfī deemed the presence of a beautiful boy necessary for a perfect performance of *sama*," or the practice of hearing God's instruction.[65] The same word, *sama*, is used to mean listening to music,[66] which has also been a powerful way for Ṣūfīs to connect with God: "there is a common saying among Ṣūfīs that earthly beauty with its appreciation, is a bridge to the universal beauty."[67] There also seems to be a preference for young boys:

> The brief period between childhood and entry into the world of adult males was a time when gender boundaries were not yet fully formed, and young men were in an ambiguous situation. . . . in Arabic homoerotic literature the appearance of a beard signaled the end of a youth's desirability.[68]

Schimmel placed the love of boys alongside the spiritual path of the Ṣūfīs: "their *qibla* (direction of prayer and remembrance of God) consisted of *shikam*, *sham* and *shahid*: stomach, candles (in festivities), and a beautiful boy."[69] Ṣūfī commentators have used a saying of the prophet Muḥammad to justify these relationships: "I saw my Lord in the shape of a beautiful young man with his cap awry."[70]

Same-sex love in Ṣūfīsm has more often than not given a veil of heterosexuality in order to satisfy heteronormativity: sometimes the relationships between men and boys are characterized as platonic or simply washed over completely. Modern writers, Kugle has alleged, even change the gender of young men—into young women—in order to expunge the same-sex, mixed-age attraction from the record.[71] In reckonings of Ṣūfī lore and history, same-sex love is often minimized or eraced in tacit acceptance of the idea that true love must be heterosexual and that same-sex acts must be devoid of love. The prolific Persian Ṣūfī writer Ahmad Kasravi (d. 1946) wrote a blistering account of some Ṣūfī practices in which he stated that Ṣūfīs "coined a good name for each evil act of theirs."[72] Kasravi uses the story of Sheikh Owhad al-Dīn Kermāni as an example,

> In *Nafahat al-Ons*, the name of one of the great Ṣūfīs, Sheikh Owhad al-Din Kermani (May God Most High bless him) is mentioned. It states, "In witnessing the Truth he used to turn to manifestations of the upper body, and he witnessed Absolute Beauty in fixed forms." The author wants to say Sheikh Kermani was a homosexual, but he clothes his ugly acts in other garments. He says, "He contemplated the beauty of God in the faces of the youth."[73]

Kasravi dismisses the existence of same-sex love as an appreciation of the ultimate beloved, God, and indicates his own reluctance to the issues because it does not fit Kasravi's ideals of Islamic masculinity.

Al-Rouayheb recalled numerous stories which affirm the claim that same-sex activity was prevalent in Islamic history, but more often than not it was seen as an "evil." He narrated the time when the prophet Muḥammad had seated a handsome man from the tribe of Qays behind him so as to avoid looking at him, the time when Sufyan al-Thawri (d. 778) fled from a handsome boy in a bath because he said that a devil was with every woman and 17 devils were with every beardless youth. He also told of the time when the legal scholar Abu Hanifa (d. 767) seated a handsome student behind him for "fear of betrayal of the eye."[74] Al-Rouayheb gives detailed summaries of the views that legal scholars held on the issue of *liwat* (same-sex intercourse) but concludes that, although it would be correct to state that this practice was forbidden by all legal schools, it was practised by many:

> Having established that the recognized interpreters of Islamic law held that an act was not permissible, we are faced with abundant evidence that it was nevertheless indulged in openly, by belletrists who had close personal ties with religious scholars, and often by religious scholars themselves.[75]

The intersection of love and law poses a challenge to Ṣūfīs, who continually feel that they need to negotiate their Islamic understanding in relation to the Islamic legalists yet often find their own actions contradicting institutional structures. The ideal and reality can be difficult to bring into union. Kugle has written an extensive essay on "sexuality, diversity and ethics" in which his main point is that the Qur'ān is silent on the issue of homosexuality because there is no such term used in the Arabic language; he further argues the term is a late addition to Western vocabulary. He states that anti-homosexual sentiment has developed in Islamic culture as a result of narrow interpretation by Qur'ān scholars; in modern times, he argues, one must adopt a "sexuality-sensitive interpretation" of the Qur'ān which acknowledges the fact that there are multiple sexualities in society.[76] In a 2005 essay he questions whether the Prophet Muḥammad even saw homosexuality as a crime to punish:

> The Prophet certainly did encounter people in his Arab society in Mecca and Medina who had uncommon sexual identities and practices that contradicted the heterosexual norm. Researchers in pre-Islamic and early Islamic Arabic literature have uncovered a wealth of examples. Salah al-Din Munajjad has documented that same-sex practices existed among both men and women in pre-Islamic Arabia. . . . These people were ambiguous in their gender and in their sexuality. Yet, the Prophet is not known to have censured any of them for sexual acts or sexuality in the wider sense. There is no report of the Prophet having any of them burned or stoned for sexual practices.[77]

In an Islamic tradition which is largely heterocentric and family-focused, alternative forms of masculine sexualities are often deemed un-Islamic because they allegedly threaten procreation. In the Shi'i tradition, Ali is asked by a heretic (*zindiq*) why *liwāt* is prohibited. He responds, "if carnal penetration of a boy (*ityān al-ghulām*) were permitted, men would dispense with women, and this would lead to the disruption of procreation and the inoperativeness of vaginas and from allowing this much evil would arise."[78]

The sexual act in homosexual and heterosexual relationships has often been understood in terms of "active" and "passive" partners. Such definitions have also played a role in Islamic sexualities, where the penetrating individual is considered the dominant, active, and powerful one.

> Like Greek homoeroticism, Muslim homoeroticism structured relations according to patterns of domination and submission, activity and passivity. Male sexuality was constructed as domination expressed through penetration, and domination in the sexual act signified power, honor, and status in other spheres.[79]

The very act of sex between a man and a woman in which the man penetrates—certainly not the only conceivable physical arrangement between them—has then influenced the way in which gender is constructed. The constructs of activity and passivity have been used to characterize the sexual act between two men, which in that sense challenges and disrupts heterosexual ideals of power play. In Islamic masculinity and this is another reason why homosexuality has traditionally been excluded as un-Islamic. If the sex act was to be deconstructed as an extension of the ultimate role of submission to God, then passivity is not just an alternative sexual pleasure but also a divine act:

> The passive position for adult males was considered shameful and a sign of weakness, those who enjoyed being penetrated were subject to scorn and even legal punishment. The normative role for adult males was active and insertive; passive roles were held by women, boys, and prostitutes of both sexes. Men who penetrated boys were as "masculine" as those who penetrated women, but those who submitted to penetration (and even desired it) risked humiliation and dishonor.[80]

The issue of celibacy has different implications when it comes to same-sex love and Ṣūfism. It seems that rejection of marriage need not mean rejection of sexual activity, and celibacy means only rejecting procreative forms of intercourse. Mystics may have embraced such "antisocial ways of sexual gratification" as part of their "deliberately rejectionist repertoire."[81] The existence of a distinct group of youths known as *koceks* (from Persian *kuchak*, "youngster") in the Ottoman empire, who were young, handsome cross-dressing boys for sexually provocative dance "entertainment," is certainly suggestive in this regard. However, due to the pressure of a prevalent tradition that same-sex love was un-Islamic, many opted for total abstinence.

Schimmel recalled an interesting story relating to Rumi that shows the way in which celibacy created pent-up frustration which even Rumi found unnecessary:

> Rumi was apparently of a similar opinion, holding that a temporary fulfilment was more practical for a balanced and normal life than endless yearning. He simply put it somewhat more crudely when he was told that Awhaduddin Kirmani's love for young boys was chaste (although he used to tear their frocks during sama, dancing breast to breast with them). Rumi's short remark about this kind of relation was simple: "*Kash kardi u gudhashti*" ("Wish he had done it and been done with it!").[82]

Ṣūfis, on the other hand, have long stated that same-sex relationships are a means to the beloved. This could also be said about heterosexual acts, too; however, homosexual activity has more often than not been dismissed as an "evil" among non-Ṣūfis because it was a serious challenge to the masculinist ideals that society wished to uphold.

Of the numerous colorful Ṣūfī saints in South Asian history who are revered to this very day,[83] one, in particular, encompasses and challenges the notions of sexuality that are at issue here. Shah Hussayn was born in 1539 in the Punjabi city of Lahore, current-day Pakistan.[84] He was understood to be a theologian but best known for his prolific Punjabi poetry, known as *kafi*.[85] What makes Hussayn an interesting Ṣūfī saint are his heterodoxies, about which he was fairly open. While the descriptor *gay* might not attach well to a person of this period, I join Scott Kugle, the scholar of Ṣūfism and the author of the first full length book on homosexuality in Islam, in determining that his lifestyle was all but homosexual in a modern sense. He eschewed the male household responsibilities, including marriage and children, and his romantic partner was a man.[86]

Hussayn, unlike Ghālib, was accepted as a Ṣūfī saint even though his practices would be frowned upon by the pious *Ulama* (religious scholars). Hussayn rooted his hermeneutic within Islamic traditions, organizing his life around the Qur'ānic verse "The life of the world is nothing but play and pleasurable distraction."[87] Once Hussayn struck upon the truth of this verse, he resolved to live a life of submission, which for him meant breaking free of "constraints of ascetic piety, legal rectitude, and rational seriousness; he would instead lead his life as a child at play, abandoning all pretence, hypocrisy, and ambition as well as fear of social blame."[88] A hagiographic poem records him as declaring

> Isn't it better to dance through the marketplace
> than to study knowledge without putting it to practice?
> This verse has opened wide eyes of my understanding
> that I make myself into the living interpretation of its words
> The life of this world is such a burden
> escape complaining by abandoning yourself to play![89]

Hussayn's master was outraged when he heard that he had "misinterpreted" the Qur'ānic verse. Shaykh Bahlul is said to have rushed to Lahore to urge his disciple to change his ways:

> But when he saw Hussayn in ripped red clothes, dancing and drinking wine, he realised that this was his personal path to religious sincerity. The Shaykh blessed him and returned to his home. These two diametrically opposed reactions, initial rejection followed by consideration acknowledgement and respect, would set the pattern for Hussayn's reception in the wider society.[90]

Hussayn then began to live a life of spirituality mixed with ample amounts of "play" and had the "blessing" of his master on his practices. The relationship of master and disciple is here subverted, first by the creative iconoclasm of the disciple and then by the master's ability to validate that deviance. What emerges is not just an alternative path to God but also a distinct divergence within Islamic masculinities.

Hussayn understood the Qur'ān as supportive of alternative paths of spirituality and masculinity. His masculinity did not conform to any of the ideals or roles that society had laid out for him. Society had placed many boundaries for grown men such as Hussayn, but he had no intention of upholding any of them, especially when it came to Madho Lal, a Brahmin Hindu boy with whom Hussayn fell in love. Initially the teenager Madho resisted the advances of the forty-odd-year-old Hussayn, but he finally gave in. It is said that Hussayn would follow Madho wherever he went and would spend the night on his doorstep. Their union finally came to fruition at the spring Basant festival, where the two "frolicked and played." After some difficulties involving the resistance of Madho's Brahmin family, the two began to live together in a place known as Baghabanpur, just outside of Lahore. The onlookers found this to be peculiar, but Hussayn construed their physical relationship as an especially potent way of transferring divine love.[91] Madho joined the army for a time but then returned to Hussayn. When Hussayn died at the age of sixty, Madho fell into a deep depression and spent 35 years at his lover's tomb, longing to be united with him: "He became the spiritual successor of Hussayn's saintly authority, and upon his death Madho was buried directly beside Hussayn."[92]

There is much controversy surrounding this love affair, and many wonder whether it actually existed. Kugle argues that those who deny it have their own prejudices. He gives the example of Lajwanti Ramakrishna, a contemporary scholar who dismisses the love as just a "rumour" and "un-natural."[93] Ramakrishna is also critiqued by Kugle for stating that Hussayn wanted to "possess" Madho, which Kugle shows how she excludes the element of love between the two—something she is "obviously uncomfortable with," Kugle retorts.[94] In a way, Ramakrishna is reading masculine ideals and roles into the gender-defying love story of Hussayn and Madho, but spiritual Ṣūfīs were led to a path to God which was often heterodox.[95]

In the path of submission to God, societal ideals can fall by the wayside. Hussayn used play and love as his basis for getting closer to God. It was through his true love for Madho that he felt spiritually uplifted, and he took the Ṣūfī practice of kissing to transfer "grace or spiritual power" at face value—as a physical exchange, even on an erotic level.[96] It may be that, as Kugle argues, "the medieval and early modern periods were a time of flexibility and pluralism in Islamic communities, when understandings of gender were more fluid, norms of sexuality more flexible, and boundaries of communal allegiance more permeable."[97] But there are still some very defined communities that carry this perhaps old-fashioned elasticity forward (Figure 5.1).

The abject gender play of the Qalandari Malangs

As marginalized Ṣūfīs in South Asia, the Malangs[98] are possibly one of the largest groups of individuals who challenge Islamic traditions and societies, masculinity and masculinities.[99] The Qalandars, as the Malangs call themselves, emerged as a playful force in South Asia, living with a kind of wild abandon that Shah Husseyn would have appreciated: "The Qalandars are radical Ṣūfīs, or dervishes, who stormed across Islamic boundaries of social etiquette and legal rectitude in an attempt to rescue ritual from the demands of order and restore it to its primordial status as 'play.'"[100] Qalandars reject all property (even clothing at times), are celibate, do accept employment (but alms-taking became fairly regulated), are homeless wanderers, and are thoroughly antinomian in appearance and behavior.[101] The Qalandars also use hashish as a hallucinogen.[102] However, their use of hashish plays a role in their spiritual existence and in fact underscores their insistence that one's "relationship to God need not be mediated by external rules."[103] Direct connection with the divine can come, they hold, through alternate consciousness—dreams,

Figure 5.1 A Malangi Qalandar in an ecstatic dance with the beat of Dhol (Drum) at a Sufi shrine in Pakistan

intoxication, trances. They offend some "social sensibilities through their conspicuous elevation of music and dance to the status of ritual practice."[104] Dance and music were not commonly part of religious practice or worship in Islam during early modernity. In the ninth chapter of his *Awarif al-ma'arif*, Abu Hafs Umar al-Suhrawardi (1144–1234) characterizes Qalandars as "people who are governed by the intoxication [engendered by] the tranquility of their hearts to the point of destroying customs and throwing off the bonds of social intercourse."[105] Adopting the path of a Qalandari Ṣūfī is not a simple undertaking, as it requires the followers to dislocate themselves from society.

A Qalandar "resists the conventions of the prevailing social order, the dress and etiquette of polite society. Typically, those who are identified as Qalanders live in violation of shari'at openly and publicly."[106] Malangs have an appearance that challenges stereotypes of feminine and masculine in terms of clothing and grooming.[107] They cover their hair partially, and they wear large pieces of jewelery around their necks, hands, and ears. They are outside the law which governs society, so they are also socially separate from the mainstream Ummah. ↳ androgynous group / removing from gender [roles]

> Qalandars embody this intense reaction against bourgeois notions of work, countering them with "holy waste." They renounce productive work, refuse reproduction of the family, and resist the labour it takes to conform to religious customs and law. Those who oppose Qalandars see their lives as waste—wasting their time, living as parasites off productive society, and squandering the opportunity to earn religious merit through conventional morality.[108]

The Malangs challenge the social order so drastically that they are not looked upon favorably by others who are invested in Islamic order.

The emergence of these "mendicants"[109] occurred in the Middle East,

> Two widespread movements: the Qalandariya, which first flourished in Syria and Egypt under the leadership of ethnically Iranian leaders, most notably Jamal al-Din Savi (d. c. 630/1232–3), and the Haydariyah, which took shape in Iran as a result of the activities of its eponymous founder Qutb al-Din Haydar (d. c. 618/1221–2). Both movements rapidly spread from their respective places of origin to India and to Asia Minor.[110]

However in the Indian subcontinent, the Qalandars were associated with Shaykh Usman Marandi (1177–274) of Sindh, current-day Karachi, Pakistan. He was better known as La`l Shahbaz Qalandar, La`l because of his habit of dressing in red and Shahbaz ("Royal Falcon") conferred by his shaykh. Shah Khizr Rumi and Bu Ali Walandar of Panipat, key figures who helped establish the Qalandari way in South Asia, also emerged in and around the seventh–eighth/thirteenth–fourteenth centuries.[111]

The Malangs are known to roam from shrine to shrine of long dead Ṣūfis, and their dress defies the social norms and expectations from men in South Asian society. The central meeting place for Malangs in Pakistan is at the shrine of La`l Shābaz Qalandar because they believe that their lines of spiritual descent can be traced back to him, whom they see as the spiritual and physical focus of their order.[112] At the tomb, the Malangs dance into a mystical frenzy to *dhamāl* (Ṣūfī trance music). The dhamāl is very different from the dance movements of the whirling dervishes of Turkey as there is no sequence or rotation in the Qalandari dance; it is without any structure, and the Malang may get carried away in remembrance of the beloved at any given time. *Qawwalli*, Ṣūfī devotional music, is typically played at the shrines of dead Ṣūfī saints. The songs are normally sung by groups of men, but the famous female Qawwali singer Abida Parveen, of Pakistan, is an example that goes against the male-dominated set up. The Malangs' position during Qawwalis is also interesting:

> In the space outside the *diwan khana*, the musicians sing *qawwali* and the Malangs gather, though at some shrines the space set aside for "respectable" qawwali is separated from the open space where the Malang establish themselves.[113]

Malangs are relentless in their challenge to every structure and this includes devotional Ṣūfī love music such as Qawwali which is often ritually structured by Ṣūfī orders. Malangs defy all orders, but this comes at a social cost. The cultural anthropologist, Katherine Pratt Ewing, does recall meeting one female Malang,[114] who throughout their conversation kept relating back to her spiritual masters—all men.[115] Bava Sahib, this female Malang, was not as antinomian as some Qalandars, connecting both to *be-shar* (in violation of Islamic law) Qalandari orders and also the *ba-shar* (in accordance with Islamic Law) Qadiri order.[116] Clearly, there is diversity within the Malang community, but the adherents all take commandments "directly from God or from a dead saint who requires the service of the qalandar."[117] In her case, Bhava Sahib thought these communications with her spiritual master came through dreams and visions.[118] Note that this is distinct from the *Ṣūfī pir* structure, which assumes *shari'a* as the starting point for any mystical experience.[119] The Malangs' approach to God is internal, not structured by laws constraining from without.[120] The Malangs distance themselves from the *pir* for the main reason that they are too involved in the external part of the world which includes marriage and children. It is this externality, the socially acceptable domestic path, that *requires* them to perform the ritual practices, such as ablutions, prescribed by law.[121] The Malangs circumvent all that: they have no worldly attachments and thus can forego things like basic grooming.

Eschewing the "inside," domestic world, Malangs do not even live in houses; as we have already established, they often spend their time beside the graves of Ṣūfī saints.[122] One might suspect that ignoring the Islamic law that in some ways tyrannically polices gender roles would free Malangs to express their masculinity and femininity in more fluid ways. However, Ewing argued that Malangs generally reject the home and domestic responsibilities in order to avoid the trappings of womanhood.[123] Malangs then do not embrace femininity necessarily but understand themselves as submissive relative to God—even *betrothed* to God—just as women are submissive to their husbands.[124] The use of the term *bride* in Malang theology is not metaphorical, as the men are known to dress as women and wear women's jewellery too.[125] But those behaviors would not have the same transcendent significance when performed by women, for whom wearing women's clothing and accessories is not an act of defiance or, necessarily, submission to God. So while qalandar gender expression can be seen as fluid for men, those same avenues of expression are almost neutered for women. *vs men can do more crossing-esuy*

The Qalandars of South Asia, embodying centuries of interaction between Islam and Hinduism, constitute an antinomian movement dismissive of all societal and religious structures. The contemporary case of the Malangs of Pakistan today highlights the fact that even in the face of legalists and religious orthodoxy the practices of the religious heterodox still flourish. The Malangs defy social norms in search of perfect union with God. They intoxicate themselves with *hashish* in hopes that it will release them into a religious frenzy. However, Malangs have tried to ungender their spiritual subservient position by adopting the feminine role, which they believe is the ultimate societal role of submission, but by doing this they are also conversely strengthening certain mainstream Islamic notions about gender. The Qalandari Malangs have one goal: communion with God. But their single-minded devotion to that goal, which is also central for all Muslims, "challenges the naturalness of the prevailing social order from within."[126]

Appealing to custom is often used to limit spiritualities and in turn masculinities. Indeed, tradition can bring many to feel closer to the divine, but, as Ian Netton, the British Islamicist, has argued, "for both Islam and Christianity, the Sacred may be achieved by community, *umma*. Notions of community may transform that which is merely profane."[127] Still, communities necessarily, if not actively, exclude some in order to draw boundaries that create meaningful groupings. This in turn creates a tension between the acts of a "united umma" and the marginalized few, such as the Malangs, whose practices arose in direct response to fundamentalist powers—forces that we might actually see as precursors to Mawdūdi-style Islamism. To help us better understand how communities are forged with respect to tradition—and thus how the Qalandars fit into or distinguish themselves from that process, Netton has presented four paradigms describing the tension, or struggle, that emerges when traditions conflict with spiritual activities. First, the neo-cycle of tradition, this is "the basic attempt to re-clothe- or even 're-invent' a community—in the case of Islam, the *umma*—in a more 'traditional' or 'traditionalist' guise in order to access the fundamentally sacred."[128] He explains this through the following example:

> There is a prophetic grounding (Buddha, Jesus, Paul, Muḥammad) which yields an oral and written tradition/Tradition. This, in turn, with the passing of the years, is given a liberal/modern/Modernist slant or *tafsir*, after which an animated reaction emerges: there is an attempt to return to that early tradition/Tradition, to the *salaf*, in the case of Islam.[129]

The second paradigm is the paradigm of purification, which Netton bases on the view of the influential social anthropologist Mary Douglas, that sacred things and places are to be protected from defilement.[130] The third paradigm for Netton is that of kenosis, or "emptying," whereby all the elements of modernity or liberalism in faith, society, custom, and ritual must be vacated in order to access the truly sacred and return to tradition.[131] The final paradigm is the return, which is based on the understanding that everything created has come from God and so it must return.[132] The more traditional a Muslim society tries to be, the more controlling of gender and sexuality it tends to be. It is this rigid tradition that the Qalandars reacted against and challenged as they developed their unique spiritual existence. While legal schools in Islam and formalized Ṣūfi orders have been established—and for many reasons—Qalandars have no intention of being restricted by them. The Qalandars' devotion lies to God only, and through their antisocial ways they confirm their submission to God.

Ṣūfīsm is deeply committed to achieving a mystical union with the beloved (God). The master-disciple relationship is for Ṣūfīs one means of accessing the beloved—the master is expected to help the disciple in understanding what is required in order to strengthen their spirituality. But the way in which divine oneness and submission are achieved in Ṣūfīsm varies not just from region to region but from person to person. It is for this reason that Ṣūfīsm has conflicted with a prescriptivist, legalist Islam, which, contrariwise, could be accused of losing sight of "love." If love is the guiding factor for mystical Islam, then it, like God, could be considered genderless, but Ṣūfī commentators such as Ibn al-Arabi and Ghazālī have added socially constructed gender to Ṣūfī thought and in turn supported dominant conceptions of Islamic masculinity.

As mainstream Islam uses the context of family to work out gender roles, Ṣūfī doctrine experiences friction on the matter of marriage, about which there are conflicting arguments. It is generally accepted in Ṣūfī practice that every man (and woman) has sexual needs, but it is believed that marriage is not the only means of regulating those needs. Some believe that marriage is an integral part of the path to God, whereas others believe that celibacy is the cornerstone of oneness with the beloved divine. Along with that ambivalence about marriage, Ṣūfīs have a history of same-sex relationality, usually grounded in an acceptance that loved one can help "witness" or achieve oneness with God. However, anti-Ṣūfī sentiment has sometimes fermented around the same-sex relationships, which has led to Ṣūfīs in homosexual relations to try and justify their actions through a heteronormative glaze. The power structures in a gendered society leave many forms of Ṣūfīsm in a confused state adding to the crisis of Islamic masculinities.

The case of Shah Hussayn, who fell in love with his young Hindu disciple, embodies the rejection of rules and obligations in favor of seeing the world as a "playground." It is evident from the primary sources that theirs was a relationship rooted in love and spirituality. This love and spirituality flourished beyond religious barriers and continued even after the death of Shah Hussayn, with his lover demonstrating his devotion in perpetuity. Even though historians and theologians have attempted to deconstruct their story through heteronormative masculinist eyes, pushing aside the sexual overtones to their relationship, no one has been able to conceal the fact that their love was beyond gender roles and construction.

When the Malangs dismiss all that is worldly, they aim to perfect a positive loving union with their beloved, but through this theology of absolute love they also reduce their position. The most submitted become the most vulnerable in society. Their opting for more radical appearance and behavior leaves them submissive and vulnerable not only to God but also to other human beings. In her anthropological research with the Malangs in Pakistan, Ewing found that they were equal, at times, to nothing but beggars:[133] "Qalandars are considered beyond the social pale. They are shunned for their reliance on hashish and their rejection of the outer, visible aspects of Muslim law."[134] Through its ritual laws and regulations, Muslim society attempts to structure itself very systematically. But the Qalandar troubles "even the most unexamined habits, the established hegemonies, of everyday life," such as wearing gender-appropriate clothes, or any clothes at all.[135] In contemporary Pakistani politics, where some religious and political movements are trying to establish a uniform Islamic state, the Qalandari Malangs determined failure to uphold not just the Islamic legal requirements of faith but also the societal requirements of citizenship becomes problematic—perhaps by design.

While Ṣūfism provides a space for men—and, to a lesser extent, women—in they can defy their obligations as construed by legalist Islam and play with gender and sexuality, a fluid masculinity is hardly the aim of these mystics. When the focus is on the love between God and God's people, social roles do tend to shift around that central priority; a radical approach to the one relationship reconstrues other relationships. Interactions with cultural others—Hindus, women, the abject poor, the dead—are permitted, but the traditionally sanctioned and close relationship between husband and wife, for example, withers. The Malangs are abjectly submissive to God and even a bit feminized, but despite the theoretical possibilities for gender fluidity, Ṣūfī practices still do not completely buck patriarchy. Ṣūfīs do show that more diversity-tolerant gendering can come from communities which are less focused on text and law, but a focus on communing with the beloved is not a recipe for nonnormative-gender acceptance.

-possible homosexual relationships
-Sufism + submissive gender roles
-dualistic relations
-homosexual practice has been common (but not labeled)

Conclusion

O Mankind! Be conscious of your Sustainer,
who has created you out of one living entity,
And out of it created its mate,
and out of the two spread abroad a multitude of men and women.
And remain conscious of God,
in whose name you demand [your rights] from one another,
and of these ties of kinship.
Verily, God is ever watchful over you. (Qur'ān 4:1)

An exploration of key figures in these two sites—the Qur'ān and Indian-Pakistani Islamic history—exposes the tendentiousness and precarity of tight constraints on Muslim manhood. By examining Qur'ānic arguments and the strict social responsibilities advocated along with narrow Islamic masculinities, we find that God and women (to whom Islamic men relate but are different from) often act as foils for the construction of masculinity. The constrainers of masculinity have used God and women to think with and to dominate through; they mine ineffable and highly varied relationships with the divine, in romantic, and domestic partnerships for paradigms suited to the organization of society. Rigid gender roles are the product of this misguided enterprise: the highly personal relationship between humans and God does not lend itself to the organization of society because that relationship cannot be typified and replicated.

Over the course of this investigation, we have traced the way that Islamic texts and traditions have been bridged with the lived, diverse, realities of Islamic masculinities and femininities by rejecting particular forms and understandings of Islam that are based on othering, foils, and whetstones. This has led us to view the different lives of men and women, through the very act of individual submitted faith, exposing many different forms of Islam and many different forms of Muslim. These performances are the forms and reforms of Islam that are often overlooked. A monolithic understanding of Islamic masculinity is often imbued in politics, and although it is difficult to separate religion from politics, an exploration of Islamic masculinities must be pushed to appreciate that Islamic masculinities are constructed through so much more. Most often this has been disguised using the powerful force of "tradition," Islamic law, or widespread acceptance by the mainstream Muslims under the rubric of a united Ummah, and hence a challenge to any of these is not only difficult but also at times dangerous.

The rich heritage of India and Pakistan highlights the tapestry of Muslim spiritual life, beyond Arabo-centric Islam. However, these spiritual paths have been judged by those who understand their Islam in its most narrowest and traditional form and then attempt to enforce this on all as they administer the "right" or "wrong" form of Islamic masculinity or femininity without appreciating the liberty and freedom involved in the very gray matter of faith, submission, and piety to God. Such narrow interpretations of submission to God by some have demoralized many Muslim men and women who have been forced to accept that their spiritual existences are in some way inferior. This has led many to label themselves as secular or nonreligious Muslims; they are bullied out of the religious sphere, as was the case for Ghālib. At a time when there is much debate about the necessity of a reformation in Islam, it may just be the case that one finds the buried treasures that reformers seek through unveiling and appreciating the rich diversity of Islamic traditions, societies, and cultures that are lived, formed, and reformed in the lives of Muslim men and women in the past and present.

Masculinities studies highlight the way gender is constructed through a series of reflections with the other, including other men and women. Such a dynamic creates and constructs gender based on power with catastrophic consequences, at times involving killing and bloodshed. If submission is the central idea of Islam and the fundamental awareness that all of humanity is rightly submissive to God, then this overrides particularities and divisions in a way that could be liberative for nondominant expressions of masculinity. Piety and submission to God, the ultimate other, relieve men and women from conformity to socially constructed ideals and gender roles and at the same time construct a distinctly Islamic masculinity and femininity. As God's ultimate power is essentially a personal spiritual experience, which cannot be idealized, there has been an effort to concretize this power by codifying human relationships and gender dynamics in religious law. To the likes of Mawdūdi, recognizing that Islamic law and its jurisprudence are human endeavors is itself an act of disdain for tradition. Putting law above Ḥadīth or the Qur'ān is a polarizing move with detrimental psychological effects. General citizens of any nation-state understand that law orders society, and Muslim legalists take advantage of this, commanding their position through statements attached to Islamic law that they present as divine and encompassing of Ḥadīth and the Qur'ān. Yet a more detailed and academic understanding of the Qur'ān and Ḥadīth—and, in fact, of Islamic law—appreciates these texts' ambiguous nature. For that reason, preferring the Qur'ān and/or the prophets as precedent over the accreted layers of sharia law is potentially subversive.

The history of Qur'ānic interpretation has snowballed and traveled with the text, so the Muslim feminists' impulse to shed those layers is rightheaded to an extent. The Qur'ān presents a number of problematic passages, such as wife beating and the promotion of multiple marriages for men, which complicates understandings of piety and submission. What is important to appreciate is that the message of the Qur'ān was revealed in a patriarchal society and its divine messages have more often than not been understood to uphold patriarchy. Problematic passages of the Qur'ān, in terms of gender diversity, cannot be thrown away but must be appreciated in the context of its core message of submission to God through its ambiguous nature. The labeling of specific forms of gender, especially procreating, as divine has led to a widespread understanding that there is an Islamic masculinity and Islamic femininity and to challenge such genders would be tantamount to challenging God, even though a closer examination raises the question whether such gender constructions fall into the category of *Shirk*—associating anything with God's divinity. The example of the prophet Muḥammad's life is evidence of this as his, greatly debated, marriage to the very young Aisha has raised a number of critical questions relating to his example of masculinity for Muslim men. And this is why another of the feminist scholars' major strategies—that of celebrating multiple interpretive readings all as holding a bit of the truth—is a necessary complement to the strategy of separating what the Qur'ān says from what it has, over centuries, been made to say.

We took this feminist challenge to expose diversity and variance to heart by exploring the Qur'ān that revealed a celebratory panoply of masculinities in characters that remain steadfast in their ultimate role of submission to God. It would be very difficult indeed to argue thereafter that the Qur'ān places any emphasis on uniform norms of gender, sexuality, masculinity, or femininity: its message of strengthening piety and submission is not consistently restricted to any specific form. Belief in God as the overarching power has the potential to reduce the power dynamic between creation, namely men and women, and in turn create a more egalitarian society. However, the Qur'ān presents far from perfect lives of men and women as examples of piety and submission, as is illustrated through the stories of the prophets and it utilizes multiplicity and diversity in creation (human beings, angels, men, women, religions, nations, tribes) as a means of reflecting, realizing, and upholding ethics and morality in light of God's power.

The codification of gender has also strengthened a limited understanding of Islamic masculinities through the establishment of Islamic law as it was also shaped in the deeply patriarchal culture of medieval Arabia. It is a recommendation of this book to examine the extent to which this is true through a concentrated study of Islamic law derived from the Arab lands and masculinities studies. The work of Mawdūdi, including other political Islamist leaders and movements, and his (their) ambitions in making Pakistan (or the whole world) an Islamic state under his (their) understanding of Islamic law offers a glimpse into the potential of such a question, although this book focused more on the ideological connotations of Mawdūdi's work on constructions of political Islamist masculinity in particular.

The various examples presented from India and Pakistan between the eighteenth and twentieth centuries highlight the tension between traditions, society, and culture as we explored the subjectivity of Muslim men and women. Political Islamist movements led by charismatic men have sought to support idealized understandings of an Islamic masculinity and have done so by advocating the family structure as divine. Mawdūdi used politics to develop a theology based on an East-versus-West power dichotomy that became more focused on empowering his construction of "Islam" through an idealized Islamic state and in turn losing sight of the relevance and significance of diversity. Mirzā Ghālib provided an image of masculinity that was perhaps hedonistic in its outlook but deeply obedient and submissive to God. His love for alcohol and courtesans led Ghālib to deem himself un-Islamic because he failed to be led by the power of society or traditions. This led to a discussion on the extent to which one can speak of the liberatory powers of Ṣūfism, which has often been used to support nontraditional paths to God. However, what emerged through an evaluation of Ṣūfi thought and practice is that it also remains confined to the patriarchal and idealized notions of an Islamic masculinity. Antinomian Ṣūfis, namely the Qalandari Malangs, rejected such conformist understandings of Ṣūfism and sought a radical return back to submission to God. As God's brides, they challenge sex and social norms in India and Pakistan but at times negotiate their antinomian positions in submission to patriarchal society, which they find difficult to dismiss for God.

By reading the silences and magnifying lives and phenomena that do not have an easy place in fundamentalist conceptions of Islamic masculinities, we see that the core constellations of relationships that have defined manhood in Islam shift significantly. How masculinity is worked out via women, other men, one's own gender expression, and the figure of the cultural other permutes nimbly. The embodiment of Islam comes from its living and breathing men and women who have grappled with their own personal quests toward God. We likewise ought to appreciate the quests of polar opposites such as Mawdūdi and Ghālib because both were Islamic but might not recognize the other as such. As diverse, slippery, and complicated as the use of these foils can become, none of those outworkings necessarily dictate masculinity's relationship to the ultimate other, God, which remains the central relationship in Islam.

Notes

Introduction

1 "N'importe! elle n'était pas heureuse, ne l'avait jamais été. D'où venait donc cette insuffisance de la vie, cette pourriture instantanée des choses où elle s'appuyait? . . . Mais, s'il y avait quelque part un être fort et beau, une nature valeureuse, pleine à la fois d'exaltation et de raffinements, un cœur de poète sous une forme d'ange, lyre aux cordes d'airain, sonnant vers le ciel des épithalames élégiaques, pourquoi, par hasard, ne le trouverait-elle pas? Oh! quelle impossibilité! Rien, d'ailleurs, ne valait la peine d'une recherche; tout mentait! Chaque sourire cachait un bâillement d'ennui, chaque joie une malédiction, tout plaisir son dégoût, et les meilleurs baisers ne vous laissaient sur la lèvre qu'une irréalisable envie d'une volupté plus haute," in G. Flaubert, *Madame Bovary—Moeurs De Province* (Paris: Michel Levy Freres, Libraires-Edituers, 1857), pp. 399–400.

2 G. Dawson, "The Blond Bedouin: Lawrence of Arabia, Imperial Adventure and the Imagining of English-British Masculinity," ed. M. Roper and J. Tosh, *Manful Assertions: Masculinities in Britain since 1800* (Routledge: London, 1991), p. 118.

3 Islam may be defined in many ways but as a matter of faith and practice its fundamental orientation lies in submission to God (Allah).

4 Namely, belief in God and Muḥammad, the five daily prayers, giving the alms tax to the poor, fasting during Ramadhan and making pilgrimage to Hajj.

5 For further discussions on Islam and alcohol, see: K. Kueny, *Rhetoric of Sobriety—Wine in Early Islam* (New York, NY: State University of New York Press, 2001).

6 "He (God) has forbidden to you only carrion, and blood, and the flesh of swine, and that over which any name other than God's has been invoked" (Qur'ān 2:173).

7 A. Karamustafa, "A Civilizational Project in Progress," ed. O. Safi, *Progressive Muslims on Justice, Gender and Pluralism* (Oxford: Oneworld, 2004), p. 110.

8 D. S. Ahmed, "Gender and Islamic Spirituality: A Psychological View of 'Low' Fundamentalism," ed. L. Ouzgane, *Islamic Masculinities* (London: Zed Books, 2006) pp. 11–34; 21.

9 For an anthropological and sociological discussion on masculinities and the Muslim and Arab Middle East, see: M. Ghoussoub and E. Sinclair-Webb (eds), *Imagined Masculinities—Male Identity and Culture in the Modern Middle East* (London: Saqi Books, 2000).

10 L. Ahmed, *A Quiet Revolution: The Veil's Resurgence, from the Middle East to America* (New Haven, CT: Yale University Press, 2011).

11 L. Ouzgane, "The Rape Continuum: Masculinities in Ben Jelloun's and El Saadawi's Works," ed. S. M. Whitehead, *Men and Masculinities—Critical Concepts in Sociology*, vol. V (Oxford: Routledge, 2006), p. 88.

12 For further reading on homosexual Muslim male experience see: G. S. Dhalla, *Ode to Lata* (Los Angeles, CA: Really Great Books, 2002); B. Whitaker, *Unspeakable Love—Gay and Lesbian Life in the Middle East* (London: Saqi Books, 2006); A. Kabil, *Straightening Ali* (Herndon: Star Books Press, 2007); B. Khan, *Sex, Longing and Not Belonging: A Gay Muslim's Quest for Love and Meaning* (Oakland, CA: Floating Lotus Press, 1997); A. Jama, *Illegal Citizens: Queer Lives in the Muslim World* (Los Angeles, CA: Salaam Press, 2008); A, Schmittand J. Sofer (eds), *Sexuality and Eroticism Among Males in Moslem Society* (Binghamton: Harrington Park Press, 1992); S. O. Murray and W. Roscoe (eds), *Islamic Homosexualities: Culture, History and Literature* (New York, NY: New York University Press, 1997); M. T. Luongo (ed.), *Gay Travels in The Muslim World* (Binghamton: Harrington Park Press, 2007).

13 For further reading on female homosexuality see: S. Habib, *Female Homosexuality in the Middle East—Histories and Representations* (London: Routledge, 2007).

14 All Qur'ānic translations are taken from M. Asad, *The Message of the Qur'ān* (Bristol: The Book Foundation, 2003) throughout this thesis but translations used by authors in their work are not changed in any way.

15 M. Mac an Ghaill (ed.), *Understanding Masculinities—Social Relations and Cultural Arenas* (Buckingham: Open University Press, 2000), p. 1.

16 M. Roper and J. Tosh (eds), *Manful Assertions: Masculinities in Britain since 1800* (London: Routledge, 1991), p. 8.

17 Mac an Ghaill, *Understanding Masculinities*, p. 1.

18 C. Haywood and M. Mac an Ghaill, *Men and Masculinities—Theory, Research and Social Practice* (Buckingham: Open University Press, 2003), p. 8.

19 Joseph Massad's book *Desiring Arabs* is a detailed analysis into the development of perceptions of Arabs from an Orientalist and Arab point of view. Massad, a student of Said, uses his mentor's argument on Orientalism as a way to introduce his research focus. Edward Said's *Orientalism* showed how Orientalism created the Oriental and how it shaped and still shapes the views of that Westerners hold about Arabs since the European Enlightenment. *Orientalism* generated an important body of scholarship about various kinds of Orientalism representations of Arabs and Muslims in Europe but, unfortunately, little if any scholarship was produced in its wake about Orientalist representations in the Arab world, whether in Arabic or in European languages. J. A. Massad, *Desiring Arabs* (Chicago, IL: University of Chicago Press, 2008), pp. 47–8.

20 S. Gerami, "Mullahs, Martyrs, and Men—Conceptualizing Masculinity in the Islamic Republic of Iran," ed. S. M. Whitehead, *Men and Masculinities—Critical Concepts in Sociology*, vol. V (Oxford: Routledge, 2006), p. 103.
21 D. W. Brown, *Rethinking Tradition in Modern Islamic Thought* (Cambridge: Cambridge University Press, 1996), p. 11.
22 Ibid., p. 44.
23 L. Ouzgane (ed.), *Islamic Masculinities* (London: Zed Books, 2006).
24 Ibid., p. 2.
25 R. W. Connell, *The Men and the Boys* (Oxford: Polity Press, 2000), p. 10.
26 S. Frosh, A. Phoenix and R. Pattman, *Young Masculinities: Understanding Boys in Contemporary Society* (Palgrave: Basingstoke, 2002), pp. 75–6.
27 Connell, *The Men*, p. 29.
28 Further information on seeking knowledge and Islam, see: I. R. Netton, *Seek Knowledge: Thought and Knowledge in the House of Islam* (Richmond: Curzon, 1995).
29 A. Mālik bin, *Kitāb al-Muwaṭṭa'*, trans. A. A. at-Tarjumana and Y. Johnson (Norwich: Diwan Press, 1982), p. 198.
30 S. M. Whitehead and F. J. Barrett, "The Sociology of Masculinity," ed. S. M. Whitehead and F. J. Barrett, *The Masculinities Reader* (Cambridge: Polity Press, 2001), p. 22.
31 J. Halberstam, "An Introduction to Female Masculinity: Masculinity without Men," ed. R. Adams and D. Savran, *The Masculinity Studies Reader* (Oxford: Blackwell Publishers, 2002), p. 355.
32 Scott Siraj al-Hajj Kugle, *Homosexuality in Islam: Critical Reflection on Gay, Lesbian, and Transgender Muslims* (Oxford: Oneworld, 2010).
33 Connell, *The Men*, p. 17.
34 V. J. Seidler, *Man Enough—Embodying Masculinities* (London: Sage Publications, 1997), p. 1.
35 Ahmed, "Gender and Islamic Spirituality," pp. 11–34; 17.

Chapter 1

1 A. Ahmed, *Islamic Modernism in India and Pakistan* (Oxford: Oxford University Press, 1967), p. 208.
2 The English translation of the book will be used extensively but the original, in Urdu, was also consulted. See: A. A. Mawdūdi, *Purdah* (Lahore: Islamic Publications, 2007).
3 For further reading on masculinity and politics see: M. Messner, *Politics of Masculinities: Men in Movements* (Thousand Oaks, CA: Sage, 1997); S. Dudink, K.

Hagemann, and J. Tosh (eds), *Masculinities in Politics and War—Gendering Modern History* (Manchester: Manchester University Press, 2004).
4 K. Aḥmad and Z. I. Ansari, *Mawdūdī: An Introduction to His Life and Thought* (Leicester: Islamic Foundation, 1979), p. 6.
5 Ibid.
6 Ibid., pp. 6–7.
7 Ibid., p. 7.
8 Ibid.
9 Ibid., p. 8.
10 Ibid., p. 9.
11 Ibid., p.16
12 Ibid., p. 9.
13 Aḥmed, *Islamic Modernism*, p. 208.
14 A. O. Khān, "Political and Economic Aspects of Islamisation," ed. M. A. Khān, *The Pakistan Experience—State and Religion* (Lahore: Vanguard Books, 1985), p. 140.
15 A. A. Mawdūdi, *Capitalism, Socialism and Islam*, trans. S. A. Khān (Safat: Islamic Book Publishers, 1987), p. 12.
16 Ibid., pp. 12–16.
17 Ibid., p. 31.
18 Ibid., pp. 34–5.
19 Ibid., pp. 68, 70.
20 Ibid., p. 70.
21 Ibid., p. 71.
22 Ibid., p. 73.
23 Ibid., p. 78.
24 A. A. Mawdūdi, *Human Rights in Islam*, trans. K. Ahmad (Leicester: Islamic Foundation, 1993), p. 9.
25 Ibid., p. 9.
26 Z. Aḥmed, "Maudoodi's Islamic State," ed. M. A. Khān, *The Pakistan Experience—State and Religion* (Lahore: Vanguard Books, 1985), p. 109.
27 A. Schimmel, *Islam in the Indian Subcontinent* (Leiden: E.J. Brill Publications, 1980), p. 238.
28 A. A. Mawdūdi, *The Islamic Way of Life (Islām kā Niẓām Ḥayāt),* trans. and ed. K. Ahmad and K. Murad (Leicester: Islamic Foundation, 2001), pp. 13–14.
29 Ibid., p. 16.
30 Ibid., pp. 21–3.
31 Ibid., p. 31.
32 Aḥmed, "Maudoodi's Islamic State," p. 99.
33 R. H. Dekmijian, *Islamic in Revolution—Fundamentalism in the Arab World* (Syracuse: Syracuse University Press, 1995), p. 11.
34 Ibid., pp. 10–11.

35 Ibid., p. 19.
36 Ibid., pp. 19–22.
37 Ibid., p. 19.
38 Ibid., p. 36.
39 Further information on al-Banna, see: L. Brynjar, *The Society of the Muslim Brothers in Egypt: The Rise of an Islamic Mass Movement 1928–1942* (Reading: Garnet Publishers and El Awaisi, 1998); M. Abd al-Fattah El-Awaisi, *The Muslim Brothers and the Palestine Question* (London: I.B. Tauris & Co Ltd, 1998).
40 Further information on Qutb see: S. Qutb, *Milestones* (India: Islamic Book Service, 2006); A. J. Bergesen (ed.), *The Syed Qutb Reader: Selected Writings on Politics, Religion and Society* (New York: Routledge, 2008).
41 Further information on Hawwa see: I. Weismann, "Sa'id Hawwa and Islamic Revivalism in Ba'thist Syria," *Studia Islamica*, 85 (1997), pp. 131–54
42 Further information on Farrāj and Islamism in Egypt, see: G. Kepel, *Muslim Extremism in Egypt: The Prophet and Pharaoh*, trans. J. Rothschild (Berkeley, CA: University of California Press, 1985).
43 Further information on Yakan see: S. Elsässer, "Between Ideology and Pragmatism: Fathī Yakan's Theory of Islamic Activism," *Die Welt des Islams*, 47(3–4) (2007), pp. 376–402.
44 Further information on Utaybi, see: Y. Trofimov, *The Siege of Mecca: The Forgotten Uprising in Islam's Holiest Shrine* (London: Penguin, 2008).
45 Ibid., p. 41.
46 Dekmijian, *Islamic in Revolution*, pp. 41–4.
47 For further reading on Islamism, see: P. R. Demant, *Islam Vs. Islamism: The Dilemma of the Muslim World* (Westport: Praeger Publishers, 2006); J. Calvert, *Islamism: A Documentary and Reference Guide* (Westport, CT: Greenwood Press, 2007).
48 I. Talbot, *Pakistan—A Modern History* (London: Hurst and Company, 1998), p. 27.
49 Q. M. Haq and M. I. Waley, *Allama Sir Muḥammad Iqbal—Poet-Philosopher of the East* (Scarborough: British Museum Publications, 1977), p. 9.
50 S. A. Vahid, *Iqbal—His Art & Thought* (Hyderabad: Government Central Press, 1944), p. 11.
51 M. Iqbal, *Stray Reflections: The Private Notebook of Muhammad Iqbal*, ed. J. Iqbal (Lahore: Iqbal Academy Pakistan, 1987), p. 53.
52 Ibid., p. 43
53 Waley, *Allama Sir Muḥammad Iqbal*, p. 7.
54 R. D. Lee, *Overcoming Tradition and Modernity* (Colorado: Westview Press, 1997), p. 59.
55 A. H. Syed, "Iqbal and Jinnah on Issues of Nationhood and Nationalism," ed. C. M. Naim, *Iqbal, Jinnah and Pakistan—The Vision and the Reality* (Lahore: Vanguard Books, 1984), p. 77.

56 Iqbal, *Stray Reflections*, p. 111.
57 M. S. Mir, "Religion and Politics in Pakistan," ed. A. A. Engineer, *Islam in Asia* (Lahore: Vanguard Publications, 1986), p. 157.
58 Lee, *Overcoming Tradition*, pp. 58–9.
59 Ibid., p. 80.
60 Haqandwaley, *Allama Sir Muḥammad Iqbal*, p. 9.
61 S. Irfani, "The Progressive Islamic Movement," ed. M. A. Khān, *The Pakistan Experience—State and Religion* (Lahore: Vanguard Books, 1985), p. 42.
62 S. V. R. Nasr, *Mawdūdi & The Making of Islamic Revivalism* (New York: Oxford University Press, 1996), p. 107.
63 Lee, *Overcoming Tradition*, p. 67.
64 M. Iqbal, *Shikwa and Jawab-i-Shikwa—Complaint and Answer—Iqbal's Dialogue with Allah*, trans. K. Singh (New Delhi: Oxford University Press, 2008).
65 Ibid., pp. 31–3.
66 Ibid., p. 25.
67 Ibid., pp. 73–4.
68 Ibid., p. 8.
69 T. Ali, *Can Pakistan Survive?* (Harmondsworth: Pelican Books, 1983), p. 42.
70 Ibid., p. 28.
71 K. B. Sayeed, *Pakistan—The Formative Phase 1857–1948* (Oxford: Oxford University Press, 1968), p. 11.
72 Ibid., p. 33.
73 Parsi is the name given to a Zoroastrian family that lives in India.
74 M. A. Karandikar, *Islam in India's Transition to Modernity* (Bombay: Orient Longmans Ltd., 1968), p. 256.
75 Mir, "Religion and Politics in Pakistan," pp. 158–9.
76 A. Rashid, "Pakistan: The Ideological Dimension," ed. M. A. Khān, *The Pakistan Experience—State and Religion* (Lahore: Vanguard Books, 1985), p. 81.
77 Mir, "Religion and Politics in Pakistan," p. 158.
78 Aḥmed, *Islamic Modernism*, p. 214.
79 Ibid.
80 See section on Sir Syed Aḥmed Khān in Chapter 3.
81 Ali, *Can Pakistan Survive?*, p. 28.
82 Aḥmadand Ansari, *Mawdūdī*, p. 10.
83 Ibid., p. 10.
84 Ibid.
85 Nasr, *Mawdūdi*, p. 130.
86 Ibid.
87 Mawdūdi, *Purdah*, p. 105.
88 A. A. Mawdūdi, *The Laws of Marriage and Divorce in Islam*, trans. F. Aḥmed (Safat: Islamic Book Publishers, 2000), p. 6.

89 Ibid., p. 11
90 Mawdūdi, *Purdah*, pp. 65–6.
91 Ibid., p. 66.
92 Ibid., p. 94.
93 Ibid., pp. 98–9.
94 Ibid., pp. 95–6.
95 Ibid., p. 1.
96 Nasr, *Mawdūdi*, p. 33.
97 A. A. Mawdūdi, *Towards Understanding Islam* (Leicester: Islamic Foundation, 1980), p. 108.
98 Ibid.
99 Qur'ān 51:49.
100 Mawdūdi, *Purdah*, p. 132.
101 Ibid., p. 133.
102 Ibid.
103 Ibid., p. 134.
104 Mawdūdi described the *mahram* as "a women's father, brother, son or any other relative with whom she cannot enter into matrimony" (*Purdah*, p. 146).
105 Ibid., pp. 145–7.
106 "Men shall take full care of women with the bounties which God has bestowed more abundantly on the former than on the latter, and with what they may spend out of their possessions. And the righteous women are the truly devout ones, who guard the intimacy, which God has [ordained to be guarded]. And as for those women whose ill-will you have reason to fear, admonish them [first]; then leave them alone in bed, then beat them; and if thereupon they pay you heed, do not seek to harm them. Behold, God is indeed most high, great!"
107 A. A. Mawdūdi, *Towards Understanding the Qur'ān*, trans. and ed. A. I. Ansari (Delhi: Markazi Maktaba Islami Publishers, 2005), p. 36.
108 Mawdūdi, *Purdah*, p. 149.
109 Ibid., p. 114.
110 Ibid.
111 Ibid., p. 115.
112 Ibid., p. 116.
113 Ibid., p. 117.
114 Ibid.
115 Ibid., p. 119.
116 Ibid., p. 84.
117 Mawdūdi's use of "animal instinct" in terms of men was literal. He believed that men were given divine rule over women who were like animals in men's farms. Mawdūdi interpreted the Qur'ānic verse, "He has given you wives from among yourself to multiply you, and cattle male and female" (Qur'ān 42:11) and "Your

wives are your farms" (Qur'ān 2:223) to mean, "In the first verse, mention has been made of the pairs of man and animal together, and of the common object intended thereof, that is, the propagation of the species as a result of their sex relationship. In the second verse, man has been considered separately from the other animal species, and it has been indicated that the relation between the partners of a human pair is that of a cultivator and his farm. This is a biological fact and the most appropriate illustration from the biological viewpoint of a relationship between the man and the woman" (ibid., p. 135).

118 Ibid., p. 88.

119 Ibid., p. 107.

120 Ibid., p. 15. Iqbal also said "Art is a sacred lie" in *Stray Reflections*, p. 43.

121 Mawdūdi, *Purdah*, p. 109.

122 Ibid. Mawdūdi surely overlooked the explicit "bathing scene" on the walls of the Eighth-Century Umayyad Qusayr (Palace) "Amra, which was both a fortress with a garrison and a residence of the Umayyad Caliphs." See: Museum without Frontiers (eds), *Discover Islamic Art in the Mediterranean—A Book by Museum with No Frontiers* (London: Compass Press, 2007), p. 37.

123 Mawdūdi, *Purdah*, pp. 4–17.

124 Ibid., p. 5.

125 Ibid., p. 8.

126 Mawdūdi, *Purdah*, p. 9.

127 Mawdūdi, *Capitalism, Socialism and Islam*, pp. 2–3.

128 Mawdūdi, *Purdah*, p. 12.

129 Ibid., p. 13.

130 Ibid., p. 46.

131 Ibid., p. 51.

132 Ibid., p. 58.

133 Ibid., pp. 58–9: "a physician of Baltimore has reported that within a year or so, more than a thousand cases of fornication with girls under 12 were tried in that city. This is then the first fruit of the social environment charged with sexual excitement and licentiousness."

134 Ibid., p. 59.

135 Ibid., p. 61.

136 Ibid., p. 63.

137 Ibid., p. 67.

138 Ibid., p. 19.

139 Ibid., p. 23.

140 Ibid., p. 25.

141 Ibid., p. 218.

142 Ibid., p. 125.

143 Ibid., p. 127.

144 Ibid., p. 159.
145 Ibid., p. 163.
146 Ibid., p. 164.
147 Ibid., pp. 164–5.
148 Ibid.
149 Ibid., p. 166.
150 Ibid., pp. 168–9.
151 Ibid., p. 169.
152 Ibid., p. 171.
153 Ibid., p. 173.
154 Ibid., p.175.
155 Ibid., pp. 176–7.
156 Ibid., p. 178.
157 Ibid., p. 194.
158 "O Children of Adam! We have sent down to you clothing in order to cover the shameful parts of your body and serve as protection and decoration; and the best of all garments is the garment of piety" (Qur'ān 7:26).
159 Ibid., p. 139.
160 Ibid., p. 195.
161 Ibid., p. 22.
162 Ibid., p. 132.
163 Mawdūdi, *The Laws of Marriage*, pp. 14–15.
164 Ibid., p. 15.
165 Ibid., p. 16.
166 Ibid., p. 17.
167 Ibid., p. 24.
168 Ibid., p. 19.
169 Qur'ān 4:4–6.
170 Mawdūdi, *Towards Understanding the Qur'ān*, pp. 7–8.
171 Mawdūdi, *Towards Understanding Islam*, p. 109.
172 Ibid., p. 14.
173 Ibid., p. 14.
174 Ibid., p. 120.
175 Ibid.
176 Ibid., p. 121.
177 "Behold, those whom the angels gather in death while they are still sinning against themselves, [the angels] will ask, 'What was wrong with you?' They will answer; 'We were too weak on earth.' [The angels] will say; 'Was, then, God's earth not wide enough for you to forsake the domain of evil? For such, then, the goal is hell—and how evil a journey's end!'"
178 Ibid., p. 211.

179 Ibid., p. 157.
180 Nasr, *Mawdūdi*, p. 62.
181 Mawdūdi, *Purdah*, p. 111.
182 See: H. Ansari, *The Infidel Within—Muslims in Britain since 1800* (London: C. Hurst and Co. Publishers, 2004), pp. 389–406.

Chapter 2

1 C. Brontë, "Life and Works of Charlotte Bronte and Her Sisters—an Illustrated Edition in Seven Volumes," vol. II 'Shirley' (London: Smith, Elder, & CO., 1895), p. 315.
2 Amina Wadud is an African-American Muslim feminist scholar of Islam who was born in Bethesda, Maryland, United States of America. Wadud's father was a Methodist Minister and her mother is said to have descended from "Muslim slaves" in Africa. Wadud completed her Ph.D. at the University of Michigan in 1988 and studied Arabic and Islamic Studies for a short time in Cairo, Egypt. Wadud has been a controversial figure due to her leading the prayers of a mixed-sex Muslim congregation in various cities around the world. Her books on Muslim feminism have received international coverage and she has presented her thoughts and ideas globally.
3 A. Wadud, *Inside the Gender Jihad—Women's Reform in Islam* (Oxford: Oneworld, 2006), p. 93.
4 Ibid., p. 8.
5 The term "Muslim feminist" will be used to refer to all Muslim women who have challenged the prevalent understanding and construction of Islamic masculinity and femininity regardless if they do or do not self identify with this term.
6 See Q. Amin, *The Liberation of Women—The New Woman*, trans. S. S. Peterson (Cairo: American University in Cairo Press, 2004).
7 Barlas defined it as such, "I define patriarchy in both a narrow (specific) and broad (universal) sense in order to make a definition as comprehensive as possible. Narrowly defined, patriarchy is a historically specific mode of rule by fathers that, in its religious and traditional forms, assumes a real as well as symbolic continuum between 'father/fathers'; that is, between a patriarchalized view of God as Father/male, and a theory of father-right, extending to the husband's claim to rule over his wife and children. . . . Patriarchy, broadly conceived, is based in an ideology that ascribes social/sexual inequalities to biology; that is, it confuses sexual/biological differences with gender dualisms/inequality." A. Barlas, *Believing Women in Islam—Unreading Patriarchal Interpretations of the Qur'ān* (Austin, TX: University of Texas Press, 2004), pp. 11–12.

8 Asma Barlas is a Pakistani academic who is currently a Professor of Politics and the Director of the Centre for the Study of Culture, Race and Ethnicity at Ithaca College, New York State, United States of America. Although not a Islamic Studies specialist, her book on women and Islam has received widespread coverage and ignited much discussion and debate. Barlas started her academic career at Kinnaird College for Women in Pakistan where she graduated with her B.A. in English Literature. This was followed by a Masters degree in Journalism from Punjab University and subsequently a Ph.D. at the University of Denver in International Studies. This chapter will cover key areas of discussion from her book and discuss them in relation to other Muslim women feminists through a thematic approach to understanding their construction of masculinity. Barlas, *Believing Women in Islam*, p. 132.
9 Ibid., p. 1.
10 Ibid., p. 8.
11 Ibid., p. 3.
12 Ibid., p. 167.
13 See: B. Friedan, *The Feminine Mystique* (London: Penguin, 1992).
14 Barlas, *Believing Women in Islam*, p. 167
15 Ibid., p. 154.
16 Wadud, *Inside the Gender Jihad*, p. 127.
17 F. Mernissi, *Beyond the Veil: Male-Female Dynamics in Modern Muslim Society* (Bloomington and Indianapolis: Indiana University Press, 1987), p. x.
18 Barlas, *Believing Women in Islam*, p. 132.
19 Z. Mir-Hosseini, *Islam and Gender—The Religious Debate in Contemporary Iran* (London: I.B. Tauris & Co Ltd., 1999), p. 6.
20 S. Shaikh, "A tafsīr of Praxis: Gender, Marital Violence, and Resistance in a South African Muslim Community," ed. D. McGuire and S. Shaikh, *Violence Against Women in Contemporary World Religion: Roots and Cures* (Cleveland: Pilgrim Press, 2007).
21 Wadud, *Inside the Gender Jihad*, p. 180.
22 R. Hassan, "'Jihād fi sabil Allah': a Muslim Woman's Faith Journey from Struggle to Struggle to Struggle," ed. L. Grob, R. Hassan, and H. Gordon, *Women's and Men's Liberation—Testimonies of Spirit* (Westport, CT: Greenwood Press, 1991), p. 12.
23 Ibid., p. 13.
24 Ibid., p. 14.
25 Ibid., p. 18.
26 Ibid., p. 15.
27 Ibid., p. 21.
28 Ibid.
29 Ibid., p. 22.

30 Ibid., pp. 24–5.
31 See: A. Q. Nomani, *Standing Alone: An American Woman's Struggle for the Soul of Islam* (New York, NY: HarperSanFrancisco, 2003) and A. Q. Nomani, *Tantrika: Traveling the Road of Divine Love* (New York, NY: HarperCollins Publishers, 2003).
32 Nomani, *Standing Alone*, p. 14.
33 Ibid., p. 22.
34 Barlas, *Believing Women in Islam*, p. 91.
35 N. El Saadawi, *The Hidden Face of Eve—Women in the Arab World* (London: Zed Press, 1980), p. 81.
36 B. Bhutto, *Reconciliation—Islam, Democracy, and the West* (London: Simon & Schuster UK Ltd, 2008), p. 270.
37 Ibid., p. 39.
38 B. Bhutto, *Benazir Bhutto—Daughter of the East - An Autobiography* (London: Simon & Schuster UK Ltd, 2007), p. 32.
39 Wadud, *Inside the Gender Jihad*, p. 182.
40 A. Wadud, *Qur'ān and Woman—Rereading the Sacred Text from a Woman's Perspective* (Oxford: Oxford University Press, 1999), p. 42.
41 Hassan, "The Issue of Woman-man," p. 66.
42 Barlas, *Believing Women in Islam*, p. 1.
43 Ibid., p. 80.
44 Ibid., p. 19.
45 Ibid., p. xi.
46 Ibid., p. xi.
47 This is evident in the majority of medieval *tafsīrs* (interpretation, commentary), such as Ibn Kathir and al-Tabari. See: al-Ṭabarī, *Tafsīr al-Ṭabari: Jāmi` al-Bayān 'an Ta'wīl Āy al-Qur'ān*, ed. Ṣalāḥ 'Abd al Fattāh al-Khālidī (Damascus: Dār al-Qalam; Beirut: Dār al-Shāmiyya, 1998) and Ibn Kathir, *Tafsīr Ibn Kathir* (Riyadh: Dar al-Islam, 1998).
48 Wadud, *Qur'ān and Woman*, p. 32.
49 Bhutto, *Reconciliation*, p. 19.
50 Barlas, *Believing Women in Islam*, p. 21.
51 For further autobiographies of Muslim females, see: T. Durrani, 1995) *My Feudal Lord* (Reading, UK: Corgi Publishers, 1995); S. F. Farmaian, *Daughter of Persia* (Reading, UK: Corgi Publishers, 1993); G. Karmi, *In Search of Fatima—A Palestinian Story* (London: Verso Books, 2002); S. Ali-Karamali, *The Muslim Next Door—The Qur'ān, the Media and that Veil Thing* (Ashland, Oregan: White Cloud Press, 2008), L. Ahmed, *A Border Passage: From Cairo to America—A Woman's Journey* (New York, NY: Penguin, 2012).
52 Barlas, *Believing Women in Islam*, p. 17.
53 Ibid., p. 79.

54 Ibid., p. 25.
55 Ibid., p. 35.
56 Ibid., p. 25.
57 Ibid., p. 169.
58 Wadud, *Inside the Gender Jihad*, p. 6.
59 Barlas, *Believing Women in Islam*, p. 10.
60 Ibid., p. 22.
61 Ibid., p. 148
62 Hassan, "The Issue of Woman-man," p. 70.
63 Wadud, *Inside the Gender Jihad*, p. 155.
64 Barlas, *Believing Women in Islam*, p. 132.
65 Ibid., p. 98.
66 Wadud, *Qur'ān and Woman*, p. 15.
67 Ibid., pp. 20–1.
68 "The Qur'ān first establishes that all created things are paired, then reinforces this mutual necessity by depicting theoretical pairs in the rest of creation." Ibid., p. 21.
69 Ibid., p. 22.
70 Wadud, *Qur'ān and Woman*, p. 29.
71 Qur'ān 2:223.
72 R. Hassan, "An Islamic perspective," ed. J. Becher, *Women, Religion and Sexuality* (Geneva: WCC Publications, 1990), p. 119.
73 Hassan, "An Islamic perspective," p. 75.
74 Wadud, *Inside the Gender Jihad*, p. 41.
75 Qur'ān 4:34.
76 Hassan, "An Islamic Perspective," p. 111.
77 Barlas, *Believing Women in Islam*, p. 187.
78 Hassan, "An Islamic Perspective," p. 112.
79 G. Karmi, "Women, Islam and Patriarchalism," ed. M. Yamani, *Feminism and Islam: Legal and Literary Perspectives* (Lebanon: Ithaca Press, 1996), p. 74.
80 Hassan, "An Islamic Perspective," p. 111.
81 R. El-Nimr, "Women in Islamic Law," ed. M. Yamani, *Feminism and Islam: Legal and Literary Perspectives* (Lebanon: Ithaca Press, 1996), p. 97.
82 Wadud, *Inside the Gender Jihad*, p. 200.
83 Barlas, *Believing Women in Islam*, p. 187.
84 Hassan, "An Islamic Perspective," p. 112.
85 Barlas, *Believing Women in Islam*, p. 85.
86 A. Barlas, *Believing Women in Islam*, p. 125.
87 A. Barlas, *Believing Women in Islam*, p. 153.
88 Mernissi, *Beyond the Veil*, p. 48.
89 Ibid., p. 59.

90 Wadud, *Inside the Gender Jihad*, p. 126.
91 Barlas, *Believing Women in Islam*, p. 178.
92 Ibid., p. 179.
93 Wadud, *Inside the Gender Jihad*, p. 150.
94 Ibid., p. 144.
95 Wadud, *Qur'ān and Woman*, p. 73.
96 El Saadawi, *The Hidden Face of Eve*, p. 76.
97 Further information on veil see: F. El Guindi, *Veil—Modesty, Privacy and Resistance* (Oxford: Berg Publishers, 1999) and K. Ask and M. Tjomsland, *Women and Islamization* (Oxford: Berg Publishers, 1998).
98 Qur'ān 24:30–31.
99 Barlas, *Believing Women in Islam*, p. 221.
100 Ibid., p. 54.
101 Hassan, "An Islamic Perspective," p. 121.
102 Mernissi, *Beyond the Veil*, p. 45.
103 Barlas, *Believing Women in Islam*, p. 158.
104 Bhutto, *Reconciliation*, p. 43.
105 Wadud, *Inside the Gender Jihad*, p. 219.
106 Ibid., p. 220.
107 Barlas, *Believing Women in Islam*, p. 181.
108 Ibid., p. 98.
109 For further information on "honor killings" and Muslim women see, S. Hossain and L. Welchman (eds), *Honor: Crimes, Paradigms, and Violence Against Women* (London: Zed Books, 2005) and M. Mai, *In the Name of Honor* (London: Virago Press Limited, 2007).
110 Wadud, *Inside the Gender Jihad*, p. 23.
111 Barlas, *Believing Women in Islam*, p. 143.
112 Wadud, *Inside the Gender Jihad*, p. 28.
113 Barlas, *Believing Women in Islam*, p. 13.
114 Wadud, *Inside the Gender Jihad*, p. 31.
115 See, M. Elkaisy-Friemuth, *God and Humans in Islamic Thought—'Abd al-Jabbar, Ibn Sina and al-Ghazali* (Oxford: Routledge, 2006), pp. 1–40.
116 Barlas, *Believing Women in Islam*, p. 14.
117 Wadud, *Inside the Gender Jihad*, p. 81.
118 Barlas, *Believing Women in Islam*, p. 15.
119 Hassan, "An Islamic Perspective," p. 97.
120 Ibid., pp. 114–5.
121 Ibid., p. 115.
122 Ibid.
123 Barlas, *Believing Women in Islam*, p. 122.

124 Mernissi, *Beyond the Veil*, p. 57.
125 Barlas, *Believing Women in Islam*, p. 169.
126 Wadud, *Inside the Gender Jihad*, p. 183.
127 Wadud, *Inside the Gender Jihad*, p. 256.
128 Nomani, *Standing Alone*, p. 108.
129 "For example, the patriarchal formulations of Islamic law through out history hold condescending utilitarian perspectives on women. Not only is the female looked down upon, she is treated as an object in Sharī`a discussions, not as a discussant. The woman is a recipient of its decisions, not a decision maker. Decisions made concerning her role in the family and society were made from the perspective of those who did not and could not share her experience and therefore judged on the basis of second hand perceptions." Wadud, *Inside the Gender Jihad*, p. 96.
130 Mernissi, *Beyond the Veil*, p. 18.
131 M. Siddiqui, "Law and the Desire for Social Control: An Insight into the Hanafi Concept of *Kafa'a* with Reference to the Fatāwā 'Ālamgīrī (1664–1672)'" ed. M. Yamani, *Feminism and Islam: Legal and Literary Perspectives* (Lebanon: Ithaca Press, 1996), p. 49.
132 Barlas, *Believing Women in Islam*, p. 74. For further information on family law and women, see: A. A. An-Na`im, *Toward an Islamic Reformation—Civil Liberties, Human Rights and International Law* (Syracuse: Syracuse University Press, 1996), A. A. An-Na`im, *Islamic Family Law in a Changing World: A Global Resource Book* (London: Zed Books, 2002) and L. Welchman, *Women and Muslim Family Laws in Arab States: A Comparative Overview of Textual Development and Advocacy (ISIM Series on Contemporary Muslim Societies)* (Amsterdam: Amsterdam University Press, 2007).

Chapter 3

1 Qur'ān 35:26–28.
2 Al-Kisā`i—*Tales of the Prophets*, Ibn Kathir—*Stories of the Prophets*, Ibn Saad—*Tabaqat* to name a few. For a more in depth discussion on the philosophy of prophecy see: F. Rahman, *Prophecy in Islam* (London: George Allen and Unwin Ltd. Publishers, 1958).
3 F. Rahman, *Major Themes in the Qur'ān* (Chicago, IL: Bibliotheca Islamica, 1980), p. 80. U. Rubin, "Prophet," ed. J. McAuliffe, *Encyclopedia of the Qur'ān*, vol. 4 (Leiden: Brill, 2004), p. 289.
4 F. Denny, "Meaning of Ummah in the Qur'ān," ed. C, Turner, *The Koran—Critical Concepts in Islamic Studies*, vol. 2 (Oxford: Routledge, 2006), p. 35.

5 The term *rasul* occurs 236 times in singular in 49 chapters and 95 times in plural in 36 chapters. There are a total of 331 occurrences in total in the Qur'ān. W. A. Bijlefeld, "A prophet and More Than a Prophet? Some Observations on the Qur'ānic Use of Terms 'prophet' and 'apostle,'" ed. C. Turner, *The Koran—Critical Concepts in Islamic Studies*, vol. 2 (Oxford : Routledge, 2006), p. 301.

6 B. Stowasser, *Women in the Qur'ān, Traditions, and Interpretation* (United Kingdom: Oxford University Press, 1994), p. 15.

7 T. J. O' Shaughnessy, "The Qur'ānic View of Youth and Old Age," ed. C. Turner, *The Koran—Critical Concepts in Islamic Studies* (Oxford : Routledge, 2006), p. 264.

8 "Yea, indeed, We have created you, and then formed you" (Qur'ān 7:12).

9 Ibn Ḥazm, Abū Muḥammad "ʿAlī ibn Aḥmad ibn Saʿīd," ed. M. I. Nasr and A. A. Umayra, *Kitāb al-Fasl fi al-milal wal-ahwa' wal-nihal*, vol. 5 (Jeddah: Uzak Publications, 1982), pp. 119–20.

10 M. Khaleel, "Sex, Sexuality and the Family," ed. A. Rippin, *The Blackwell Companion to the Qur'ān* (Oxford: Blackwell Publishing, 2006), p. 300.

11 Wheeler cited Suyuti as saying that the name Adam comes from the Arabic "*adim al'ard*" meaning from the "surface of the earth." Suyuti cited in B. M. Wheeler, *Prophets in the Qur'ān* (London: Continuum, 2002), p. 17.

12 C. Schock, "Adam and Eve," ed. J. McAuliffe, *Encyclopedia of the Qur'ān*, vol. 1 (Leiden: Brill, 2003), p. 22.

13 Ibn Kathir, *Stories of the Prophets*, trans. R. A. Azami (Jeddah: Darussalam Publishers 1st Edition), p. 30.

14 Qur'ān 3:59 compares the likeness of Adam with Jesus.

15 Ibn Masud cited in Wheeler, *Prophets*, p. 17.

16 According to the exegete and historian, al-Tabari, God wanted to expose Iblīs' arrogance. See al-Tabari cited in Wheeler, *Prophets*, p. 18.

17 Ibn Kathir, *Stories*, p. 16.

18 "Whoever pays heed unto the apostle pays heed unto God thereby; and as for those who turn away—we have not sent thee to be their keeper" (Qur'ān 4:80).

19 al-Kisā`i, Muḥammad Ibn Abdullah, *Tales of the Prophets*, trans. W. M. Thackston Jr (Chicago: Kazi Publications, 1997), pp. 13–14.

20 Ibid., p. 12.

21 al-Tabari cited in Wheeler, *Prophets*, p. 17.

22 Ibid., p. 16.

23 "Ibn Abbas said: Adam spoke seven hundred languages, the best of which was Arabic." in al-Kisā`i, *Tales*, p. 28. See also Qur'ān 2:31.

24 al-Tabari cited in Wheeler, *Prophets*, p. 15. There are further illustrations of this interpretation in the works of Ibn Abbas, Rabi'a b. Anas, and Tabari in Wheeler's translation.

25 Ibn Kathir, *Stories*, p. 31.

26 Ibid., p. 31.

27 "Hasan Basri commented that Iblīs was the first to draw analogous conclusions between himself, made from fire, and Adam, made from clay (see Qur'ān 17:61–65). His origin is further obscured by the saying of the Prophet Muḥammad in which he says, 'The angels are created from light, and jinn are created out of searing fire. And Adam is created from what it had been described to you.'"—Ibn Kathir, *Stories*, pp. 19–20.

28 Ibn Kathir stated that the distinction would not stand in any case, as "soil is more beneficial than fire as soil has qualities serenity, gentleness, perseverance, and growth. While in fire there are qualities of frivolity, impatience, haste and burning." Ibn Kathir, *Stories*, p. 19.

29 Stowasser, *Women in the Qur'ān*, p. 26.

30 J. Penrice, *A Dictionary and Glossary of the Koran—with Copious Grammatical References and Explanations of the Text* (Karachi: Darul-Ishaat, 1998), p. 63.

31 Ibid., p. 63.

32 See A. R. Doi, *Sharī'ah: The Islamic Law* (London: Ta Ha Publishers, 1984), pp. 114–27, A. I. N. al-Misri, *Reliance of the Traveler: A Classical Manual of Islamic Sacred Law*, trans. N. H. M. Keller (Evanston: Sunna Books, 1994), pp. 506–53, and A. Mālik bin *Kitāb al-Muwaṭṭa'*, trans. A. A. at-Tarjumana and Y. Johnson (Norwich: Diwan Press, 1982).

33 Doi, *Sharī'ah*, p. 118.

34 Ibid., p. 119.

35 Stowasser, *Women in the Qur'ān*, p. 29.

36 al-Kisā'i, *Tales*, p. 32.

37 Munabbih, Wahb Ibn, cited in Wheeler, *Prophets*, p. 23.

38 Ibn Kathir, *Stories*, p. 27.

39 Ibn Abbas, Ibn Masud, and Wahb Bin Munabbih state that Iblīs persuaded a snake-like creature, which looked like a camel with four feet, to let him enter its mouth and take him to Adam in paradise. Iblīs was unable to convince any other creature to undertake him and God was fully aware of the situation. The snake is said to have been covered and walked on four legs but God's wrath has made the snake naked and crawl on its stomach. The Muslim tradition of killing snakes is based upon the covenant the snake made with Iblīs. Ibn Abbas, Ibn Masud, and others cited in Wheeler, *Prophets*, p. 24.

40 Ubayy bin Ka'b cited in Wheeler, *Prophets*, p. 25.

41 According to Ibn Abbas, Ibn Masud, Wahb Bin Munabbih their clothes were made of light, covering their genitals. Ibn Abbas, Ibn Masud and others cited in Wheeler, *Prophets*, pp. 24–5.

42 Ibid.

43 Tabari, Ibn Abbas, Hasan al-Basri, Suddi, Abu al-Aliyah all stated that when Adam was sent to earth he was dropped in India. Ibn Abbas states that Eve was cast down in Jeddah. Ibn Abbas, Ibn Masud and others cited in Wheeler, *Prophets*, pp. 25–7.

44 Ibid., p. 29.
45 Ibn Kathir, *Stories*, p. 38.
46 Ibid., p. 46.
47 Ibid., p. 42.
48 Ibid., p. 231.
49 S. Goldman, "Joseph," ed. J. McAuliffe, *Encyclopedia of the Qur'ān*, vol. 1 (Leiden: Brill, 2003), p. 227.
50 al-Kisā'i, *Tales*, p. 32.
51 Ibn Kathir, *Stories*, p. 230.
52 Ibn Kathir said that al-Aziz's wife was called Ra'el Ibn al-Walid. Tha'labi said her name was Fakka Ibn Yunis. It is widely accepted amongst the classical exegetes that Zulaykha was her nickname. Ibn Kathir and Tha'labi cited in Wheeler, *Prophets*, p. 132.
53 Ibn Kathir stated that Zulaykha's invitation was an "act of seduction." She was said to dress in her most elegant clothes and was beautiful. Zulaykha's attraction was only "because of his handsome youth and of his awesome appearance." Ibn Kathir, *Stories*, p. 238. Stowasser cited al-Tabari's comments on what happened between the two of them, "Joseph unfastened the belt of his trousers and sat before her 'as the circumciser sits'; she lay down for him and he sat between her legs; she lay down on her back and he sat between her legs and loosened his garment (or her garment); he dropped his pants to his buttocks; he sat with her as a man sits with his wife, etc." Stowasser, *Women in the Qur'ān*, p. 52.
54 Ibn Kathir commented, "his Lord saved him from committing indecency and protected him from women's evil plot" and further states "what is important for our belief is that God saved him from that indecent act and protected him from the evil of that woman." Ibn Kathir, *Stories*, p. 239. In contrast Tabari places great emphasis in his commentary on Zulaykha's "true love" for Joseph—Stowasser, *Women in the Qur'ān*, p. 53.
55 al-Kisā'i, *Tales*, pp. 174–5.
56 Ibn Kathir states, "in a report about the Prophet's night journey the prophet saying, 'I passed by Joseph and he had been given half of the beauty.' Suhayli and other scholars say that the meaning of this is that Joseph has half the beauty of Adam because God created Adam with his own hands, blew his breath into him, and he was the ultimate of human beauty. Because of this, the inhabitants of paradise enter paradise with the stature of Adam and beauty of Joseph. Joseph had the half that was the beauty of Adam. Between them there is none more beautiful, and likewise there are no two after Eve and Sarah, the wife of Abraham who resembled Eve." Ibn Kathir, *Stories*, p. 242.
57 Ibn Kathir, *Stories*, p. 239.
58 Stowasser, *Women in the Qur'ān*, p. 52.

59 Ibid., p. 53.

60 Ibid., p. 52.

61 Qur'ān 12:30.

62 K. Ali, *Sexual Ethics and Islam—Feminist Reflections on Qur'ān, Hadith and Jurisprudence* (Oxford: Oneworld Publications, 2006), p. 147. Ali recalls the Ṣaḥīḥ Bukhārī ḥādīth at the beginning of her chapter on the prophet Muḥammad, "Aisha narrated that the prophet married her when she was a girl of six and he consummated the marriage when she was a girl of nine." Bukhārī, *Ṣaḥīḥ al-Bukhārī*, trans. M. M. Khan, vol. VII, Ḥādīth Number 64 (Lahore: Kazi Publications, 1986), p. 50.

63 M. Lings, *Muḥammad—His Life Based on the Earliest Sources* (London: Islamic Texts Society, 1983), p. 21. (Martin Lings biography of the prophet Muḥammad is based on the writings of Ibn Ishaq—*Sirat Rasul Allah*, Ibn Sa'ad—*Kitāb al-Tabaqat al-Kabir*, Waqidi—*Kitāb al-Maghazi*, Azraqi—*Akhbar Makkah*, Tabari—*Ta'rikh ar-Rasul wa'l-Muluk and Suhayli—ar-Rawd al-unuf.*)

64 Lings, *Muḥammad*, p. 21.

65 Ibid., p. 22.

66 Ibid., p. 26.

67 S. al-Mubarakpuri, *Ar-Raheeq al-Makhtum—Biography of the Noble Prophet* (Riyadh: Maktaba Dar-us-Salam, 1996), p. 60.

68 The main story is narrated by Ibn al-Kalbi (d. 204/820) and appears in Ibn Sa'd's Tabaqat al-Kubra (Beirut: Dār Ṣadir edition, 8:151 ff) and in later sources as well, but there are other versions with slight differences in wording and detail. The story is narrated by Ibn al-Kalbi (d. 204/820), who told it directly to Ibn Sa'd, who put it in his Tabaqat al-kubra in Umm Hani's biography. The story tells of the Prophet telling how he had proposed to her before the revelation, but that she had rejected him for Hubayra bin Wahb, who became her husband. After the conquest of Mecca, she became Muslim but her husband did not (he fled to Najran), and the Prophet proposed again. She said, "Indeed I loved you in the Jahiliyya, so what about in Islam? But I am a women with young children."

69 M. Lings, *Muḥammad*, p. 33.

70 al-Mubarakpuri, *Ar-Raheeq al-Makhtum*, p. 62.

71 Muslim, *Ṣaḥīḥ Muslim*, trans. A. H. Siddiqi, vol. II, Ḥādīth Number 3458 (Lahore: Ashraf Publishers, 1993), p. 749.

72 Bukhārī, *Ṣaḥīḥ al-Bukhārī*, trans. M. M. Khan, vol. VII, Ḥādīth Number 4 (Lahore: Kazi Publications, 1986), p. 4. Bukhārī, *Ṣaḥīḥ al-Bukhārī*, trans. M. M. Khan, vol. VII, Ḥādīth Number 2, 3, 4 (Lahore: Kazi Publications, 1986), p. 3.

73 Al-Mubarakpuri, *Ar-Raheeq Al-Maktum*, p. 126.

74 W. M. Watt, *Muḥammad—Prophet and Statesman* (London: Oxford University Press, 1961), p. 131.

75 For further information on the wives of the Prophet Muḥammad see, C. Bennet, *In Search of Muḥammad* (London: Cassell Publications, 1998), pp. 249–52.

76 Watt, *Muḥammad*, p. 132.

77 A more detailed analysis of this verse will be covered in subsequent chapters of this thesis.

78 Al-Mubarakpuri, *Ar-Raheeq Al-Maktum*, p. 44.

79 F. Rahman, *Major Themes of the Qur'ān* (Chicago, IL: Bibliotheca Islamica, 1980), p. 48.

80 Ibid., p. 48.

81 A. S. Roald, *Women in Islam—The Western Experience* (London: Routledge, 2001), p. 202, and also mentioned by H. Motzki, "Marriage," ed. J. McAuliffe, *Encyclopedia of the Qur'ān*, vol. 3 (Leiden: Brill, 2003), p. 278.

82 Bukhārī, *Ṣaḥīḥ al-Bukhārī*, p. 5.

83 "Sabra Juhanni reported: Muḥammad permitted temporary marriage for us. So I and another person went out and saw a woman of Bana 'Amir, who was like a young long-necked she-camel. We presented ourselves to her (for contracting temporary marriage), whereupon she said: What dower would you give me? I said: My cloak. And my companion also said: My cloak. And the cloak of-my companion was superior to my cloak, but I was younger than he. So when she looked at the cloak of my companion she liked it, and when she cast a glance at me I looked more attractive to her. She then said: Well, you and your cloak are sufficient for me. I remained with her for three nights, and then Muḥammad said: He who has any such woman with whom he had contracted temporary marriage, he should let her off." Muslim, *Ṣaḥīḥ Muslim*, trans. A. H. Siddiqi, vol. II, Ḥādīth Number 3252 (Lahore: Ashraf Publishers, 1993), p. 706.

84 T. P. Hughes, *A Dictionary of Islam* (Calcutta: Rupa & Co., 1988), p. 400.

85 Muslim, *Ṣaḥīḥ Muslim*, trans. A. H. Siddiqi, vol. II, Ḥādīth Number 3371 (Lahore: Ashraf Publishers, 1993), pp. 732–3.

86 See R. Bell, *The Origins of Islam in its Christian Environment* (London: Macmillan & Co. Ltd, 1926) and M. Ata'ur Rahim and A. Thomson, *Jesus—Prophet of Islam* (London: Ta Ha Publishers, 1996).

87 N. Robinson, "Jesus,"" ed. J. McAuliffe, *Encyclopaedia of the Qur'ān*, vol. 2 (Leiden: Brill, 2003), p. 22.

88 T. Khalidi, *The Muslim Jesus* (Cambridge, MA: Harvard University Press, 2003), p. 14.

89 H. Goddard, *Christians and Muslims—from Double Standards to Mutual Understanding* (Cornwal, UK: Curzon Press, 1995), p. 19.

90 K. Cragg, *Jesus and the Muslim—an Exploration* (Oxford, UK: Oneworld Publications, 1999), p. 25.

91 Khalidi, *The Muslim*, p. 14.

92 L. Ridgeon, *Crescents on the Cross* (Glasgow: Trinity St. Mungo Press, 1999), p. 46.

93 N. Robinson, *Christ in Islam and Christianity* (New York, NY: State University of New York, 1991), p. 37.

94 Jesus' prayer from Abū Ḥamīd al-Ghazālī's Iḥyā' `Ulūm al-Dīn (vol. 2), cited in J. Nurbakhsh, *Jesus in the Eyes of Ṣūfīs*, trans. T. Graham, L. Lewisohn, and H. Mashkuri (London: Khaniqahi-Nimatullahi Publications, 1992), p. 71.

95 Ridgeon, *Crescents*, p. 46.

96 Khalidi, *The Muslim*, p. 10.

Chapter 4

1 R. Russel, "Getting to Know Ghālib," ed. R. Russell, *The Oxford India Ghālib: Life, Letters and Ghazals* (India: Oxford University Press, 2005), p. 319.

2 A. Schimmel, "Foreword," ed. D. Rahbar, *Urdu Letters of Mirzā Asadu'llah Khān Ghālib* (New York, NY: State University of New York), p. x.

3 Those who observe a strict dress code (for women), grown their beards, pray five times a day, and refrain from alcohol are just some examples of the ritualistic Islamic practices which this alludes to.

4 Further information on King Zafar, see: W. Dalrymple, *The Fall of a Dynasty, Delhi, 1857—The Last Mughal* (London: Bloomsbury Publications, 2007).

5 P. K. Varma, *Ghālib: The Man and Times* (India: Penguin, 1989), p. 41.

6 P. Spear, "Ghālib's Delhi," ed. R. Russell, *The Oxford India Ghālib: Life, Letters and Ghazals* (India: Oxford University Press, 2005), p. 277.

7 Ibid., p. 277.

8 Ibid., p. 279.

9 Spear, "Ghālib's Delhi," pp. 293–4.

10 Ibid.

11 R. Russel and K. Islam, "Ghālib: Life and Letters," ed. R. Russell, *The Oxford India Ghālib: Life, Letters and Ghazals* (India: Oxford University Press, 2005), p. 105.

12 M. A. H. Hali, *Yādgār-i-Ghālib*, trans. K. H. Qadiri (Delhi: Idarah-I Adabiyāt, 1990), p. 111.

13 In this case Varma is alluding to the physical separation of the sexes, as opposed to the head veil that will be discussed at length later in this thesis.

14 Varma, *Ghālib*, p. 112.

15 Ibid., p. 48.

16 Ibid., p. 47.

17 Ibid., pp. 48–9.

18 N. Prigarina, *Mirzā Ghālib: A Creative Biography*, trans. M. O. Faruqi (Karachi: Oxford University Press, 2004), pp. 96–9.

19 Varma, *Ghālib*, p. 113.
20 A virgin female is understood as a reward to pious men in heaven in some Islamic traditions.
21 Prigarina, *Mirzā Ghālib*, p. 261.
22 Ghālib's pension was said to come from here.
23 Spear, "Ghālib's Delhi," p. 164.
24 Hali, *Yādgār-i-Ghālib*, p. 111.
25 Ibid.
26 Ibid.
27 Ibid., p. 113.
28 K. Islam and R. Russell, *Three Mughal Poets—Mir, Sauda, Mir Hasan* (Delhi: Oxford University Press, 2006), pp. 98–9.
29 Islam, "Ghālib," pp. 43–4.
30 Prigarina identified one occasion when lenders took Ghālib to court in order to receive their dues from him. On one such occasion the Mufti (Azurda) was known to be Ghālib's friend and when he asked Ghālib why he was being dragged to court for debt repayment. Ghālib responded, "we used to drink by borrowing, even though we knew that drinking, when we were starving, would bring us problems one day." The Mufti burst out laughing at this and then proceeded to pay the amount on behalf of Ghālib. (*Mirzā Ghālib*, p. 213).
31 Islam, "Ghālib," p. 3.
32 Ibid., p. 3.
33 See Qur'ān 8: 1–75, 'al-`Anfāl—The Spoils of War.
34 See J. Renard, *Islam and the Heroic Image* (Macon, GA: Mercer University Press, 1999).
35 K. C. Kanda, *Mirzā Ghālib: Selected Lyrics and Letters* (New Delhi: New Dawn Press, 2007), p. 281.
36 Hali, *Yādgār-i-Ghālib*, p. 14.
37 Ibid., p. xxiii.
38 Ibid., p. 14.
39 Ibid., p. 16.
40 Schmidt stated, "In the generation between 1827 and 1857, Delhi College contributed to the development of Urdu prose through its teaching, sponsorship of translations, and the publication of its students, and encouraged the development of new literary forms such as the novel, short story, essay and literary criticism." R. L. Schmidt, "Urdu," ed. G. Cardona and D. Jain, *The Indo-Aryan Languages* (London: Routledge, 2003), p. 289.
41 Ibid., p. 38.
42 Kanda, *Mirzā Ghālib*, p. 310.
43 Schimmel, "Foreword," p. xxxii.

44 Varma, *Ghālib*, p. 133.
45 Prigarina, *Mirzā Ghālib*, p. 119.
46 Varma, *Ghālib*, p. 138.
47 D. Rahbar, *Urdu Letters of Mirzā Asadu'llah Khān Ghālib* (New York, NY: State University of New York, 1987), p. xviii.
48 Schimmel, "Foreword," p. xi.
49 Hali, *Yādgār-i-Ghālib*, p. 99.
50 Prigarina, *Mirzā Ghālib*, p. 239.
51 Ibid., pp. 273–4.
52 Ibid., pp. 240–1.
53 Ibid., p. 280.
54 Hali, *Yādgār-i-Ghālib*, pp. 64–5
55 M. A. H. Hali, *Hali's Musaddas—The Flow and Ebb of Islam,* trans. C. ShackleJ. Majeed (Delhi: Oxford University Press, 1997), p. 2.
56 Further information on the East India Company see: J. Keay, *The Honorable Company: History of the English East India Company* (London: HarperCollins Publishers, 1991).
57 A. Aḥmed, *Islamic Modernism in India and Pakistan* (London: Oxford University Press, 1967), p. 31.
58 Ibid., p. 37.
59 U. Sanya, *Ahmad Riza Khan Barelwi—in the Path of the Prophet* (Oxford: Oneworld Publishers, 2005), pp. 44–5.
60 S. Irfani, "The Progressive Islamic Movement," ed. M. A. Khan, *The Pakistan Experience—State and Religion* (Lahore: Vanguard Books, 1985), p. 37.
61 Ibid., p. 106.
62 Ibid., p. 35.
63 Islam, "Ghālib," p. 93.
64 Ibid., p. 174.
65 Ibid., p. 174.
66 Ibid., p. 173.
67 D. W. Brown, *Rethinking Tradition in Modern Islamic Thought* (Cambridge: Cambridge University Press, 1996), p. 37.
68 Islam, "Ghālib," p. 70.
69 Ibid.
70 Ghālib writes about his Hindu friend, Mahesh Das, "But these days in Delhi foreign wine is very dear and my pockets are empty. What would I have done had not my stalwart God-fearing . . . friend, the generous and bounteous Mahesh Das sent me wine made from sugar cane (possibly rum), matching French in colour and excelling it in fragrance . . . In short he is a good man, who does good to his fellow men and leads a good life amidst music and wine." and Islam, "Ghālib," p. 136.

71 Russel, "Getting to Know Ghālib," p. 302.
72 Ibid., p. 70.
73 It should be noted that the culture of Mughal courtesans does draw parallels within other regions such as the Geishas in Japan, but the Geishas do not have sex with their clients in the way that the courtesans of Mughal India did.
74 Islam, "Ghālib," p. 296.
75 It is important to note that Pakeezah is a fictional movie and Umrao Jaan is based on a true story.
76 b. 1857 in Lucknow, India.
77 M. M. H. Ruswa, *Umrao Jan Ada*, trans. K. Singh and M. A. Husaini (Delhi: Disha Books, 1982) pp. v–vi.
78 literary meaning: virgin, pure.
79 http://film.guardian.co.uk/Century_Of_Films/Story/0,,71138,00.html (accessed on April 14, 2013)
80 Ibid.
81 Ibid., p. 151.
82 Prigarina, *Mirzā Ghālib*.
83 Islam, "Ghālib," p. 296.
84 Ibid., pp. 18–19.
85 Ibid., p. 296.
86 Kanda, *Mirzā Ghālib*, p. 197.
87 Prigarina, *Mirzā Ghālib*, p. 103.
88 Islam, "Ghālib," p. 18.
89 Ibid., p. 18.
90 Ibid.
91 Ibid., p. 49. Indeed Ghālib's poetry also reflected this, Azad, a contemporary of Ghālib, stated in a poem, "what is the point of writing verse which only you can understand? A poet feels the thrill of joy when others too can understand; We understand the verse of Mir, we understand what Mirzā wrote; But Ghālib's verse!—Save he and God, we know not who can understand!" Islam, "Ghālib," p. 47.
92 Hali, *Yādgār-i-Ghālib*, p. 17.
93 Most likely a courtesan.
94 Islam, "Ghālib," p. 158.
95 Ibid., p. 5.
96 Ibid., p. 7.
97 For further reading on Ghālib's verses on "Love," see: M. A. K. Ghālib, *Love Sonnets of Ghālib*, trans. S. K. Niazi (New Delhi: Rupa & Co., 2006); M. A. K. Ghālib, *Ghazals of Ghālib—Versions from the Urdu*, ed. A. Aḥmad (New Delhi: Oxford University Press, 2007); and M. A. K. Ghālib, *Divan-e-Ghālib*, trans. K. R. S. Rana (New Delhi: Anmol Publications, 2005).

98 Russel, "Getting to Know Ghālib," p. 305.
99 K. C. Abraham and A. K. Abraham, "Homosexuality: Some Reflections From India," *The Ecumenical Review*, 50(1) (January 1998), p. 23.
100 R. Vanita, "Preface," ed. R. Vanita and S. Kidwai, *Same-Sex Love in India: Readings from Literature and History* (New York, NY: Palgrave Publishing, 2001), p. xx.
101 Ibid., p. xxi.
102 S. Kidwai, "Introduction: Medieval Materials in the Perso-Urdu Tradition," ed. R. Vanita and S. Kidwai, *Same-Sex Love in India: Readings from Literature and History*, (New York, NY: Palgrave Publishing, 2001), p. 120.
103 Ibid., p. 124.
104 Ibid.
105 Islam, "Ghālib," p. 34.
106 Ibid.
107 Ibid., p. 295.
108 Ibid., p. 189.
109 Ibid., p. 295.
110 Gulzar, *Mirzā Ghālib—A Biographical Scenario* (Delhi: Rupa & Co Publishers, 2006), p. 45.
111 S. Kidwai, "Mir Taqi 'Mir': Autobiography (Persian) and Poems (Urdu)," ed. R. Vanita and S. Kidwai, *Same-Sex Love in India: Readings from Literature and History* (New York, NY: Palgrave Publishing, 2001), p. 189.
112 C. M. Naim, *Zikr-I Mir: The Autobiography of the Eighteenth Century Mughal Poet: Mir Muḥammad Taqi Mir, Translated, Annotated and with an Introduction* (New Delhi: Oxford University Press, 1999), p. 201.
113 Ibid., p. 199.
114 Ibid., p. 198.
115 Ibid., p. 203.
116 Russel, "Getting to Know Ghālib," p. 302.
117 Islam, "Ghālib," p. 103.
118 Ibid., p. 221.
119 Hali, *Yādgār-i-Ghālib*, p. 91.
120 A. Bausani, "Ghālib's Persian Poetry," ed. R. Russell, *The Oxford India Ghālib: Life, Letters and Ghazals* (India: Oxford University Press, 2005), p. 462.
121 Ibid.
122 Russell interpreted "tomorrow" as the life after death, "you" as God, "the angel" as Iblīs and "we" as humankind, the descendant of Adam. R. Russel, "Ghālib's Urdu Verse," ed. R. Russell, *The Oxford India Ghālib: Life, Letters and Ghazals* (India: Oxford University Press, 2005), pp. 358–9.
123 Islam, "Ghālib," p. 45.
124 Hali, *Yādgār-i-Ghālib*, p. 10.

125 Islam, "Ghālib," pp. 45–6.
126 Russel, "Ghālib's Urdu," p. 347.
127 R. Russell, "Ghālib–A Self Portrait," ed. R. Russell, *The Oxford India Ghālib: Life, Letters and Ghazals* (India: Oxford University Press, 2005), p. 20.
128 Ibid.
129 Islam, "Ghālib," p. 34.
130 Ibid., p. 36.
131 Ibid., p. 44.
132 Ibid., p. 45.
133 Ibid., p. 46.
134 Russel, "Getting to Know Ghālib," p. 304.
135 Ibid., p. 304.
136 Islam, "Ghālib," p. 260.
137 Russel, "Getting to Know Ghālib," p. 307.

Chapter 5

1 F. Iraqi, *Divine Flashes*, trans. W. C. Chittick and P. Wilson (New York, NY: Paulist Press, 1982), p. 85.
2 b. 1207–d. 1273.
3 R. A. Nicholson, *The Mystics of Islam* (London: Routledge and Kegan Paul Ltd., 1963), p. 107.
4 For further insight into Rumi's life see: A. R. Arasteh, *Rumi the Persian—The Ṣūfī* (London: Routledge and Kegan Paul Ltd., 1974).
5 For further information on the rituals that Ṣūfīs practice, such as *dhikr* (litany) and *sama'* (mystical concert) see: I. R. Netton, *Ṣūfī Ritual—The Parallel Universe* (Surrey, UK: Curzon Press, 2000).
6 Nicholson, *The Mystics*, p. 29.
7 Ibid., p. 28.
8 A. Hujwiri, *Kashf al-Mahjub of al-Hujwiri*, trans. R. A. Nicholson (London: Luzac and Co.), p. 45.
9 b. 1909–d. 2005.
10 b. 1336–d. 1406.
11 M. Lings, *What is Ṣūfīsm?* (Surrey: George Allen and Unwin Ltd., 1975), p. 45.
12 R. A. Nicholson, *The Mystics of Islam* (London: Routledge and Kegan Paul Ltd., 1963), p. 80. For further reading on al-Hallaj's work see his most renowned work on understanding and knowing God: al-Hallaj, *Kitab al-Tawasin* (Paris: Geuthner, 1913).
13 M. Lings, *The Book of Certainty—The Ṣūfī Doctrine of Faith, Vision and Gnosis* (Cambridge: Islamic Texts Society, 1996), pp. 17–18.

14 Nicholson, *The Mystics*, p. 78.

15 M. Malamud, "Gender and Spiritual Self-Fashioning: The Master-Disciple Relationship in Classical Ṣūfism," *Journal of the American Academy of Religion*, 64(1) (Spring 1996), p. 94.

16 Ibid., p. 103.

17 J. J. Elias, "Female and the Feminine in Islamic Mysticism," *The Muslim World*, 78,(3–4) (October 1998), p. 210.

18 A. Schimmel, "Eros – Heavenly and Not So Heavenly – In Ṣūfī Literature and Life," *Ṣūfī*, 29 (Spring 1996), p. 35.

19 C. A. Helminski, *Women of Ṣūfism—A Hidden Treasure, Writings and Stories of Mystic Poets, Scholars and Saint* (Boston: Shambhala Publications, 2003), p. 102.

20 M. Alam, *The Languages of Political Islam—India 1200–1800* (Chicago, IL: University of Chicago Press, 2004), p. 82.

21 See: D. N. Lorenzen (ed.), *Bhakti Religion in North India: Community, Identity and Political Action* (Albany, NY: State University of New York Press, 1995) and K. K. Klostermaier, *A Survey of Hinduism* (Albany, NY: State University of New York Press, 1989).

22 A. A. Engineer, "A Muslim View of Hinduism," ed. P. Schmidt-Leukel and L. Ridgeon, *Islam and Inter-Faith Relations—The Gerald Weisfeld Lectures 2006* (London: SCM Press, 2007), p. 172.

23 Further reading on Akbar the Great see: V. A. Smith, *Akbar the Great Moghal 1542–1605* (Oxford: Clarendon Press, 1917).

24 The idea of a divine faith has been rejected by some, "while many scholarly works on the Mughal period claim that Akbar invented a new religion known as Din-I Ilahi, this is an older view based on mistranslations of Abu al-Fazl's writings about Akbar. In fact, the Din-I Ilahi was a discipleship order intended to bind the highest ranking nobles in complete loyalty to the emperor, not unlike the relationship that bonded the first Safavid ruler Ismail (r.1501–24) and his Qizilbish supporters. Akbar was seen as a master (*pir*) in the Ṣūfī sense and his devotees were like students (*murids*)." C. B. Asher and C. Talbot (eds), *India before Europe* (Cambridge: Cambridge University Press, 2006), p. 130.

25 D. E. Streusand, *The Formation of the Mughal Empire* (Delhi: Oxford University Press, 1989), p. 23.

26 On February 15, 2008 a Bollywood movie directed by Ashutosh Gowariker was released under the title *Jodha Akbar*. There was much protest about the name of this movie as experts argued that the name Jodha had not been mentioned in any text from that period of Indian history. Professor Shirin Moosvi, a historian at Aligargh Muslim University in India, argued that Jodha was called Maryam Zamani and had converted to Islam. *Fact, myth blend in re-look at Akbar-Jodhabai*, December 10, 2005 http://timesofindia.indiatimes.com/articleshow/1326242.cms (date accessed: April 17, 2013).

27 For further information on Aurungzeb's life see: J. F. Richards, *The Mughal Empire* (Cambridge: Cambridge University Press, 1995) and A. Schimmel, *The Empire of the Great Mughals: History, Art and Culture* (London: Reaktion Books, 2006).

28 S. Kugle, *Ṣūfīs and Saints' Bodies—Mysticism, Corporeality, and Sacred Power in Islam* (Chapel Hill: North Carolina Press, 2007), p. 223.

29 R. A. Nicholson, *The Mystics of Islam* (London: Routledge and Kegan Paul Ltd., 1963), p. 32.

30 O'Halloran.

31 Nicholson, *The Mystics*, p. 103.

32 M. Malamud, "Gender and Spiritual Self-Fashioning: The Master-Disciple Relationship in Classical Ṣūfism," *Journal of the American Academy of Religion*, 64(1) (Spring, 1996), p. 110.

33 "The image of the child at the breast symbolises the utter dependence of the novice on the sheikh, a dependence that is analogous to his reliance on a gentle and loving God." M. Malamud, "Gender and Spiritual Self-Fashioning: The Master-Disciple Relationship in Classical Ṣūfism," *Journal of the American Academy of Religion*, 64(1) (Spring 1996), p. 97.

34 Ibid., p. 90.

35 Ibid., p. 91.

36 Ibid., p. 105.

37 S. Kugle, *Ṣūfīs and Saints' Bodies—Mysticism, Corporeality, and Sacred Power in Islam* (Chapel Hill: North Carolina Press, 2007), p. 277.

38 Ibid., p. 93.

39 Ibid., p. 94.

40 Ibid., p. 95.

41 Ibid.

42 Malamud, "Gender and Spiritual," p. 108.

43 A. Schimmel, "Eros—Heavenly and Not So Heavenly—In Ṣūfī Literature and Life" *Ṣūfī*, 29 (Spring 1996), pp. 32–3.

44 Ibid., p. 32.

45 Ibid., p. 33.

46 Hujwiri, *Kashf al-Mahjub*, p. 363.

47 Schimmel, "Eros," pp. 32–3.

48 Ibid.

49 S. Murata, *The Tao of Islam—A Sourcebook on Gender Relationships in Islamic Thought* (New York, NY: State University of New York Press, 1992), p. 190.

50 Ibid., pp. 191–2.

51 M. Ibn Arabi, *Fusus Al-Hikam*, trans. B. Rauf, vol. 4 (Oxford: Muhyiddun Ibn Arabi Society, 1991), p. 1059.

52 Malamud, "Gender and Spiritual," p. 109. For further reading on Ghazālī see: M. Ghazālī, *Ihya 'ulum al-din* (Cairo: Matba'at al-Amirat al-Sharafiyya, 1908–1909).

53 Schimmel, "Eros," p. 30.
54 Ibid., p. 34.
55 Hujwiri, *Kashf al-Mahjub*, p. 362.
56 Ibid., pp. 361–2.
57 Ibid., p. 364.
58 J. J. Elias, "Female and the Feminine in Islamic Mysticism," *The Muslim World*, 78(3–4) (October 1998), p. 210.
59 Ibid.
60 Ibid., pp. 212–13.
61 Ibid., p. 217.
62 Malamud, "Gender and Spiritual," p. 99.
63 al-Shadhili, Abu-al-Mawahib, *Illumination in Islamic Mysticism—A translation, with an introduction and notes, Based upon a critical edition of Abu-al-Mawahib Al-Shadhili's treatise entitled Qawanin Hikam al-Ishraq*, trans. J. A. Jurji (Princeton, NJ: Princeton University Press, 1938), p. 36.
64 F. Iraqi, *Divine Flashes*, trans. W. C. Chittick and P. Wilson, (New York, NY: Paulist Press, 1982), pp. 38–9.
65 Schimmel, "Eros," p. 39.
66 W. C. Chittick, *Ṣūfism—A Short Introduction* (Oxford: Oneworld Publications, 2000), p. 78. See also H. G. Farmer, *A History of Arabian Music* (India: Goodword Books, 2001).
67 A. M. A. Shushtery, "Traditional Ṣūfism—Ideas and Teachers, Philosophy, Training, Orders and Ethics," ed. N. P. Archer, *The Ṣūfī Mystery* (Kent: Octagon Press, 1980), p. 74.
68 Ibid., p. 107.
69 Schimmel, "Eros," p. 32.
70 Malamud, "Gender and Spiritual," p. 99.
71 S. Kugle, *Ṣūfis and Saints' Bodies—Mysticism, Corporeality, and Sacred Power in Islam* (Chapel Hill: North Carolina Press, 2007), p. 196.
72 L. Ridgeon, *Ṣūfī Castigator: Ahmad Kasravi and the Iranian Mystical Tradition* (Oxford UK: Routledge, 2006), p. 79.
73 Ibid.
74 K. Al-Rouayheb, *Before Homosexuality in the Arab-Islamic World, 1500–1800* (Chicago, IL: Chicago University Press, 2005), p. 113.
75 Ibid., p. 147.
76 S. Kugle, "Sexuality, Diversity, and Ethics," ed. O. Safi, *Progressive Muslims—On Justice, Gender and Pluralism* (Oneworld: Oxford, 2005), p. 203.
77 Ibid., p. 222.
78 Ibid., p. 129.
79 Malamud, "Gender and Spiritual," p. 106.
80 Ibid., pp. 106–7.

81 A. T. Karamustafa, *God's Unruly Friends—Dervish Groups in the Islamic Middle Period 1200–1500* (Oxford: Oneworld Publications, 2006), pp. 20–1.

82 Schimmel, "Eros," p. 36.

83 See: Types of Ṣūfī orders around the world are presented by A. M. A. Shushtery, "Traditional Ṣūfism—Ideas and Teachers, Philosophy, Training, Orders and Ethics," ed. N. P. Archer, *The Ṣūfī Mystery* (London: Octagon Press, 1980), pp. 57–77, S. A. A. Rizvi, *History of Ṣūfism in India* (Delhi: Munishiram Manoharlal, 1989). See also the life of the Sarmad, Persian mystic of the seventeenth century, understood to be a Jew who converted to Islam but then alleged to have renounced Islam to Hinduism. Sarmad became known as the naked mystic who smoked *bhang* (marijuana), believed in the Hindu Gods, and had fallen in love with a Hindu boy called Abhai Chand in N. Katz, "The Identity of a Mystic: The Case of Sa'id Sarmad, a Jewish-Yogi-Ṣūfī Courtier of the Mughals," *Numen*, 47(2) (2000), pp. 142–60.

84 Further information on Shah Hussayn's life: The most in depth biography was written by Shaikh Mahmud ibn Muḥammad Pir (ca. 1662), *Haqiqat al-Fuqara* (The Truth of Those Impoverished by Love), housed at Punjabi University Library, Pakistan, number 3253/248 Farsi. S. T. Mirzā, *Shah Hussayn* (Islamabad: Lok Wirsa Isha'at Ghar, 1989).

85 See: G. Y. Anwar (trans.), *The Paths Unknown: Kafiyan Shah Hussain* (Lahore: Majlis Shah Hussain, 1966).

86 S. Kugle, *Ṣūfīs and Saints' Bodies—Mysticism, Corporeality, and Sacred Power in Islam* (Chapel Hill: North Carolina Press, 2007), p. 184.

87 (Qur'ān 6:32, echoed in Qur'ān 29:64 and Qur'ān 47:36).

88 Kugle, *Ṣūfīs and Saints' Bodies*, pp. 185–6.

89 Ibid.

90 Ibid., p. 211.

91 Ibid., p. 194.

92 Ibid., p. 198.

93 L. Ramakrishna, *Punjabi Ṣūfī Saints* (New Delhi: Ashajanak Publications, 1973).

94 Kugle, *Ṣūfīs and Saints' Bodies*, p. 197. See also for further discussion on this: S. Alhaq, *Forgotten Vision: A Study of Human Spirituality in the Light of the Islamic Tradition* (London: Minerva, 1996).

95 Kugle, *Ṣūfīs and Saints' Bodies*, p. 196.

96 Ibid., p. 194.

97 Kugle, *Ṣūfīs and Saints' Bodies*, p. 222.

98 Platts translated the Urdu word "Malang" as, a kind of Mohammadan derwish, who lets the hair of his head grow to its full length, and leaves it uncombed and dishevelled;—a derwish in a state of ecstasy; a religious enthusiast;—a careless or inconsiderate person;—a tall, robust fellow;—a kind of bird." J. T. Platt, *A Dictionary of Urdū Classical Hindi and English* (New Delhi: Manohar, 2006), p. 1066.

99 Karamustafa used the word "marginalised," A. T. Karamustafa, *God's Unruly Friends—Dervish Groups in the Islamic Middle Period 1200–1500* (Oxford: Oneworld Publications, 2006), p. 102.

100 Kugle, *Ṣūfīs and Saints' Bodies*, p. 199. "At a more popular level, Ṣūfism developed several offshoots, absorbing some local Hindu features. The Gurzmars a branch of the Rifa'is, carried maces, and with them inflicted wounds upon themselves; the Jalalis took hashish, ate snakes and scorpions, and allowed their leaders sexual promiscuity with female members of the order. The Qalanders shaved their heads and facial hair, used intoxicants, and sometimes roamed naked; the Madaris consumed hashish, rubbed ash on their bodies, and wandered naked. The Haidaris adorned themselves with iron necklaces and bracelets and wore a ring attached to a lead bar piercing their sexual organs, there by eliminating the possibility of sexual intercourse. Like a number of other heterodox orders that developed outside India, these locally influenced Ṣūfī orders paid little care to regular Islamic rituals and prayers. The violation of Islamic norms and the absorption of the evidently anti-Islamic features were, however, glaringly blatant." M. Alam, *The Languages of Political Islam—India 1200–1800* (Chicago, IL: University of Chicago Press, 2004), pp. 90–1.

101 A. T. Karamustafa, *God's Unruly Friends—Dervish Groups in the Islamic Middle Period 1200–1500* (Oxford: Oneworld Publications, 2006), pp. 16–17.

102 Ibid., p. 19.

103 Ibid., p. 215.

104 Ibid., p. 20.

105 Ibid., p. 34.

106 K. P. Ewing, *Arguing Sainthood: Modernity, Psychoanalysis, and Islam* (Durham, NC: Duke University Press, 1997), p. 203.

107 Ibid., p. 204.

108 Kugle, *Ṣūfīs and Saints' Bodies*, p. 200.

109 Ibid., p. 4.

110 Ibid., p. 3.

111 Ibid., p. 59.

112 K. P. Ewing, "Malangs of the Punjab: Intoxication or Adab as the Path to God?" ed. B. Metcalf, *Moral Conduct and Authority: The Place of Adab in South Asian Islam* (Berkeley, CA: University of California Press, 1984), p. 364.

113 Ibid., p. 367.

114 K. P. Ewing, *Arguing Sainthood: Modernity, Psychoanalysis, and Islam* (Durham, NC: Duke University Press, 1997), pp. 209–17.

115 Ibid., p. 213.

116 Ibid., p. 214.

117 Ibid.

118 Ibid., p. 215.

119 Ewing, "Malangs of the Punjab," p. 360.
120 Ibid.
121 Ibid., p. 361.
122 Ibid., p. 362.
123 Ibid. The case of the female Malang, Bhava Sahib, as highlighted earlier in this chapter.
124 Ibid., p. 363.
125 Ibid.
126 Ibid., p. 217.
127 I. R. Netton, *Islam, Christianity and Tradition—A Comparative Exploration* (Edinburgh: Edinburgh University Press, 2006), p. 145.
128 Ibid., p. 144.
129 Ibid.
130 Ibid.
131 Ibid.
132 Ibid., p. 145.
133 Ibid., p. 206.
134 Ibid., p. 201.
135 Ibid., p. 217.

Bibliography

Abraham, K. C. and Abraham, A. K., "Homosexuality: Some Reflections From India," *The Ecumenical Review*, 50(1), pp. 22–9 (January 1998).

ad-Dīn, A. B. S. (M. Lings), *The Book of Certainty—The Sufi Doctrine of Faith, Vision and Gnosis* (Cambridge: Islamic Texts Society, 1996).

Adams, R. and Savran, D. (eds), *The Masculinity Studies Reader* (Oxford: Blackwell Publishers, 2002).

Aḥmad, K. and Ansari, Z. I., *Mawdūdī: An Introduction to His Life and Thought* (Leicester: Islamic Foundation, 1979).

Aḥmed, A., *Islamic Modernism in India and Pakistan* (London: Oxford University Press, 1967).

Ahmed, D. S., "Gender and Islamic Spirituality: A Psychological View of 'Low' Fundamentalism," ed. L. Ouzgane, *Islamic Masculinities* (London: Zed Books, 2006), pp. 11–30.

Aḥmed, Z., "Maudoodi's Islamic State," ed. M. A. Khān, *The Pakistan Experience—State and Religion* (Lahore: Vanguard Books, 1985), pp. 95–113.

Alam, M. and Subrahmanyam, S. (eds), *The Mughal State—1526–1750* (Delhi: Oxford University Press, 1998).

— *The Languages of Political Islam—India 1200–1800* (Chicago, IL: University of Chicago Press, 2004).

Ali, K., *Sexual Ethics and Islam—Feminist Reflections on Qur'ān, Hadith and Jurisprudence* (Oxford: Oneworld Publications, 2006).

Ali-Karamali, S., *The Muslim Next Door—The Qur'ān, the Media and that Veil Thing* (Ashland, Oregan: White Cloud Press, 2008).

Ali, T., *Can Pakistan Survive?* (Harmondsworth: Pelican Books, 1983).

al-Hallaj, *Kitab al-Tawasin* (Paris: Geuthner, 1913).

al-Misri, A. I. N., *Reliance of the Traveler: A Classical Manual of Islamic Sacred Law*, trans. N. H. M. Keller (Evanston: Sunna Books, 1994).

al-Mubarakpuri, S., *Ar-Raheeq al-Makhtum—Biography of the Noble Prophet* (Riyadh: Maktaba Dar-us-Salam, 1996).

al-Rouayheb, K., *Before Homosexuality in the Arab-Islamic World, 1500–1800* (Chicago, IL: Chicago University Press, 2005).

al-Shadhili, Abu-al-Mawahib, *Illumination in Islamic Mysticism—A Translation*, with an Introduction and Notes, based upon a *Critical Edition of Abu-al-Mawahib*

Al-Shadhili's Treatise Entitled Qawanin Hikam al-Ishraq, trans. J. A. Jurji (Princeton, NJ: Princeton University Press, 1938).

al-Ṭabarī, *Tafsīr al-Ṭabari: Jāmi` al-Bayān 'an Ta'wīl Āy al-Qur'ān*, ed. Ṣalāḥ 'Abd al Fattāh al-Khālidī (Damascus: Dār al-Qalam; Beirut: Dār al-Shāmiyya, 1998).

Amin, Q., *The Liberation of Women—The New Woman*, trans. S. S. Peterson (Cairo: American University in Cairo Press, 2004).

An-Na`im, A., A., *Toward an Islamic Reformation—Civil Liberties, Human Rights and International Law* (Syracuse: Syracuse University Press, 1996).

— *Islamic Family Law in a Changing World: A Global Resource Book* (London: Zed Books, 2002).

Ansari, H., *The Infidel Within—Muslims in Britain since 1800* (London: C. Hurst and Co. Publishers, 2004).

Anwar, G. Y. (trans.), *The Paths Unknown: Kafiyan Shah Hussain* (Lahore: Majlis Shah Hussain, 1966).

Arasteh, A. R., *Rumi the Persian—The Sufi* (London: Routledge and Kegan Paul, 1974).

Asad, M., *The Message of the Qur'ān* (Bristol: The Book Foundation, 2003).

Asher, C. B. and Talbot, C. (eds), *India before Europe* (Cambridge: Cambridge University Press, 2006).

Ask, K. and Tjomsland, M. (eds), *Women and Islamization* (Oxford: Berg Publishers, 1998).

Ata'ur Rahim, M. and Thomson, A., *Jesus—Prophet of Islam* (London: Ta Ha Publishers, 1996).

Barlas, A., *Believing Women in Islam—Unreading Patriarchal Interpretations of the Qur'ān* (Austin:University of Texas Press, 2004).

Bausani, A., "Ghālib's Persian Poetry," ed. R. Russell, *The Oxford India Ghālib: Life, Letters and Ghazals* (India: Oxford University Press, 2005), pp. 390–414.

Bell, R., *The Origins of Islam in its Christian Environment* (London: Macmillan & Co. Ltd, 1926).

Bennet, C., *In Search of Muhammad* (London: Cassell Publications, 1998).

Bergesen, A. J. (ed.), *The Syed Qutb Reader: Selected Writings on Politics, Religion and Society* (New York: Routledge, 2008).

Beynon, J., *Masculinities and Culture* (Buckingham: Open University Press, 2002).

Bhutto, B., *Benazir Bhutto—Daughter of the East—An Autobiography* (London: Simon & Schuster UK Ltd, 2007).

— *Reconciliation—Islam, Democracy, and the West* (London: Simon & Schuster UK Ltd, 2008).

Bijlefeld, W. A., "A Prophet and More than a Prophet? Some Observations on the Qur'ānic Use of Terms 'Prophet' and 'Apostle'," ed. C. Turner, *The Koran—Critical Concepts in Islamic Studies*, vol. 2 (Oxford, UK: Routledge, 2006), pp. 295–322.

Bonde, H., “Masculine Sport and Masculinity in Denmark at the Turn of the Century,” ed. S. Ervø and T. Johansson, *Among Men—Moulding Masculinities*, vol. 1 (Aldershot: Ashgate Publishing, 2003), pp. 81–115.

Brown, D. W., *Rethinking Tradition in Modern Islamic Thought* (Cambridge: Cambridge University Press, 1996).

Brynjar, L., *The Society of the Muslim Brothers in Egypt: The Rise of an Islamic Mass Movement 1928–1942* (Reading, UK: Garnet Publishers, 1998).

Bukhārī, *Ṣaḥīḥ al-Bukhārī*, trans. M. M. Khan, vol. VII, Ḥādīth Number 64 (Lahore: Kazi Publications, 1986).

Calvert, J., *Islamism: A Documentary and Reference Guide* (Westport, CT: Greenwood Press, 2007).

Chittick, W. C., *Sufism—A Short Introduction* (Oxford: Oneworld Publications, 2000).

Connell, R. W., *The Men and the Boys* (Oxford: Polity Press, 2000).

— *Gender* (Cambridge: Polity Press, 2002).

Cragg, K., *Jesus and the Muslim—An Exploration* (Oxford, UK: Oneworld Publications, 1999).

Crone, P. and Cook, M., *Hagarism—The Making of the Muslim World* (Cambridge: Cambridge University Press, 1977).

Dalrymple, W., *The Fall of a Dynasty, Delhi, 1857—The Last Mughal* (London: Bloomsbury Publications, 2007).

Dawson, G., “The Blond Bedouin: Lawrence of Arabia, Imperial Adventure and the Imagining of English-British Masculinity,” ed. M. Roper and J. Tosh, *Manful Assertions: Masculinities in Britain since 1800* (Routledge: London, 1991), pp. 113–44.

Dekmijian, R. H., *Islamic in Revolution—Fundamentalism in the Arab World* (Syracuse: Syracuse University Press, 1995).

Demant, P. R., *Islam vs. Islamism: The Dilemma of the Muslim World* (Westport, CT: Praeger Publishers, 2006).

Denny, F., “Meaning of Ummah in the Qur'ān,” ed. C. Turner, *The Koran—Critical Concepts in Islamic Studies*, vol. 2 (Oxford: Routledge, 2006), pp. 19–53.

Dhalla, G. S., *Ode to Lata* (Los Angeles, CA: Really Great Books, 2002).

Doi, A. R., *Sharī'ah: The Islamic Law* (London: Ta Ha Publishers, 1984).

Dudink, S., Hagemann, K., and Tosh, J. (eds), *Masculinities in Politics and War—Gendering Modern History* (Manchester: Manchester University Press, 2004).

Durrani, T., *My Feudal Lord* (Reading, UK: Corgi Publishers, 1995).

El Awaisi, A. A. M., *The Muslim Brothers and the Palestine Question* (London: I.B. Tauris & Co Ltd., 1998).

El Fadl, K. A., *Speaking in God's Name—Islamic Law, Authority and Women* (Oxford: Oneworld Publications, 2003).

El Guindi, F., *Veil—Modesty, Privacy and Resistance* (Oxford: Berg Publishers, 1999).

Elias, J. J., "Female and the Feminine in Islamic Mysticism," *The Muslim World*, 78(3–4) (October 1988), pp. 209–24.

Elkaisy-Friemuth, M., *God and Humans in Islamic Thought—'Abd al-Jabbar, Ibn Sina and al-Ghazali* (Oxford: Routledge, 2006).

El-Nimr, R., "Women in Islamic Law," ed. M. Yamani, *Feminism and Islam: Legal and Literary Perspectives* (Lebanon: Ithaca Press, 1996), pp. 87–102.

El Saadawi, N., *The Hidden Face of Eve—Women in the Arab World* (London: Zed Press, 1980).

Elsässer, S., "Between Ideology and Pragmatism: Fathī Yakan's Theory of Islamic Activism," *Die Welt des Islams*, 47(3–4) (2007), pp. 376–402.

Engineer, A. A., "A Muslim View of Hinduism," ed. P. Schmidt-Leukel and L. Ridgeon, *Islam and Inter-Faith Relations—The Gerald Weisfeld Lectures 2006* (London: SCM Press, 2007), pp. 165–79.

Ewing, K. P., "Malangs of the Punjab: Intoxication or Adab as the Path to God?," ed. B. Metcalf, *Moral Conduct and Authority: The Place of Adab in South Asian Islam* (Berkeley, CA: University of California Press, 1984), pp. 357–71.

— *Arguing Sainthood: Modernity, Psychoanalysis, and Islam* (Durham, NC: Duke University Press, 1997).

Farmaian, S. F., *Daughter of Persia* (Reading, UK: Corgi Publishers, 1993).

Farmer, H. G., *A History of Arabian Music* (India: Goodword Books, 2001).

Faruki, K. A., "Pakistan: Islamic Government and Society," ed. J. L. Esposito, *Islam in Asia—Religion, Politics and Society* (New York: Oxford University Press, 1987), pp. 53–78.

Flaubert, G., *Madame Bovary—Moeurs De Province* (Paris: Michel Levy Freres, Libraires-Edituers, 1857).

Franklin II, C. W., *The Changing Definition of Masculinity* (New York: Plenum Press, 1986).

Friedan, B., *The Feminine Mystique* (London: Penguin, 1992).

Frosh, S., Phoenix, A., and Pattman, R., *Young Masculinities: Understanding Boys in Contemporary Society* (Palgrave: Basingstoke, 2002).

Gerami, S., "Mullahs, Martyrs, and Men—Conceptualizing Masculinity in the Islamic Republic of Iran," ed. S. M. Whitehead, *Men and Masculinities—Critical Concepts in Sociology*, vol. V (Oxford: Routledge, 2006), pp. 257–74.

Ghālib, M. A. K., *Divan-e-Ghālib*, trans. K. R. S. Rana (New Delhi: Anmol Publications, 2005).

— *Love Sonnets of Ghālib*, trans. S. K. Niazi (New Delhi: Rupa & Co., 2006).

— *Ghazals of Ghālib—Versions from the Urdu*, ed. A. Aḥmad (New Delhi: Oxford University Press, 2007).

Ghazālī, M., *Ihya 'ulum al-din* (Cairo: Matba'at al-Amirat al-Sharafiyya, 1908–9).

Ghoussoub, M. and Sinclair-Webb, E. (eds), *Imagined Masculinities—Male Identity and Culture in the Modern Middle East* (London: Saqi Books, 2000).

Goddard, H., *Christians and Muslims—From Double Standards to Mutual Understanding* (Cornwal, UK: Curzon Press 1995).

Goldman, S., "Joseph," ed. J. McAuliffe, *Encyclopedia of the Qur'ān*, vol. III (Leiden: Brill, 2003), pp. 55–7.

Gulzar, *Mirzā Ghālib—A Biographical Scenario* (Delhi: Rupa & Co Publishers, 2006).

Gutterman, D. S., "Postmodernism and the Interrogation of Masculinity," ed. S. M. Whitehead and F. J. Barrett, *The Masculinities Reader* (Cambridge: Polity Press, 2001), pp. 56–71.

Habib, S., *Female Homosexuality in the Middle East—Histories and Representations* (London: Routledge, 2007).

Halberstam, J., "An Introduction to Female Masculinity: Masculinity without Men," ed. R. Adams and D. Savran, *The Masculinity Studies Reader* (Oxford: Blackwell Publishers, 2002), pp. 355–74.

Hali, M. A. H., *Yādgār-i-Ghālib*, trans. K. H. Qadiri (Delhi: Idarah-I Adabiyāt, 1990).

— *Hali's Musaddas—The Flow and Ebb of Islam*, trans. C. Shackle and J. Majeed (Delhi: Oxford University Press, 1997).

Haq, Q. M. and Waley, M. I., *Allama Sir Muḥammad Iqbal—Poet-Philosopher of the East* (Scarborough: British Museum Publications, 1977).

Hassan, R., "An Islamic Perspective," ed. J. Becher, *Women, Religion and Sexuality* (Geneva: WCC Publications, 1990), pp. 93–128.

— "The Issue of Woman-Man Equality in the Islamic Tradition," ed. L. Grob, R. Hassan, and H. Gordon, *Women's and Men's Liberation—Testimonies of Spirit* (Westport, CT: Greenwood Press, 1991), pp. 65–82.

— "'Jihād Fi Sabil Allah': A Muslim Woman's Faith Journey from Struggle to Struggle to Struggle," ed. L. Grob, R. Hassan, and H. Gordon, *Women's and Men's Liberation—Testimonies of Spirit* (Westport, CT: Greenwood Press, 1991), pp. 11–30.

Haywood, C. and Ghaill, M. M., "Schooling Masculinities," ed. M. M. Ghaill, *Understanding Masculinities* (Buckingham: Open University Press, 2000), pp. 50–60.

— *Men and Masculinities—Theory, Research and Social Practice* (Buckingham: Open University Press, 2003).

Helminski, C. A., *Women of Sufism—A Hidden Treasure, Writings and Stories of Mystic Poets, Scholars and Saint* (Boston: Shambhala Publications, 2003).

Horrocks, R., *Masculinity in Crisis* (New York: St Martin's Press, 1994).

Hossain, S. and Welchman, L. (eds), *Honor: Crimes, Paradigms, and Violence Against Women* (London: Zed Books, 2005).

Hughes, T. P., *A Dictionary of Islam* (Calcutta: Rupa & Co., 1988).

Hujwiri, *Kashf al-Mahjub of al-Hujwiri*, trans. R. A. Nicholson (London: Luzac and Co., 1911).

Ibn Arabi, M., *Fusus Al-Hikam*, trans. B. Rauf, vol. 4 (Oxford: Muhyiddun Ibn Arabi Society, 1991).

Ibn Ḥazm, Abū Muḥammad ʿAlī ibn Aḥmad ibn Saʿīd., *Kitāb al-Fasl fi al-milal wal-ahwa' wal-nihal*, ed. M. I. Nasr and A. A. Umayra, vol. 5 (Jeddah: Uzak Publications, 1982).

Ibn Kathir, *Stories of the Prophets*, trans. R. A. Azami (Jeddah: Darussalam Publishers, first edn).

— *Tafsīr Ibn Kathir* (Riyadh: Dar al-Islam, 1998).

Ibn Sa'd, *Tabaqat al-Kubra* (Beirut: Dār Ṣadir edition, 8:151 ff).

Iraqi, F., *Divine Flashes*, trans. W. C. Chittick and P. Wilson (Paulist Press: New York, 1982).

Irfani, S., "The Progressive Islamic Movement," ed. M. A. Khan, *The Pakistan Experience—State and Religion* (Lahore: Vanguard Books, 1985), pp. 31–68.

Islam, K. and Russell R., *Three Mughal Poets—Mir, Sauda, Mir Hasan* (Delhi: Oxford University Press, 2006).

Iqbal, M. *Stray Reflections: The Private Notebook of Muhammad Iqbal*, ed. J. Iqbal (Lahore: Iqbal Academy Pakistan, 1987).

— *Shikwa and Jawab-i-Shikwa—Complaint and Answer—Iqbal's Dialogue with Allah*, trans. K. Singh (New Delhi: Oxford University Press, 2008).

Jama, A., *Illegal Citizens: Queer Lives in the Muslim World* (Los Angeles, CA: Salaam Press, 2008).

Kabil, A., *Straightening Ali* (Herndon: Star Books Press, 2007).

Kanda, K. C., *Mirzā Ghālib: Selected Lyrics and Letters* (New Delhi: New Dawn Press, 2007).

Karamustafa, A., "A Civilizational Project in Progress," ed. O. Safi, *Progressive Muslims on Justice, Gender and Pluralism* (Oxford: Oneworld, 2004), pp. 98–110.

Karamustafa, A. T., *God's Unruly Friends—Dervish Groups in the Islamic Middle Period 1200–1500* (Oxford: Oneworld Publications, 2006).

Karandikar, M. A., *Islam in India's Transition to Modernity* (Bombay: Orient Longmans Ltd., 1968).

Karmi, G., "Women, Islam and Patriarchalism," ed. M. Yamani, *Feminism and Islam: Legal and Literary Perspectives* (Lebanon: Ithaca Press, 1996), pp. 65–85.

— *In Search of Fatima—A Palestinian Story* (London: Verso Books, 2002).

Katz, N., "The Identity of a Mystic: The Case of Sa'id Sarmad, a Jewish-Yogi-Sufi Courtier of the Mughals," *Numen*, 47(2) (2000), pp. 142–60.

Kaufman, M. (ed.), *Beyond Patriarchy: Essays by Men on Pleasure, Power and Change* (Oxford: Oxford University Press, 1987).

Keay, J., *The Honorable Company: History of the English East India Company* (London: HarperCollins Publishers, 1991).

Kepel, G., *Muslim Extremism in Egypt: The Prophet and Pharaoh*, trans. J. Rothschild (Berkeley, CA: University of California Press, 1985).

Khaleel, M., "Sex, Sexuality and the Family," ed. A. Rippin, *The Blackwell Companion to the Qur'ān* (Oxford: Blackwell Publishing, 2006), pp. 298–307.

Khalidi, T., *The Muslim Jesus* (Cambridge: Harvard University Press, 2003).

Khān, A. O., "Political and Economic Aspects of Islamisation," ed. M. A. Khān, *The Pakistan Experience—State and Religion* (Lahore: Vanguard Books, 1985), pp. 127–63.

Khan, B., *Sex, Longing and Not Belonging: A Gay Muslim's Quest for Love and Meaning* (Oakland, CA: Floating Lotus Press, 1997).

Kidwai, S., "Introduction: Medieval Materials in the Perso-Urdu Tradition," ed. R. Vanita and S. Kidwai, *Same-Sex Love in India: Readings from Literature and History* (New York: Palgrave Publishing, 2001), pp. 107–25.

— "Mir Taqi 'Mir': Autobiography (Persian) and Poems (Urdu)," ed. R. Vanita and S. Kidwai, *Same-Sex Love in India: Readings from Literature and History* (New York: Palgrave Publishing, 2001), pp. 184–90.

Kimmel, M. S., "The Contemporary 'Crisis' of Masculinity," ed. H. Brod, *The Making of Masculinity* (London: Allen and Unwin, 1987), pp. 121–53.

Klostermaier, K. K., *A Survey of Hinduism* (Albany, NY: State University of New York Press, 1989).

Kueny, K., *Rhetoric of Sobriety—Wine in Early Islam* (New York, NY: State University of New York Press, 2001).

Kugle, S., "Sexuality, Diversity, and Ethics," ed. O. Safi, *Progressive Muslims—On Justice, Gender and Pluralism* (Oneworld: Oxford, 2005), pp. 190–234.

— *Sufis and Saints' Bodies—Mysticism, Corporeality, and Sacred Power in Islam* (Chapel Hill, NC: North Carolina Press, 2007).

Landolt, H., "Two Types of Mystical Thought in Muslim Iran—An Essay on Suhrwardī Shaykh al-Ishrāq and Aynulquẓāt-I Hamadānī," *The Muslim World*, 68(3) (July 1978), pp. 187–204.

Lee, R. D., *Overcoming Tradition and Modernity* (Colorado: Westview Press, 1997).

Lings, M., *What is Sufism?* (Surrey: George Allen and Unwin Ltd., 1975).

— *Muhammad—His Life Based on the Earliest Sources* (London: Islamic Texts Society, 1983).

Lorenzen, D. N. (ed.), *Bhakti Religion in North India: Community, Identity and Political Action* (Albany, NY: State University of New York Press, 1995).

Luongo, M. T. (ed.), *Gay Travels in the Muslim World* (Binghamton: Harrington Park Press, 2007).

Mac an Ghaill, M. (ed.), *Understanding Masculinities—Social Relations and Cultural Arenas* (Buckingham: Open University Press, 2000).

Maḥmūd Ibn Muḥammad Pīr, *Haqīqat al-Fuqarā'* (*The Truth of Those Impoverished by Love*), number 3253/248 Farsi.

Mai, M., *In the Name of Honor* (London: Virago Press Limited, 2007).
Malamud, M., "Gender and Spiritual Self-Fashioning: The Master-Disciple Relationship in Classical Sufism," *Journal of the American Academy of Religion*, 64(1) (Spring 1996), pp. 89–117.
Mālik bin A., *Kitāb al-Muwaṭṭa'*, trans. A. A. at-Tarjumana and Y. Johnson (Norwich: Diwan Press, 1982).
Massad, J. A., *Desiring Arabs* (Chicago, IL: University of Chicago Press, 2008).
Mawdūdi, A. A., *Towards Understanding Islam* (Leicester: Islamic Foundation, 1980).
— *Capitalism, Socialism and Islam*, trans. S. A. Khān (Safat: Islamic Book Publishers, 1987).
— *Human Rights in Islam*, trans. K. Ahmad (Leicester: Islamic Foundation, 1993).
— *The Laws of Marriage and Divorce in Islam*, trans. F. Aḥmed (Safat: Islamic Book Publishers, 2000).
— *The Islamic Way of Life (Islām kā Niẓām Ḥayāt)*, trans. and ed. K. Ahmad and K. Murad (Leicester: Islamic Foundation, 2001).
— *Purdah*, trans. Al-Ash`ari (Lahore: Islamic Publications, 2004).
— *Towards Understanding the Qur'ān*, trans. and ed. A. I. Ansari (Delhi: Markazi Maktaba Islami Publishers, 2005).
— *Purdah—Urdu* (Lahore: Islamic Publications, 2007).
McInnes, J., *The End of Masculinity* (Buckingham: Open University Press, 1998).
Mernissi, F., *Beyond the Veil: Male-Female Dynamics in Modern Muslim Society* (Indiana: 1987).
— *Women and Islam—An Historical and Theological Enquiry* (Oxford: Blackwell Publishing, 1994).
Messner, M., *Politics of Masculinities: Men in Movements* (Thousand Oaks, CA: Sage, 1997).
Mir, M. S., "Religion and Politics in Pakistan," ed. A. A. Engineer, *Islam in Asia* (Lahore: Vanguard Books, 1985), pp. 145–70.
— *Islam and Gender—The Religious Debate in Contemporary Iran* (London: I.B. Tauris & Co. Ltd., 1999).
Mirzā, S. T., *Shah Hussayn* (Islamabad: Lok Wirsa Isha'at Ghar, 1989).
Mohamed, S., "Challenging Moral Guardianship in Pakistan," ed. G. Misra and R. Chandiramani, *Sexuality, Gender and Rights—Exploring Theory and Practice in South and Southeast Asia* (New Delhi: Sage Publications, 2005).
Motzki, H., "Marriage," ed. J. McAuliffe, *Encyclopedia of the Qur'ān*, vol. 3 (Leiden: Brill, 2003), pp. 276–81.
Murata, S., *The Tao of Islam—A Sourcebook on Gender Relationships in Islamic Thought* (New York, NY: State University of New York Press, 1992).
Murray, S. O. and Roscoe, W. (eds), *Islamic Homosexualities: Culture, History and Literature* (New York, NY: New York University Press, 1997).

Museum without Frontiers (eds), *Discover Islamic Art in the Mediterranean—A Book by Museum with No Frontiers* (London: Compass Press, 2007).

Muslim, *Ṣaḥīḥ Muslim*, trans. A. H. Siddiqi, vol. II, Ḥādīth Number 3458 (Lahore: Ashraf Publishers, 1993).

Naim, C. M., *Zikr-I Mir: The Autobiography of the Eighteenth Century Mughal Poet: Mir Muhammad Taqi Mir, Translated, Annotated and with an Introduction* (New Delhi: Oxford University Press, 1999)

Nasr, S. V. R., *Mawdūdi & the Making of Islamic Revivalism* (New York: Oxford University Press, 1996).

Netton, I. R., *Seek Knowledge: Thought and Knowledge in the House of Islam* (Richmond: Curzon, 1995)

— *Sufi Ritual—The Parallel Universe* (Surrey, UK: Curzon Press, 2000).

— *Islam, Christianity and Tradition—A Comparative Exploration* (Edinburgh: Edinburgh University Press, 2006).

Nicholson, R. A., *The Mystics of Islam* (London: Routledge and Kegan Paul Ltd., 1963).

Nomani, A. Q., *Tantrika: Traveling the Road of Divine Love* (New York, NY: HarperCollins Publishers, 2003).

— *Standing Alone: An American Woman's Struggle for the Soul of Islam* (New York, NY: HarperSanFrancisco, 2006)

Nurbakhsh, J., *Jesus in the Eyes of Sufis*, trans. T. Graham, L. Lewisohn, and H. Mashkuri (London: Khaniqahi-Nimatullahi Publications, 1992).

O'Halloran, F. X., "A Catholic Among the Sufis," ed. N. P. Archer, *The Sufi Mystery* (London, UK: Kent Octagon Press, 1980), pp. 27–8.

O'Shaughnessy, T. J., "The Qur'ānic View of Youth and Old Age," ed. C. Turner, *The Koran—Critical Concepts in Islamic Studies* (Oxford, UK: Routledge, 2006).

Ouzgane, L. (ed.), *Islamic Masculinities* (London: Zed Books, 2006).

— "The Rape Continuum: Masculinities in Ben Jelloun's and El Saadawi's Works," ed. S. M. Whitehead, *Men and Masculinities—Critical Concepts in Sociology*, vol. V (Oxford: Routledge, 2006), pp. 87–101.

Pearl, M., *A Mighty Heart: The Daniel Pearly Story* (London: Virago Press Ltd., 2004).

Penrice, J., *A Dictionary and Glossary of the Koran—With Copious Grammatical References and Explanations of the Text* (Karachi: Darul-Ishaat, 1998).

Plath, S., *Collected Poems*, ed. T. Hughes (London: Faber and Faber, 1981).

Platt, J. T., *A Dictionary of Urdū Classical Hindi and English* (New Delhi: Manohar, 2006).

Pleck, J. H., "The Theory of Male-Sex Role Identity: Its Rise and Fall, 1936 to the Present," ed. H. Brod, *The Making of Masculinity* (London: Allen and Unwin, 1987), pp. 21–38.

Prigarina, N., *Mirzā Ghālib: A Creative Biography*, trans. M. O. Faruqi (Karachi: Oxford University Press, 2004).

Queen, C. and Schimel, L. (eds), *Pomosexuals—Challenging Assumptions about Gender and Sexuality* (San Francisco, CA: Cleis Press, 1997).

Qutb, S., *Milestones* (India: Islamic Book Service, 2006).

Rahbar, D., *Urdu Letters of Mirzā Asadu'llah Khān Ghālib* (New York, NY: State University of New York, 1987).

Rahman, F., *Prophecy in Islam* (London: George Allen and Unwin Ltd. Publishers, 1958).

— *Major Themes in the Qur'ān* (Chicago, IL: Bibliotheca Islamica, 1980).

Ramakrishna, L., *Punjabi Sufi Saints* (New Delhi: Ashajanak Publications, 1973).

Rashid, A., "Pakistan: The Ideological Dimension," ed. M. A. Khān, *The Pakistan Experience—State and Religion* (Lahore: Vanguard Books, 1985), pp. 69–94.

Renard, J., *Islam and the Heroic Image* (Macon, GA: Mercer University Press, 1999).

Richards, J. F., *The Mughal Empire* (Cambridge: Cambridge University Press, 1995).

Ridgeon, L., *Crescents on the Cross* (Glasgow: Trinity St. Mungo Press, 1999).

— *Sufi Castigator: Ahmad Kasravi and the Iranian Mystical Tradition* (Oxford, UK: Routledge, 2006).

Rizvi, S. A. A., *History of Sufism in India* (Delhi: Munishiram Manoharlal, 1989).

Roald, A. S., *Women in Islam—The Western Experience* (London: Routledge, 2001).

Robinson, N., *Christ in Islam and Christianity* (New York, NY: State University of New York, 1991).

— "Jesus," ed. J. McAuliffe, *Encyclopedia of the Qur'ān*, vol. 3 (Leiden: Brill 2003), pp. 7–20

Roper, M. and Tosh, J. (eds), *Manful Assertions: Masculinities in Britain since 1800* (London: Routledge, 1991).

Rubin, U., "Prophet," ed. J. McAuliffe, *Encyclopedia of the Qur'ān*, vol. 4 (Leiden: Brill, 2004), pp. 289–307.

Russel, R., "Getting to Know Ghālib," ed. R. Russell, *The Oxford India Ghālib: Life, Letters and Ghazals* (India: Oxford University Press, 2005), pp. 283–325.

— "Ghālib's Urdu Verse," ed. R. Russell, *The Oxford India Ghālib: Life, Letters and Ghazals* (India: Oxford University Press, 2005), pp. 327–90.

— "Ghālib—A Self Portrait," ed. R. Russell, *The Oxford India Ghālib: Life, Letters and Ghazals* (India: Oxford University Press, 2005), pp. 1–27.

Russel, R. and Islam, K., "Ghālib: Life and Letters," ed. R. Russell, *The Oxford India Ghālib: Life, Letters and Ghazals* (India: Oxford University Press, 2005), pp. 29–262.

Ruswa, M. M. H., *Umrao Jan Ada*, trans. K. Singh and M. A. Husaini (Delhi: Disha Books, 1982).

Said, E., *Orientalism* (London: Penguin Books, 2003).

Salahi, A., *Muḥammad—Man and Prophet* (Leicester: The Islamic Foundation, 2002).
Sanya, U., *Ahmad Riza Khan Barelwi—In the Path of the Prophet* (Oxford: Oneworld Publishers, 2005).
Sayeed, K. B., *Pakistan—The Formative Phase 1857–1948* (Oxford: Oxford University Press, 1968).
Schmidt, R. L., "Urdu," ed. G. Cardona and D. Jain, *The Indo-Aryan Languages* (London: Routledge, 2003), pp. 286–350.
Schmitt, A. and Sofer, J. (eds), *Sexuality and Eroticism among Males in Moslem Society* (Binghamton: Harrington Park Press, 1992).
Schimmel, A., *Islam in the Indian Subcontinent* (Leiden: E.J. Brill Publications, 1980).
— "Foreword," ed. D. Rahbar, *Urdu Letters of Mirzā Asadu'llah Khān Ghālib* (New York, NY: State University of New York, 1987), pp. xi–xv.
— "Eros—Heavenly and Not So Heavenly—In Sufi Literature and Life," *Sufi*, 29 (Spring 1996), pp.30–42.
— *The Empire of the Great Mughals: History, Art and Culture* (London: Reaktion Books, 2006).
Schock, C., "Adam and Eve," ed. J. McAuliffe, *Encyclopedia of the Qur'ān*, vol. 1 (Leiden: Brill, 2003), pp. 22–6.
Sedgwick, E. K., *Between Men: English Literature and Male Homosocial Desire* (New York: Columbia University Press, 1985).
Seidler, V. J., *Man Enough—Embodying Masculinities* (London: Sage Publications, 1997).
Shaikh, S., "A Tafsīr of Praxis: Gender, Marital Violence, and Resistance in a South African Muslim Community," ed. D. McGuire and S. Shaikh, *Violence against Women in Contemporary World Religion: Roots and Cures* (Cleveland: Pilgrim Press, 2007), pp. 66–89.
Shushtery, A. M. A., "Traditional Sufism—Ideas and Teachers, Philosophy, Training, Orders and Ethics," ed. N. P. Archer, *The Sufi Mystery* (London: Kent Octagon Press, 1980), pp. 57–77.
Siddiqui, M., "Law and The Desire for Social Control: An Insight into the Hanafi Concept of *Kafa'a* with Reference to the Fatāwā 'Ālamgīrī (1664–1672)," ed. Yamani, M., *Feminism and Islam: Legal and Literary Perspectives* (Lebanon: Ithaca Press, 1996), pp. 49–68.
Smith, V. A., *Akbar the Great Moghal 1542–1605* (Oxford: Clarendon Press, 1917).
Spear, P., "Ghālib's Delhi," ed. Russell, R., *The Oxford India Ghālib: Life, Letters and Ghazals* (India: Oxford University Press, 2005), pp. 262–81.
Stowasser, B., *Women in the Qur'ān, Traditions, and Interpretation* (Oxford, UK: Oxford University Press, 1994).
Streusand, D. E., *The Formation of the Mughal Empire* (Delhi: Oxford University Press, 1989).

Syed, A. H., "Iqbal and Jinnah on Issues of Nationhood and Nationalism," ed. C. M. Naim, *Iqbal, Jinnah and Pakistan—The Vision and the Reality* (Lahore: Vanguard Books, 1984).

Talbot, I., *Pakistan—A Modern History* (London: Hurst and Company, 1998).

Tosh, J., *Manliness and Masculinities in Nineteenth Century Britain* (New York, NY: Pearsons Longman, 2005).

Treadwell, P., "Biological Influences on Masculinity," ed. H. Brod, *The Making of Masculinity* (London:Allen and Unwin, 1987), pp. 259–85.

Trofimov, Y., *The Siege of Mecca: The Forgotten Uprising in Islam's Holiest Shrine* (London: Penguin, 2008).

Vahid, S. A., *Iqbal—His Art & Thought* (Hyderabad: Government Central Press, 1944).

Vanita, R., "Preface," ed. R. Vanita and S. Kidwai, *Same-Sex Love in India: Readings from Literature and History* (New York, NY: Palgrave Publishing, 2001), pp. xiii–xxiv.

Varma, P. K., *Ghālib: The Man and Times* (India: Penguin, 1989).

Wadud, A., *Qur'ān and Woman—Rereading the Sacred Text from a Woman's Perspective* (Oxford: Oxford University Press, 1999).

— *Inside the Gender Jihad—Women's Reform in Islam* (Oxford: Oneworld, 2006).

Watt, W. M., *Muhammad—Prophet and Statesman* (London: Oxford University Press, 1961).

— *Muḥammad's Mecca—History in the Qur'ān* (Edinburgh: Edinburgh University Press, 1988).

Weismann, I., "Sa'id Hawwa and Islamic Revivalism in Ba'thist Syria," in *Studia Islamica*, 85 (1997), pp. 134–54.

Welchman, L, *Women and Muslim Family Laws in Arab States: A Comparative Overview of Textual Development and Advocacy (ISIM Series on Contemporary Muslim Societies)* (Amsterdam: Amsterdam University Press, 2007).

Westwood, S., "Feckless Fathers: Masculinities and the British State," ed. M. Mac an Ghaill, *Understanding Masculinities—Social Relations and Cultural Arenas* (Buckingham: Open University Press, 2000), pp. 21–34.

Whitehead, S. M. and Barrett, F. J., "The Sociology of Masculinity," ed. S. M. Whitehead and F. J. Barrett, *The Masculinities Reader*, (Cambridge: Polity Press, 2001), pp. 1–26.

Whitaker, B., *Unspeakable Love—Gay and Lesbian Life in the Middle East* (London: Saqi Books, 2006).

Wheeler, B. M., *Prophets in the Qur'ān* (London: Continuum, 2002).

Index

Page numbers in **bold** refer to illustrations.

76803138R00135

Made in the USA
Columbia, SC
26 September 2019